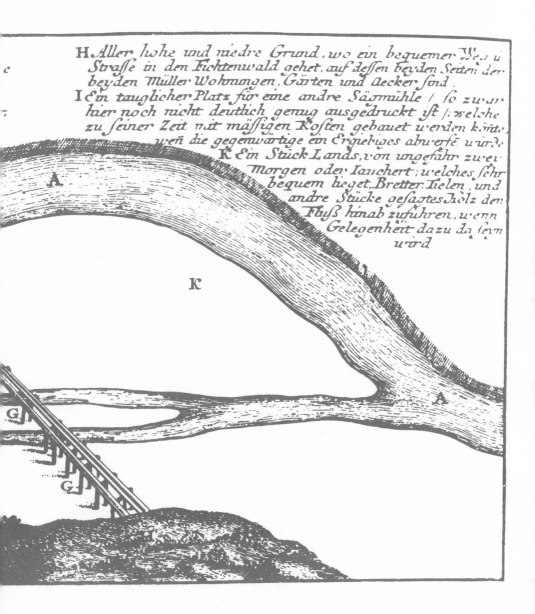

H. Aller hohe und niedre Grund, wo ein bequemer Weg u.
Straße in den Fichtenwald gehet, auf deßen beyden Seiten der
beyden Müller Wohnungen, Gärten und Aecker sind.

I. Ein tauglicher Platz für eine andre Sägmühle / so zu ar
hier noch nicht deutlich genug ausgedruckt ist / welche
zu seiner Zeit mit mäßigen Kosten gebauet werden könte
weñ die gegenwärtige ein Ergiebiges abwerfe würde

K. Ein Stück Lands, von ungefähr zwei
Morgen oder Jauchert; welches sehr
bequem lieget, Bretter, Dielen, und
andre Stücke gesagtes Holz den
Fluß hinab zuführen, wenn
Gelegenheit dazu da seyn
wird

A

K

G

G

A

DETAILED REPORTS

on the

SALZBURGER EMIGRANTS

Who Settled in America

VOLUME 18, 1744–1745

Translated and Edited by

George Fenwick Jones
and
Renate Wilson

PICTON PRESS
CAMDEN, MAINE

An 18th century reproduction of the 1744 plans for the Salzburger mills are shown on the endsheets.

First Printing October 1995

This volume and the set are available from:

Picton Press
PO Box 250
Rockport, ME 04856-0250

Visa/MasterCard orders: (207) 236-6565
Fax: (207) 236-6713

Manufactured in the United States of America
Printed on 60# acid-free paper

Contents

INTRODUCTION

In introducing this volume of the *Detailed Reports of the Salzburgers Who settled in Georgia,* we first wish to acquaint the reader who is unfamiliar with the Salzburger story with some of the background to this series.[1]

When about 19,000 Protestants were expelled from the Salzburg Archbishopric in 1731 not all the exiles went to East Prussia and other Protestant lands in Europe: a small number, some two hundred, were taken to the colony of Georgia, then in its second year. Georgia, the last of Britain's thirteen North American colonies, was founded according to the grandiose schemes of a group of benevolent gentlemen in London, the Georgia Trustees, who wished to provide a new home for impoverished Englishmen and persecuted foreign Protestants, to protect the more northerly British colonies from the Spaniards in Florida, and to provide raw materials for English manufacture.

The first Salzburger transport, or traveling party, consisted of recent exiles who had been residing in and around Augsburg, a Swabian city just northwest of Salzburg. This group arrived in Georgia in 1734 and settled some twenty-five miles northwest of Savannah, where they founded a settlement which they named Ebenezer. By the time a second transport joined them a year later, they had realized that their land was infertile and inaccessible and the stream on which it was built, Ebenezer Creek, was unnavigable. When a third transport arrived in 1736, composed mostly of Upper Austrian and Carinthian exiles, the survivors at Ebenezer joined them at the Red Bluff on the Savannah River, bringing the name of the earlier settlement with them. The original site, which became the Trustees' cowpen or cattle ranch, was henceforth called Old Ebenezer.

A fourth and last transport, consisting of Salzburger exiles who had been sojourning in Augsburg and other Swabian cities, arrived in 1741. The Salzburgers were joined by Swiss and Palatine settlers from Purysburg, a Swiss settlement a short way down the Savannah River on the Carolina side, as well as by Palatine servants donated by the

---

[1] Most of this material has been extracted from the previous volumes of the *Detailed Reports* (Vols. 1-17, University of Georgia Press, Athens, Ga., 1966-1992) and the reader of these volumes may wish to disregard it.

Trustees. Finding insufficient fertile land on the Red Bluff, many Salzburgers moved their plantations to an area along Abercorn Creek, an almost blocked channel of the Savannah River, where the lowland was flooded and enriched each winter. After some gristmills and sawmills were built on Abercorn Creek, it was usually called the Mill River (*Mühl-Fluss*).

Despite considerable sickness and mortality and the hardships incident to settlement in a wilderness, the Salzburgers became the most successful community in Georgia. This relative success was largely due to the skill, devotion, and diligence of their spiritual leader, Johann Martin Boltzius, the author of most of these reports, and to the network of missionary and commercial interests that supported this Pietist settlement in North America. Boltzius and the other divines leading the Ebenezer congregation, Israel Christian Gronau, Herman Lemcke, Christian Rabenhorst and Christoph Friedrich Triebner, had been trained at the Friedrich University at Halle in Brandenburg-Prussia. All had taught there at the Francke Foundations, a charitable institution that was to have great influence on the development of Ebenezer.

Although Boltzius was at heart a minister, his secular responsibilities in Georgia molded him into a skillful administrator, economist, and diplomat. Some of the early reports were written by Boltzius' admiring younger colleague Gronau, who officiated whenever Boltzius was away, in Savannah or elsewhere, until his untimely death in 1745.

Boltzius' and his colleagues' journals were first edited contemporaneously by Samuel Urlsperger, the Senior of the Lutheran Ministry in Augsburg. Comparison of original extracts from the diaries surviving in Halle with Urlsperger's published edition shows that he took considerable liberty in deleting unpleasant reports and suppressing proper names, which he replaced with N. or N. N. There is reason to believe that Boltzius made an entry for every day, as he and all Halle missionaries had been instructed to do prior to their departure, and that Urlsperger made major deletions and some emendations for both diplomatic and practical reasons. In some cases he simply consolidated the material for two or more days into one. Urlsperger's deletions are not very logical: he often deleted a name in one passage even though it appears in another one, or else the person in question can be easily recognized. In the case of the present diaries for parts of 1744 and 1745, Urlsperger and his associates in Halle and London decided against publication altogether, for reasons which we shall discuss below.

As more German-speaking settlers moved to Ebenezer, the inhabitants began clearing land and moving to areas along the Mill River or Abercorn Creek, where their farms were called "the Plantations," as opposed to "the Town." Others established their farms along Ebenezer Creek. Whereas the Trustees had envisioned a colony of yeoman farmers, Boltzius gradually shifted to silk culture and lumber processing, activities encouraged by James Habersham, George Whitefield's orphanage manager and later a merchant and President of the Council, who became the Salzburgers' chief champion in Savannah. Ebenezer's dependencies continued to grow. The planters along Abercorn Creek built and maintained Zion Church, larger than Jerusalem Church in Ebenezer.

Despite his many secular duties, Boltzius remained primarily a man of God and worked diligently to keep his flock well instructed in Pietist practice. In view of the high infant mortality, it is not surprising that he sought to convince his listeners that God is an all-loving God who does everything for our own good, even if His purpose is beyond our human comprehension. He also had to free many parishioners from *Anfechtungen*, the temptation to doubt that God, through the merits of Christ, can save even the worst sinner if he repents and crawls into the wounds of Jesus. As a good Pietist, Boltzius constantly contrasts "the Law" of the Old Testament and the "Grace" of the New.

The present volume is No. 18 of the *Detailed Reports*. The material covers the year 1744 and the spring of 1745. The volume thus belongs chronologically between Volumes 10 and 11, but at the time the manuscripts for 1743 and 1747 were being translated and edited, excerpts for the years 1744 to 1746 could not be found. They had become separated from the other volumes in the archives of the Francke Foundation in Halle and had not been published in the German series of reports on the Salzburgers in America [1]. Thanks to the kind suggestion of Professor Kurt Aland (deceased) and Dr. Beate Köster, who at the time were editing the

---

[1] *Ausführliche Nachricht(en) von den Sal(t)zburgischen Emigranten, die sich in America niedergelassen haben...*, herausgegeben von Samuel Urlsperger, des evangelischen Ministerii in Augspurg Seniore und Pastore (der Hauptkirche zu Sankt Annen), Halle und Augsburg, in Verlegung des Halleschen Waisenhauses, 1.-18. Continuation, 1735 to 1753, and *Americanisches Ackerwerk Gottes, der zuverlässigen Nachrichten, den Zustand der americanischen erbauten Pflanzstadt Ebenezer In Georgien betreffend, aus dahere eingeschickten glaubwürdigen Diarien genommen...*, herausgegeben von Samuel Urlsperger, Augsburg, 3 Teile, 1753, 1755, 1759, and by Johann August Urlsperger, Teil 4, 1766.

letters of Heinrich Melchior Mühlenberg[1], we consulted an inadequate photostat dating to 1932 in the Library of Congress, from which an even poorer copy could be made. Since this copy of a copy was nearly illegible to the eyes of the present translators and editors, Dr. Peter Nolte of the Humboldt University of Berlin kindly transcribed the text for us as best he was able. Subsequently, we were able to locate the original documents, written in a relatively clear but minuscule hand, in the Halle archives; and the editors have checked Dr. Nolte's transcription against the original. However, since this English translation could not rely on a printed German version, as was true for the other volumes in this series, we felt that it would be pedantic and of little use to the reader to annotate each and every doubtful phrase or word. Instead, we have relied on the fit of names and events as reported in these diaries with those of the surrounding volumes. The editors and readers of the Salzburger story nonetheless look forward to a fully annotated and textually intact German edition of this and other materials from the Pietist settlements in North America.

The diaries in this volume cover the period from February 24 to November 1, 1744, and January 1 to 18 and March 2 to April 10, 1745, respectively. A brief excerpt was found from the diaries for 1746, which we have included, as well as the 1744 plans for the Salzburger mills, which are shown in an 18th century reproduction on the endsheets. This volume also reproduces several previously unknown documents in context. The entries for February 29 and May 20, 1744, contain extensive quotes from letters of December 14, 1743, and March 15, 1744, written by Heinrich Melchior Mühlenberg after his first year in Pennsylvania.[2] Also, many pages are devoted to the arrival and adventures of Johann Ulrich Driesler, a clergyman procured from Halle for Oglethorpe's indentured servants at Frederica. Driesler's letters are

[1] Aland, Kurt, and Köster, Beate, editors. *Die Korrespondenz Heinrich Melchior Mühlenbergs. Aus der Anfangszeit des Deutschen Luthertums in Nordamerika.* Texte zur Geschichte des Pietismus, im Auftrag der historischen Kommission zur Erforschung des Pietismus herausgegeben von Kurt Aland, Karl Gottschick and Erich Peschke vol. 1, 1740-1752, vol. 2, 1753-1762, vol. 3, 1763-1768, vol. 4, 1769-1776. Berlin, de Gruyter, 1986, 1987, 1990, 1992.

[2] These letters were lost and are only preserved in excerpt in the 1744 diaries. Both excerpts were printed, together with part of the diary entries, in volume 1 of *Die Korrespondenz Heinrich Melchior Mühlenbergs*, pp. 122-123 and 129-131. They appear in English translation in *The Correspondence of Heinrich Melchior Mühlenberg*, Vol. 1 (1740-1747), ed. and trans. by John W. Kleiner and Helmut T. Lehmann. Picton Press, 1993, pp. 144-145 and pp. 149-151.

quoted liberally, possibly reflecting the fact that in the absence of his very sick colleague, Christian Israel Gronau, Johann Martin Boltzius had secured the help of the newly arrived Johann Ludwig Mayer to copy his own diaries, quite likely using outside correspondence as a filler. The lingering illness and eventual death of Gronau is described quite movingly and clearly in Boltzius' own words.

The Ebenezer diaries were published for the edification of European evangelical Protestants. Their audience included many in the cities and towns of the Holy Roman Empire of the German Nation. Men and women in the nobility, merchants, and other Pietist groups followed the story of the transoceanic missions of the Halle Orphanage Foundations in detailed reports from British North America and the Danish East Indies. In 1747, in his preface to volume 13 of the *Ausführliche Nachricht(en),* Samuel Urlsperger, who is often referred to as one of the Fathers of the Salzburger settlement, explained the two-year lapse in publishing this annual series as follows:

> Those who have known from the outset how closely divine providence has linked my heart to the fate of the plantation town of Ebenezer ... well understand that only a number of important obstacles could have prevented me from making good on my promise in the preface to the 12th continuation of 15 September 1745 and the next volume of the Ebenezer diaries of 25 April 1746.... I do not think it necessary to recount these obstacles and their causes...[1]

It is the last sentence that gives us some clue as to the disappearance of the diaries. For, while losses of mail at sea were common throughout, careful transatlantic correspondents made sure that copies were kept at the place of origin and that these were recopied in case of loss. This was the rule in Ebenezer as well, and it appears from these diaries that in addition an English version was exacted by the Georgia Trustees.[2]

However, there was indeed good reason for not publishing the diaries. In 1744 and 1745, the Georgia colony was troubled both abroad and on these shores. Financial support was waning in central Europe during the Silesian Wars between Prussia and the House of Habsburg, the Georgia Trustees found themselves under attack by men like Thomas

---

[1] Preface to the 13th Continuation, Part 1, p.3.

[2] These translations, which placed an additional burden on the ministers, are not in any of the archives accessible to the editors. It is not known, therefore, whether they were kept continuously.

Stephens and the Savannah Malcontents, and James Oglethorpe had come under the shadow of the 1745 Jacobite uprising. But a greater and more direct danger for the Ebenezer enterprise was that the American environment had begun to take its toll. Because of the wars with Spain, the high rate of mortality normal for newcomers to the Southeastern shores could not be set off by new transports of continental immmigrants; in fact, the first large replacement had to wait until 1749. As a result, Ebenezer suffered, as did the rest of Georgia, from a severe labor shortage, and lacking the inclination and the capital to acquire slaves, the inhabitants were unable or unwilling to serve in the double role of independent farmers and of unpaid laborers at the orphanage, which was the economic and the spiritual center of the settlement.

As the reader will learn from the largely unedited material for these years, there was a gentle revolt in which the farmers demanded that their minister and leader, Johann Martin Boltzius, release the few women and children and single males from the orphanage and assign them as servants to their farms. But this news, not surprising to the American colonial mind familiar with similar labor shortages, would have endangered the financial support that Ebenezer received as a foreign outpost of the Halle Orphanage, which obtained its support in the form of philanthropic donations and bequests from patrons interested in the spiritual welfare of their protegees. This welfare, and further support, could not tolerate a rejection of the bonds of social order, labor discipline, and deference that characterized the charitable reform movements of the period.

However, while the Ebenezer community and its leaders faced internal conflicts in these years, they nonetheless maintained a pattern of growth while most of the surrounding English settlements were in decline. In contrast to the numerous and far more populous settlements in the Middle Colonies where the young Heinrich Melchior Mühlenberg underwent his trial by fire, Ebenezer continued to receive substantial and extraordinary support from sponsors on the European continent. And, in addition to charitable and religious motives, we can ever more clearly discern in these diaries the presence of a strong commercial element, above all in the references to the business interests of the Augsburg banker Christian von Münch. It is largely due to his support of the mills and sericulture, and to the resilience and never-ending willingness of Johann Martin Boltzius to engage in a series of agricultural and manufacturing experiments, that the internal strife of the years 1744-45 was settled by mutual compromise on the distribution of labor and other resources.

In concluding this series, we wish to point to a previously little noticed strand in the Salzburger story, the personal involvement of the ministers' wives. Usually referred to by their husbands as their nameless "helpmeets," Gertraud Boltzius and her sister Katharina Gronau, both née Kröhr, played a major if unacknowledged role in the *oeconomia* of Ebenezer. In particular, they were at the core of developing the skills required in silk manufacture, and their work can be traced from the year 1745 to the successful 1750s, when Ebenezer equalled if not surpassed Savannah in the production of cocoons and spun silk.

For a fuller understanding of the circumstances and activities of the Georgia Salzburgers and other German-speaking inhabitants of Ebenezer during the years 1744 and 1745, we refer the reader to the previous volumes and to several publications addressing specific aspects of the Georgia Salzburger settlement and its Pietist background.[1]

The support of the R. J. Taylor Jr. Foundation in Atlanta, Georgia, for part of the work on the 1744/45 manuscripts is gratefully acknowledged. The editors wish to thank the present and former Archivists of the Francke Foundations in Halle, Dr. Thomas Müller and Mr. Jürgen Storz, and the staff at the Library of Congress, Washington, D.C. for their help.

George Fenwick Jones   Renate Wilson

Baltimore, February 1995

---

[1] In particular, *The Georgia Dutch* and *The Salzburger Saga*, both by George F. Jones, Athens, University of Georgia Press, 1984 and 1992, and "Public works and piety: The missing Salzburger Diaries for 1744/45" by Renate Wilson, *Georgia Historical Quarterly*, 77: 336-366 (Summer 1993). The medical aspects referred to throughout this volume are set out in greater detail by Renate Wilson and Hans Joachim Poeckern, in "A continental system of medical care in colonial Georgia," *Medizin, Gesellschaft und Geschichte*. Jahrbuch des Instituts für Geschichte der Medizin der Robert Bosch Stiftung 9(1990): 99-126, 1992 and in a forthcoming monograph on Pietist medicine in North America. For the chronology of the relations between the Halle Pietists and their English associates, see most recently Renate Wilson, "Continental Protestant Refugees and their Protectors in Germany and London: Commercial and Denominational Networks," *Pietismus und Neuzeit* 20:101-118, 1994.

NOTE ON SOURCES

This volume is a translation of materials in the Library of Congress, Facsimiles from German Archives, *Missions-Bibliothek des Waisenhauses, Halle, Abteilung H IV (Nordamerika)* Fach J No. 8: 2/24/1744 to 11/1/1744; No. 9: 1/1/1745 to 4/16/1745.   The originals in the Francke Foundations in Halle are located in Missionsarchiv der Franckeschen Stiftungen, Series 5D9 and 5D12.   The material for 1746 is likewise in Missionsarchiv der Franckeschen Stiftungen, 5A11, pp. 280-84, item 67.   Text in brackets has been added by the editors to identify persons and places.

The titles of German books referred to in the diaries (mainly edification literature) are translated in the text to give some idea of their content, while the original titles and brief bibliographic information are given in the footnotes.   On the other hand, the titles and verses of hymns are left intact in the text or the footnotes, and their meanings and authors, when known, are given in Appendix III.   Biblical passages, when recognized, are rendered with the words of the King James version, even if the wording differs somewhat from that of the Luther translation.

FEBRUARY 1744

The 24th of February. The Lord has made this day a day of joy for us, for I have had much refreshment today from the company of our dear Pastor Driesler.[1] In both our churches, Zion and Jerusalem, he has preached the sweet and dear gospel of Christ on Galatians 11:20, which the Lord has brought so close to the hearts of our listeners that many have been moved and uplifted and some brought to tears.

Because our listeners know that, in the course of his voyage, Pastor Driesler suffered many losses in regard to his books and other belongings[2] and that several necessities cannot be had easily or only with many difficulties in Frederica, our listeners have been particularly eager to bring to my house so much fresh butter, lard or rendered butter, eggs, and meat that we have been much surprised and well impressed.

Pastor Driesler takes this rightly as a sign of the providence of our Heavenly Father and as the fulfillment of the verse: "I will never leave thee, nor forsake thee."[3] Together with the adjoined and following lessons from Hebrews 5:5-6, I have given him this as a message to take with him. Prior to my departure for Savannah, we had sung in the evening prayer meeting the first eight verses from the beautiful song: *O Jesu, Du bist mein*; and in today's prayer meeting, in which Mr. Driesler addressed the congregation and led the prayer, we followed with verses 9-12. They apply in particular to this dear man, as is known to everyone who knows his circumstances, including his temper and emotions in the face of the trials of his journey.

After the prayer meeting, we readied our package for mailing so that my dear colleague can take it to Savannah tomorrow and deliver it to Secretary Stephens.[4] He will accompany Mr. Driesler there and to the orphanage at that place [Bethesda]. In addition to the letters listed under date of February 8, we have enclosed letters to Mr. Verelst, Court

---

[1] After long delays and much red tape, Ulrich Driesler was finally sent as pastor to the German congregation at Frederica, on St. Simons Island. He soon visited Ebenezer and Savannah, where he preached to the Lutherans there.

[2] The boat on which he was traveling had capsized in the Rhine near Düsseldorf.

[3] Hebrews 13:5. Cf. Joshua 1:5.

[4] William Stephens, the Trustees' secretary in Georgia from 1737 to 1751.

Chaplain Ziegenhagen, Senior Urlsperger, Prof. [G. A.] Francke, Mr. Albinus, and several letters from members of our community.

We took leave of each other with much emotion. May the Lord bless this occasion in eternity. Mr. Driesler told us that his congregation consists of sixty-two souls, who truly use the benefits of his office. I have sent to these through their shepherd the 62nd chapter of Isaiah, for quiet contemplation.[1] When I later reread this text, it both impressed and edified me considerably, and I begged the Lord to fulfill its promise in us, for Frederica, and for our dear German homeland and also in East India.[2]

Our exchanges, the labor spent on preparing the package, and the time spent in taking leave took until around midnight; and many of our people would have liked to say goodbye to Pastor Driesler personally and to bear witness to the good that the Lord had given them through his service, if only there had been enough time. Still, he quickly wrote a letter to a patron and friend in Germany, which will be included in our package to London.

Saturday, the 25th of February. Among the letters just arrived is the written description of the gifts for Ebenezer which have flowed into the hands of Senior Urslperger from the Fountain of Divine Benevolence during the year from September 1742 to September last. Because there are many edifying points in this letter that deal with our orphanage, I have shared several important matters with adults and children this afternoon. We have used this occasion for singing and prayer. Particularly edifying were those letters that were sent along with the gifts to our dear Senior and which we read.

We were much impressed with the words of a patron and benefactor from Gera in November 1742: "The dear Salzburgers are in my mind night and day, and I hope that we will hear of our Savior's miracles of charity and beneficence although we learn that all of Georgia has been ruined by the Spaniards." Another dear friend wrote in that very month: "I hope that the clamor occasioned by the Spanish incursion will raise some attention in Europe and cause many more charitable deeds to be raised than previously." How must these dear friends have felt upon the

---

[1] It was a custom of the Pietists and other Evangelicals to send Bible verses to their friends for their contemplation.

[2] Boltzius is alluding to the Pietist missions in the Danish East Indian colony of Tranquebar.

news that the enemy could not touch us and was forced to beat an ignominious retreat?[1]

We in turn have been much fortified in our faith and led to great praise of the Lord. And, as much as He has truly fulfilled for these our friends their intercession, wishes, and hopes concerning our fate in His wisdom, goodness, and almighty power, He will fulfill what another friend wrote in January of last year in sending his charitable gift of love: "I fully believe that Ebenezer will become a great thing, so that it will be said that from the Ebenezer Zion the beautiful light of the Lord will rise over all of America, Amen! May this come true!"

This noble patron, too, could not have known at the time of his writing that our great Lord had given us not only Jerusalem but also Zion Church and thus has shown in this, as in many other things which at first were small or entirely lacking, that His plans for Ebenezer are manifold for His glory and the extension of His Kingdom. He has always started with humble matters or from nothing. For He can make something of nothing, much from little, and great things from small beginnings. It is this which fortifies us in our current endeavor, for the Lord is prepared to give us in the orphanage a spacious instead of a small building, and He has given us much proof on other occasions that He has plans for the orphanage and for the entire congregation which we cannot foresee at this point. For its not only for material things that He has led us on this long path to Georgia from such weighty circumstances.

May He give those of us who belong to Ebenezer the grace not to impede His works and intentions, but may He make us instead into vessels of His compassion and tools of His grace. The last part of what was read today concerned the desire of a lying-in woman for us to humbly praise Him for the divine help which had mercifully maintained her and her child, and also help her implore the Lord for His continued help and grace for herself and her child. The lessons learned from this may well serve to comfort Mrs. Kalcher and Mrs. Kogler, who are lying in at the orphanage in circumstances that cause us much apprehension. For the Lord, who has not abandoned nor forsaken others, still lives. After the prayer to this dear Lord we sang: "The Lord has never, nor

---

[1] Oglethorpe had defeated the Spaniards at the battle of Bloody Marsh on July 7, 1742.

ever shall, be separated from His people. He remains their assurance, their life, salvation, and peace. He leads with a motherly hand, etc."[1]

The 27th of February. For some time now, the water in the river has risen high enough to flood the low-lying banks, to the point that Kieffer's and Roek's[2] fields that lie across from us in South Carolina have been completely flooded. This will spoil all their European crops[3] planted in the fall and spring, which misfortune has now occurred several years in a row. The shoemaker Roeck will probably give up this piece of land entirely and move across to join us or else go to Port Royal. He had some heads of cattle, cows, and calves on this land; and all would have perished if our people had not swum them across with much difficulty and ferried them in our big boat. Since the orphanage has served him and continues to serve him well in these circumstances and his cattle have been brought here for herding and care, he and his wife are rendering us loving service by showing us the proper way to handle silkworms so that they may yield good and plentiful silk for reeling. I hear that they are now learning about many advantages they did not know of before.

Because we have had warm weather throughout, the mulberry trees have borne plentiful leaves and the worms have come out of their eggs or seeds, although in past years they did so only in March. Although the Trustees have ordered the Italian woman in Savannah,[4] who receives good a yearly salary in return for little work, to instruct two of our young women in making and reeling silk, nothing seems to come of it. She is ready to take in apprentices, but it is clear that they would not learn anything because she is unwilling to instruct others in her art.

A couple of clever and industrious women stand ready to go to Savannah for instruction, if only the authorities could make her teach others her art willingly and honestly. She is so envious that she will not permit her reeling wheel to be copied. But I shall see to it that I get it, even if I have to pay a large sum to a man who lives close to Savannah and has made a wheel. Yet I shall ask the authorities for their advice

---

[1] *Der Herr ist noch und nimmer nicht von seinem Volk geschieden. Er bleibt ihre Zuversicht, ihr Leben, Heil und Frieden. Mit Mutterhänden leitet er, etc.* From strophe 5 of the hymn *Sei Lob und Ehr dem höchsten Gut*, by Johann Jacob Schultze.

[2] Jacob Reck (or Roeck) had come to Ebenezer in 1740 as a non-commissioned officer to recruit Salzburgers for Oglethorpe's Florida campaign but had only succeeded in recruiting some indentured "Palatine" servants.

[3] Wheat, barley, rye, and oats as opposed to the native crops maize, beans, and sweet potatoes.

[4] Mary Camuse (Maria Camuso), the silk expert in Savannah.

first. For, if we cannot reel the silk at our place, it is hardly worth making the people put any work into it, for the Lord Trustees will give only 2 sh per pound of cocoons, or silk balls, although from the start they have paid 4 sh a pound, from which the people in Purysburg have long made the greatest profit. I have been told that in Charleston reeled silk is paid at £10 of their currency, that is, £1 8 sh. 7 pence Sterling, although that is hard to believe. One pound Sterling would be a good price that would encourage our people to show more industry in this endeavor.

Whichever way this goes, the many trees at the orphanage will not have been planted in vain, but we hope to profit from them as much as the Lord will bless them for us. If more people, and among them servants, were to come here, many would profit from silk making, brick making, and the planting of grapes. Now we must be content with small beginnings, since every family head, including Kalcher with his helpers, has his hands full with planting and tending the crops and the cattle, not to speak of miscellaneous work and many obstacles. If we could hire just one man for making silk and paid him just one shilling for a day's work (for no one, not even a woman, will give a day's work unless the meals are included) this would at most take six weeks or forty-two days, for this is the time it takes until the silkworms spin their cocoons.

If we had more people here and the daily wages were set according to the work done, as is only reasonable, many useful enterprises could be undertaken in this comfortable climate. If through the kind providence of our heavenly Father, we reach the point that our inhabitants can devote themselves more to European than to local crops and can prepare their fields in the fall and early spring with a plow, they will have more time to attend to their silkworms. Now they must plant their Indian corn during the silk worm season, and all must help - men, women, and the older children - if they are to have a sufficient crop. In this country the orphanage cannot keep children long after they are grown, for they return either to their mothers or to other relatives to help them keep house. Or else other good people who have small children ask the orphanage to let them have the grown girls for housework, and the larger boys are trained for men's work so that we have little help from them. We recount these circumstances for the sake of our friends who, as I have noticed, find it hard to accept that silk making and other useful enterprises do not progress as swiftly as they would wish.

Tuesday, the 28th of February. Yesterday I heard that a sickly man and his family lacked meat, and we were much touched by their plight.

Therefore I came to think of how I could help this man and other poor people with some of the blessings that have arrived here recently from Augsburg. Last night, before going to sleep, I had drawn up a little list of the poorest among them and calculated a little assistance for their daily food. This morning our orphanage manager, Kalcher, told me that he had seized a dangerous ox last night that was endangering the cattle on our plantations. The ox is one of the cattle that I bought in Savannah from the heirs of the deceased Maillet. We would have liked to get rid of this ox long ago, but we did not manage to catch it. However, now that we need meat for our poor, this animal must have come here on its own, and we are now able to help our needy better than with money by giving direct gifts of food. For, after all the cattle deaths,[1] meat has become quite scarce. I thought of the dear words "For so he giveth his beloved sleep."[2] The gifts of the Lord are all the sweeter if He offers them to us in such circumstances that so clearly speak to His fatherly providence. Here too it is written: "For when the weak came, thou quickly thought of them,"[3] likewise, "Thou art free on earth, the assurance of the pious. In tribulation and hardship, thou dost not forsake thine own."[4]

We find in our dear Senior Urlsperger's letters that a certain person of rank and great station in Germany has promised our dear Ebenezer a hundred ducats if the Lord will let him return home in peace and with His blessing. If I should be empowered to dispose of this gift at my discretion, this sum will, God willing, be used to buy several cows for the poor among us who have lost most of their cattle through the plague. May the Lord grant this distinguished benefactor his and our wishes; and we shall implore Him for this before His throne with prayers, sighs, wishes, and words of thanks.

Wednesday, the 29th of February. This morning my dear colleague [Gronau] returned in good health by way of Abercorn. He brought me letters from Reverend Mühlenberg and Mr. Vigera,[5] in which we learned

---

[1] Ebenezer had recently lost many cattle to a cattle disease, apparently blackwater.

[2] Psalms 127:2. Luther's rendition fits this context better: *Denn seinen Freunden gibt er's schlafend.*

[3] *Denn als die Schwachen kamen, hast du gar bald an sie gedacht.* From the third strophe of the hymn *Man lobt dich in der Stille*, by Johann Rist.

[4] *Du bist doch frei auf Erden, der Frommen Zuversicht. In Trübsal und Beschwerden, lasst Du den Deinen nicht.* From a hymn.

[5] Heinrich Melchior Mühlenberg had stopped off for a few days at Ebenezer on his way to Philadelphia to report to Boltzius as the senior of the Pietist missions. Johann Vigera, a citizen of Strassburg, had conducted the fourth Salzburger transport to

of much misfortune that requires our intercession and prayer. His [Mühlenberg's] letter is dated December 14 and written in Philadelphia,[1] and his ardent desire for letters from Court Chaplain Ziegenhagen and our other Fathers[2] speaks from every line he writes. Since he did not receive as much as a single line during his entire first year (which he had just finished at the time of his writing), the people there became suspicious that Mr. Mühlenberg had not received a proper call. This suspicion was fanned by the idle words of a recently arrived German preacher, Johann Conrad Andrea, who had been dismissed from his office in Zweibrücken yet brought good recommendations from eleven universities. As a result, our dear brother Mühlenberg found himself in considerable difficulty since he has been beset by the creditors for the debts arising from the church construction. He will write his own account of the matter.

Last year thirteen boatloads of German people arrived in Philadelphia and five in New York, who have brought with them, in addition to this Andrea, two fine young Swedish students as their preachers. These came equipped with a license or power of attorney from the Bishop of London permitting them to assume their office. Such a certificate counts for much in Philadelphia. Another preacher, Mr. Wagner,[3] who had gone to New England with a party of Württembergers, has now arrived in Philadelphia with his wife and children and assumed office on the Indian frontier. Mr. Mühlenberg has good hopes for him. He is displacing a disorderly man, named [Johann] Caspar Stöver, who has been discharged by his parishioners. It is to this Stöver that Pastor Driesler sent the letter he had brought for Mr. Mühlenberg. I much regret this mistake, of which I have written to Court Chaplain Ziegenhagen.

The above-mentioned Andrea is causing much trouble for poor Mr. Mühlenberg and much division in the congregation through his calumny,

---

Ebenezer and was now at Philadelphia.

[1] This letter was lost and is preserved only in excerpt in the 1744 diaries. See Introduction, p. viii, n. 2.

[2] The "Reverend Fathers" of the Georgia Salzburgers were Samuel Urlsperger, Senior of St. Ann's Church in Augsburg, Gotthilf August Francke, head of the Francke Foundations in Halle, and Friedrich Michael Ziegenhagen, court chaplain in London.

[3] The American editors of *The Correspondence of H. M. Mühlenberg* give the name as Tobias Wagner. For a full description of the Lutheran and Reformed Churches in Pennsylvania and the middle colonies, including names and brief biographies of ordained ministers of the Lutheran and Reformed faith, both with a calling and interlopers, see Charles H. Glatfelter, *Pastors and People: German Lutheran and Reformed Churches in the Pennsylvanian Field, 1717-1793*. Kutztown Publishers, 1980.

insults, promises, and smooth words in his sermons. But the Lord is on the side of the truth and helps our dear brother bear his great burden, under which he sighs yet continues his work and carries on with but little means because the church construction has saddled him with a great debt. After reporting on much strife in Pennsylvania in both secular and ecclesiastical matters, he adds the following:

> Alas, dear Brother. Please tell your congregation of the great advantages you enjoy compared to us. You cannot in all eternity render sufficient thanks to God for the fact that you and your flock are sitting all by yourself in your remote corner and are provided so abundantly for your souls and adequately for your bodies. Here it is like a nest of wasps and bees, with much flying about and much noise. Many are deprived of their eternal salvation by the unbounded liberty prevailing here. I have often wished to be just a schoolmaster or catechist in Ebenezer, but I must be what the Lord has called me to be. The Lord gives more blessing to your dear Salzburgers than to any other people in the world, but He shall also call to account those who refuse to be led to repentance by God's goodness.

In his letter of December 5, Mr. Vigera writes that he left Charleston on November 7 on board a Dutch sloop and arrived well and healthy in New York on the 19th of that month. He stayed there for three days and then departed for Philadelphia, traveling by land and sea, and arriving there on the first of Advent, namely the 27th of November. Who was happier than Pastor Mühlenberg at receiving this friend? He has taken him as a guest into his little rented house and is giving him much good in his want.

Mr. Zwiffler[1] is said to have left the Herrnhuters[2] and is now quite neutral in religious matters, that is, he believes almost nothing. Thus one judgment follows another upon disloyalty and ingratitude toward the spiritual gifts of God.

---

[1] Andreas Zwiffler had come as apothecary with the first Salzburger transport but left in 1737 for Pennsylvania, where he advertised his apothecary's shop in the *Pennsylvania Gazette*.

[2] A missionary sect led by Count Nikolaus Ludwig von Zinzendorf and known in England and America as the Moravian Brethren or *Unitas Fratrum*.

MARCH 1744

Thursday, the 1st of March. Although I promised Mr. Thilo[1] to pay those men who would chop wood for him and build a kitchen, he asked again yesterday evening whether anything would come of it. I noticed that he mistrusted me and doubted that I would pay for the work when it was done. Therefore he asked to have it in writing. Also, he asserted that three or four years ago he had been forced to pay someone five shillings for transplanting and pruning his peach trees, although I had promised to pay for that. I know nothing of either the eight pence or the five shillings, and I am a bit surprised that he should have kept such a trivial matter in his memory for so long and that this should have been the cause of his suspicions against me.

I shall give him the five shillings and eight pence, whatever the true story is. I also gave him a written authorization signed by me, but I stated therein that this document was only to assure the men who are cutting wood for the medico Thilo and building his kitchen that they will be duly paid. That is why he brought the piece of paper back to me and demanded that I add two words: "by me." I have heard elsewhere that he is collecting money for travel to Pennsylvania. He does not seem to think of himself as being a tenacious person and lover of money. Since our last conversation, he and his wife have attended both sermons and prayer meetings on a regular basis. Today he said that his wife found much edification on these occasions but, if he were not to receive cut wood without payment on his part, he would be forced to stay away from the prayer meetings, since he would have to use the time to cut wood on his own just before sunset and also during the morning hours. We shall ask him about that, and may God grant that he finally recognize his own nature.

Yesterday he stayed away from the prayer meeting and missed much that would have been good for his soul. Surgeon [Ludwig] Mayer[2] has received a letter from Mr. Vigera in Philadelphia, of which he told me the following details: He had a difficult journey from Charleston to Philadelphia by way of New York and New Brunswick, which had brought him much adversity and inconvenience on both land and water.

---

[1] Ernst Christian Thilo had arrived in 1738 to be the Salzburgers' physician. He was a student of Johann Junker, the head of the medical institutions of the Halle orphanage, and tended to be at odds with Boltzius for medical and financial reasons.

[2] Johann Ludwig Mayer, or Meyer, had come with the fourth Salzburger transport on the recommendation of a patron in South Germany. He served as a surgeon and practiced in competition with Thilo, but in addition he became justice of the peace and served as a trading agent for the banker von Münch.

He would not advise anyone to undertake such a journey during the winter. There is little to the profit that people there expect to gain by using English copper coins, and it is not true that a ha'penny is worth a full pence there. True, everything in foodstuffs is to be had there as in Germany, but at a high price; and lodging is very dear. Much has to be spent on clothing, since one can not be dressed poorly as in Georgia, for this puts one at risk of being despised by others.

He writes that people there live in boundless liberty so that there is great danger of being misled into error, and there is a large measure of confusion in religious matters. However, he fears little in this respect since he did not go much into company. He has heard from conscientious people, and from the Reverend Mühlenberg, that Mr. Zwiffler, now that he has left the Herrnhuters, has ceased to believe in anything and has become a mocker of religion and an atheist. He is practicing as a pharmacist and can hardly make a living even as a single man. Mr. Vigera wrote me that, shortly before his arrival, a whole boat load of Herrnhuters had arrived from Rotterdam. A German newspaper sent to Mr. Mayer reported that the Count[1] had announced a general synod at a certain place where all his bishops are to convene from all parts of the world.

Wednesday, the 7th of March.   The widow of the late Matthias Bacher[2] told me recently with much sorrow that in Germany she had let other servants seduce her into sinning against the sixth commandment[3] by taking food and drink belonging to her masters too freely. I told her that she should in turn refresh other poor Christians with the material goods that the Lord would gradually grant her on her land and that she should also pray for the masters whom she had thus offended. Since then she has been disturbed on this account, and today she came and brought me £3 Sterling, which I should distribute among pious poor folk according to my own discretion. They should pray for her that God grant her mercy and forgive her her sins and also free her from indolence of spirit.

---

[1] The reference is to Count Ludwig von Zinzendorff, founder of the Herrnhuter sect (often referred to as the Moravian Brethren or Unitas Fratrum). Zinzendorff, a pupil of the Halle orphanage, competed with the Halle Pietists both in Germany and in the American colonies.

[2] Maria Bacher served as midwife at Ebenezer.

[3] Following Luther (and Roman Catholic usage) Boltzius numbers this the seventh commandment, the one against stealing, not adultery.

Her son-in-law, honest Theobald Kieffer [Jr.], had a bad nightmare the other night, when he felt that he had seen the devil in his ugly shape distributing foodstuffs to a large crowd. He himself had at first followed him but then he had withdrawn into the wounds of the Lord Jesus, which had caused the devil to rage all the more at him. With his honest wife he cried when he recounted this dream, and the good widow was much impressed by this. This, too, the Lord sends us as a reminder before our Feast of Remembrance and Thanksgiving so that we may recognize His goodness and so that the pious among us may be moved to His praise.

During this and the last week He has shown to all His children newly born among us His grace by means of Holy Baptism, although they themselves were unable to pray for this. To the adults, therefore, goes the command: "Step up to me comforted to see the seat of mercy. Nothing can come to you from the Son of God but love and mercy, indeed He is waiting with longing."[1]

Thursday, the 8th of March. This afternoon I had to bring a little gift of money to young [Johann Georg] Mayer on his plantation. I took this opportunity to speak to him concerning the verse "I will not fail thee, nor forsake thee"[2] and other related truths like John 1 and Hebrews 13. His wife was not at home but had gone with Mrs. Lackner[3] to visit that bearer of the cross, Mrs. Zant. I do not doubt that what they hear and see there will be to their Christian profit.

Young Mayer[4] has cultivated his land. This caused him much backbreaking pain at the beginning, but the good plantation he was able to acquire so miraculously has given him courage; and his strength has grown with his work. Thus he was able to use this first year to prepare a good tract of land for planting and to erect a long and durable fence with the help of his neighbors, which will last him many a year. With regard to this Mayer, I had many initial worries that he would have little success here since he would not be able to practice his trade.[5] But, now

---

[1] *Tretet mir getrost zum Throne, da den Gnadenstuhl zu sehen. Es kann auch von Gottes Sohn, nichts als Lieb und Huld geschehen, ja er wartet mit verlangen....* From a hymn.

[2] Joshua 1:5

[3] Boltzius uses the variant form Lechner, but the family later appears only as Lackner.

[4] Johann Georg Mayer had come with his older brother Johann Ludwig with the fourth Salzburger transport in 1741. Trained as a purse-maker, and finding little work at Ebenezer, he sought work elsewhere and does not appear in the *Detailed Reports* until returning and establishing a plantation.

[5] The Salzburgers had little need for purses.

that I see the opposite to be true, I am all the more relieved. I recited to him the verse: "What I do thou knowest not now; but thou shalt know hereafter."[1] God will have His good and salutary reason why He beckoned to him to give up his life as a traveling artisan and brought him to this wilderness.

Lackner is his neighbor, and I learned from both him and Mayer that the Lord has crowned with His grace my recent instructions from the Lord's word to the young Mrs. Lackner. It seems that she is clearly on the road to Christian improvement. I showed them my happiness on this account and left some needed advice with the husband. If he follows it and becomes obedient through God's grace, he will be better able to guide his wife.

Senior Urlsperger had remembered this Lackner in his letter, and I read him the greetings and wishes of his young stepson; and the words seem to have made a good impression on him. Young Schrempf in Augsburg hopes that his late mother's [Mrs. Lackner's] blessings and prayers might be of benefit to them. I left for him and his absent young wife the verse that our dear Senior used with regard to those of the fourth transport who were ill and have recovered: That they might now praise him since "He died for them and rose again."[2]

At the time of our Thanksgiving and Memorial Feast it was again most appropriate for us to take the occasion to read publicly a letter from our dear Father in Christ [Urlsperger], which was well suited to prepare us for the forthcoming ceremony. For, in this letter, many of the spiritual and material benefits that our Lord has bestowed upon us so far and continues to bestow upon us are recounted; and, in particular, express mention is made of last year's Thanksgiving and Memorial Day: "I and many others have shared in our hearts your joy at the generosity shown during and after the Spanish attack and at the time of your commemorative ceremony. Thus it has likewise been a great joy to read in your letters that the word of the Lord was already being preached in the Zion Church. May the Lord be praised that there, too, 'the sparrow hath found a house, and the swallow a nest for herself.'"[3]

In what follows, the venerable Senior [Urlsperger] lets us know that our dear Lord has already provided for the future of our church, school, and orphanage. May God be praised on high. We all rejoice together, and our faith is strengthened and the glory of the Lord exalted at these

---

[1] John 13:7.

[2] 2 Corinthians 5:15.

[3] Psalms 84:3.

words of our dear Senior: "The costs of the Zion Church are moderate, and the Lord will discharge the cost of £31." And that which our dear Senior hoped for, believed in, and wrote to us has in fact taken place even before his letter arrived here. For, through the Lord's munificence, the debts for both the churches are fully paid, and enough remains to pay for a graceful yet sturdy fence encircling the church, with two gates and latches, which was erected instead of a churchyard wall.

Once our carpenters have free time, they will finish the top floor of the Zion Church and also install proper benches, window frames, shutters, and glass windows as well as a pulpit, for all of which the Lord will provide in His time. The bulk of the boards needed for this work have been prepared and paid for, and comfortable seats for the parishionners and a raised platform with a table for the minister have been prepared ad interim. During today's repetition hour, our dear Lord gave us much edification from the gospels in the important words addressed to the sick who have been made well. Thus we read in this connection 2 Corinthians 5:14-16, and an application was made from this text.

An equal blessing was received from the repetition, by way of instruction, of the words from Judith 9:3-4. Those Christians who remain separate from public service and make do on their own with reading, meditation, and prayer are truly standing in their own light and are depriving themselves of much edification. For in their private readings they fail to see much that is of importance in the word, and our benevolent Lord calls out something in public which leaves a useful impression and characterizes the ministerial office as His divine order. Among our listeners, this should be carefully noted above all others by Mr. Thilo, who now also attends the reading of the letters.

Saturday, the 10th of March. Today, the weather being pleasant and comfortable, we celebrated our annual week of remembrance and thanksgiving, on which occasion our listeners, both men and women, assembled in large numbers at the Jerusalem Church. The Lord blessed and strengthened in body and soul both of us who read His word, and He has given us much spiritual joy and nourishment from the rich treasure of His Son's grace.

In the morning, we began Jeremiah 5:23-24, from which we heard of the evil conduct of the children of the world in their use of divine benevolence. By contrast, we were impressed by the beautiful text in 2 Samuel 17:18, which presents the prudent conduct of one of the Lord's children in partaking of the Lord's benevolence.

In the exordium, my dear colleague spoke to the words in Isaiah 52:7 "Zion, thy God reigneth;" and, in accordance with the dear words of the Lord from Zephania 3:14-17, he instructed us in the good that we would enjoy in the spiritual land of Zion under the reign of His Kingdom of Grace. Also, on the occasion of discussing these important texts, with the help of the Holy Spirit, we have not only recalled the many spiritual and material benefits which the Lord has bestowed upon us and continues to grant us in these ten years of pilgrimage in this country. For the good Lord has also talked to us of the many things in the distant future, in that (as we were told in a letter addressed to us) He has a whole sackful of gifts which He is just about ready to bestow on us.

We compare in these circumstances 2 Samuel 9:7-8 so that we may recognize, after the example of David, not only the great munificence and indescribable bounty of the Lord Jesus, but also our duty, like David and Mepsiboseth, to humbly accept the promised gifts with a heart full of gratitude while aware of our lack of merit.

God in His fatherly wisdom had arranged the conjunction of several very pleasant circumstances which could not but increase our edification, rejoicing in the Lord's bounty, and heartfelt praise: For

1). This morning at the break of dawn young Mrs. Lackner in the orphanage has given birth to a healthy and well-formed son, with the very special assistance of the Lord, to whom she and Mrs. Kalcher have dedicated themselves with body and soul. Lackner himself informed me of this before morning service with much joy and praise of the Lord.

2). Unexpectedly, our heavenly father has brought back to health His maidservant, Mrs. Zant (the widow of the late Piltz) and her sick child and has so strengthened them that she could attend church today and fulfill her wish to celebrate with us this joyous feast of remembrance and thanksgiving.

3). Contrary to all our expectations, the Lord has seen to it that, in the order of worship, the 118th Psalm was read in our public Bible reading at the outset of today's service. This psalm fits our circumstances right well, and we garnered from it much instruction and comfort for our future lives. I reminded my listeners before the sermon that this coincidence had left a salutary impression upon me and had informed them of what I know from our blessed Luther in regard to this psalm. For he cherished it especially because it had often offered him much comfort and had helped him in the most hopeless straits from which no angel or man, even if he had been the greatest monarch on earth, could have delivered him.

And that is why he was wont to say, of this 118th Psalm in particular, "This is my psalm." And we here have just the same right to this psalm and should therefore read it with prayerful reverence and ask the Lord for its right use. Moreover, since in reading the text from 2 Samuel 7:17-18, we learned that our dear David was a great and true lover of the divine word and a servant of the Lord and of public divine service, so today, on three occasions, we read the following 119th Psalm as is customary with us, that is before and after the sermon and during catechisation. Here, we could recognize from the manifold professions of David the true and dear treasure that we have in the word of the Lord and that we thus must use it well both night and day and in the various circumstances of our lives.

4). The children recited the 84th Psalm in the morning and the 132nd Psalm in the afternoon, which they had been instructed to learn by heart.

5). I demonstrated from the life of David, in comparison with Genesis 32:10 and the example of Joseph, the meaning of the important words of David, i.e., "Who am I, oh my God, and what is my house, that thou hast brought me hither" (2 Samuel 7:18); and I applied these words to our experience of the Lord's rich bounty on our journey, and in both Old and New Ebenezer and on the Mill and Ebenezer Creek. Then I read the last part of Pastor Mühlenberg's letter which we have already quoted in our diary entry of February 29, so that young and old could recognize the manifold gifts the Lord has bestowed upon us, and what duties are incumbent upon us and the serious accounting we must render if we make ill use of these gifts.

6). After the afternoon service, and in the presence of the entire congregation, the child born this morning was baptized; and this baptism could not but be most impressive and edifying after all the edifying things we had previously sung, read, and heard. Surely the Lord Jesus has fulfilled His wonderful and mysterious great promise from Zephaniah 3:14-17 in this little child, which He has marked with the sign of the cross on its breast and forehead as His lamb and property. This year, beginning with the first of January, fourteen children have been born and baptized in Ebenezer and survive to this day. Christians care much about the baptisms that are experienced not only among their own but among the children of others, but in the past and in the present.

7). The hymns that were sung in the morning and afternoon were both important and edifying. Thus, in the morning, we sang *Nun danket all, und bringet ihr*; *O, dass ich tausend Zungen hätte*, and the 1st and

5th verses of *Solt' ich meinem Gott nicht singen?* In the afternoon, we had *Lobe den Herrn, den mächtigen König der Ehren; Lasset uns den Herrn preisen und vermehren*, and *Man lobt dich in der stille.*

8). In our prayers to the Lord we also thought of our dear Fathers, benefactors, and friends; and my dear colleague and all of us wished upon them all the good that has been promised to them from a full heart and mouth by the Lord our God and the King of their souls, the mighty Savior, who is with us and with them. For this promise is clear from our afternoon text, Zephania 3:14-17. And may He also fortify His faithful servants in their hard labors and many sufferings in East India and let them taste and relish the strength and the sweetness of the above text and of the 118th Psalm. Finally, we held the repetition hour; and at its close we prayed for ourselves, our land, our German homeland, and both known and unknown benefactors. In that hour, we sang with much pleasure the incomparably beautiful hymn *Lobe, lobe meine Seele, den der heist Herr Zebaoth.*

Thursday, the 15th of March. Yesterday I was able to finish my business with the authorities and in other places in Savannah early enough to be able to leave this morning after two o'clock. By twelve o'clock, I was again with my family; and the boat will be at the mill before nightfall.[1] Our dear Lord has worked much good through the service of Pastor Driesler among the German people in and around Savannah so that they have experienced much love for him and desire either him or another honest man as a preacher. He reached his people in Frederica safely in a few days. He felt a bit ill on his return but has improved since, as I gather from his own letter to the German butcher Altherr in Savannah.[2]

He also mentions in his letter that Frederica has been full of fear and apprehension since the news arrived that the Spaniards are now ready for another attack on Savannah. Colonel Stephens and another friend who saw the commanding officer [Horton] in Frederica told me of this matter as follows: "The large English man of war with forty cannon which is stationed in Port Royal ran aground on a rock and sank off Providence[3] after it had captured a Spanish boat loaded with silver. The many sailors

---

[1] Boltzius must have debarked at Abercorn and returned home on horseback to save time.

[2] Johann Altherr, or Alther, was a Swiss from St. Gall.

[3] There were several colonial settlements in the Caribbean area named Providence. This cannot be the one in Rhode Island but may have been New Providence in the Bahamas.

aboard tried to save their lives on the long boats as best they could when they sighted a Spanish sloop in the vicinity which the English sailors seized and sailed to Providence. Thence they were brought to Charleston on English vessels.

On the Spanish sloop they found letters informing the governor in St. Augustine that seven thousand men were ready on board ship and smaller vessels to attack the English coast near St. Augustine in strength. Col. Stephens does not lend much credence to this news, but Pastor Driesler reported it quite seriously and with much worry. The Lord, who has until now given us protection through His arms and who has given us food for soul and body through His gentle hand daily and truly, will be with us if we only cleave to him in faith. He will not render us as a spoil to the teeth of the enemy.[1] May He work a good effect in the hearts of the people with this cry of war.

In Frederica, there is now an abundance of victuals, so that the beef and pork which several men from our community had sent there for sale would not have found a buyer had not General Oglethorpe left orders to buy at a good price everything that the people of Ebenezer might send there or bring on their own.

A good friend in London sent me in all confidence the journal of Colonel Stephens, which has been printed in London. The journal covers the period from the end of 1740 to the end of the following year. The journal contains many insulting and obviously wrong accusations against the person, the teaching, and the orphanage of Mr. Whitefield [Bethesda].[2] Therefore it is small wonder that the Lord Trustees have a poor view of Mr. Whitefield and his people in Bethesda. The teaching of rebirth and justification which Mr. Whitefield has presented here is called in this journal an empty and abstruse doctrine. It speaks of the Divine service of the New Testament in such a manner that it is clear that the author is no friend of the truth of the gospels and of those who preach them honestly and obey them. This volume does not contain one word about Ebenezer, but I have been told that I and my congregation are mentioned in the previous volume, which my friend did not have before him.

I rightly fear that the gentlemen in Savannah will proceed with us as they have done with Mr. Whitefield and his associates in their orphan-age; that is, they appear friendly and give us good assurances and praise

---

[1] Cf. Psalms 124:6.

[2] George Whitefield had established an orphanage on the Halle model ten miles south of Savannah.

to our face, but in secret they write many stories to the Lord Trustees. The worst about this is that the Trustees in turn keep such matters to themselves, and therefore the innocent cannot defend themselves and demonstrate their innocence through the truth. For these printed journals are kept quite secret, and it is quite likely that nobody in London but the Lord Trustees are aware of their contents. Perhaps the esteemed Mr. Ziegenhagen would consider it worth his while to seek knowledge of these journals, so that, if we are mentioned *malo sensu*, he could correct these impressions for the Lord Trustees and other friends.

I have often asked the gentlemen in Savannah to let me know in all frankness whenever they find fault with me or my congregation so that we both might give a full explanation and improve matters. But I have learned on a number of occasions that they will not accede to this request and secretly harbor some ill will against us. Recently, I asked the second counsellor, Mr. Watson, if he had revealed his mind to Mrs. Rheinländer, to the effect that now that General Oglethorpe and Mr. [Thomas] Jones, our patrons, have left the country, I no longer hold any power in Ebenezer. Whoever has a complaint should come to Savannah, where he will find support. While he denied this, he was quite cool in his answer.

The Italian woman [Maria Camuso] who is in charge of the silk enterprise in Savannah will take in two girls to teach them the art of silk-making and reeling, but she told me that the President and his Assistants had advised her that not Ebenezer but Savannah should have pride of place. Only if she could not find any girls there would our apprentices be considered.

In the meantime, one week passes after the other, and the girls cannot learn by watching her how to deal with the silkworms from the very start of the season. Colonel Stephens has promised me to let me know shortly if and when I should send the two women for silk-making and reeling to Savannah. Also, I have urgently requested that they decide in council whether or not I should have the power to adjudicate some civil matters in Ebenezer and to deter, within Christian love and seriousness, the wicked from their offending ways. I was asked whether I had written to the Lord Trustees in this regard; I answered, "No," but I would do it if they should consider it necessary. I do not much like the idea of complaining of our local authorities to the Lord Trustees, although I have many an occasion to do so. May God turn it all to the best advantage.

This evening, we read the first part of the letter of Pastor Mühlenberg from Philadelphia. Previously, for the memory of the congregation, we had repeated through question and answer some of the important points that had been impressed upon us before my voyage in the important letter of Court Chaplain Ziegenhagen. We learned that our wise and benevolent Lord instructs our dear Fathers and friends in mind and pen when they write us and that He has indeed often caused such advice to reach us just when our circumstances required particular counsel and comfort. Thus we can clearly see His fatherly providence and care for us.

The letter from our dear Senior Urslperger was so designed as to fit most perfectly into the preparation for our day of remembrance and thanksgiving. And thus it is with the points which we considered in our dear letter from Court Chaplain Ziegenhagen, on two occasions: Monday in the Jerusalem church and Tuesday in the Zion Church. He most strongly and lovingly reminded us that the Lord has so far extended His arm to protect us and has extended His gentle hand to provide for our spiritual and material needs. Now that there is again much talk here of a renewed Spanish attack on this colony, we recognize why our prudent and benevolent Lord has caused these important and pleasing matters which we have experienced through His divine power and grace to be impressed on our minds: to wit, that we shall firmly grasp this powerful hand of the Lord in faith and humble ourselves under His hand, or yet flee into the fortress of which it is said, the name of the Lord is a mighty fortress,[1] the just shall flee there and find refuge.

Said letter also stated that the believers are part of the testament which the Father has bequeathed with His Son and our dearest Savior. And whosoever shall attack the testament of this strong Savior in fact attacks Christ Himself. And part of this testament are the fourteen children who were born and baptized among us this year and whom He has marked on their chest and their brow as His own. In the 84th Psalm it is said that "the Lord God is a sun and shield; the Lord will give grace and glory: No good thing will He withhold from them that walk uprightly."[2] Our Lord Zebaoth, "blessed is the man that trusteth in thee."[3]

On Tuesday in the Zion Church we also noted the dear words of the Lord in Jeremiah 31:2: "Thus saith the Lord, The people which were left

---

[1] Probably an allusion to Luther's hymn *Ein feste Burg*.
[2] Psalms 84:11.
[3] Psalms 84:10.

of the sword found grace in the wilderness; even Israel, when I went to cause him to rest." Those who will not fear the Lord must fear their enemies. But whosoever fears the Lord in truth, must not fear anyone but comfort himself in saying: "I will not be afraid what man can do unto me."[1] He has said, "I will never leave thee, nor forsake thee."

Sunday, the 18th of March. On coming Good Friday, which we usually celebrate as a high holy day with public services, the congregation will go to the Lord's Supper. For this reason, I today invited the confessants, as is our custom, to sign up publicly. Also, among the children, most of those who have attended the preparation hours with considerable benefit express a great desire to take the Lord's Supper and be confirmed prior to this celebration. Therefore these children sought me in my study after catechisation, where I briefly instructed and prayed with them before sending them home. I shall talk to them as well as to their families so that we can exercise all possible caution in this holy enterprise.

I pray the Lord to incline my soul to those children whom He finds useful and ready to go to the Lord's table with regard to the present and the future. I would prefer for some of these children to take more time to attend the preparation hour so as to be better founded in their souls in the articles of faith of our Christian religion. But many of them live with their parents on the plantations or cultivate them, for their labor is much needed in view of the lack of servants among us. They lose much time from work to come here from these plantations, but with God's blessing they have come to a free recognition of divine truth and will find enough occasion in the edification hours and from our sermons to make up for what they lack in understanding. Some of them are in a truly free state of mind, and the others give good grounds for hope.

Monday, the 19th of March. The last crates from Halle and Augsburg contained a goodly number of tracts with the title *Concise Passsion Story of Christ's Martyr Week*,[2] which were distributed among the congregation along with some other books. We are now using the important contents of these tracts during our evening prayer meetings; we made a blessed beginning with this last night. Our dear Savior has already given me a blessing from this, and I hope that He is intending more than one blessing for all of us. It is most edifying to learn what

---

[1] Psalms 56:11.

[2] *Kurzgefasste Passions = Geschichte der Marter Woche J.C.* A little tract published in Halle, author unknown.

passed, according to the four evangelists, with our dearest Savior from Palm Sunday to the day of Easter and beyond.

Friday, the 23rd of March. As Good Friday has been a blessed high holy day in previous years of our pilgrimage in Ebenezer, we have reason today to praise the special and entirely undeserved bounty of the Lord, who has truly edified us from His dear word three times in our public meetings. Much blessing has flown upon us from the wounds of our Savior who died on the cross and in a Holy Communion which was partaken by ninety persons who have tasted and seen the goodness of the Lord.[1] Yesterday morning we held a sermon on the appropriate text for Maundy Thursday in the Zion Church prior to Holy Communion; in Jerusalem church, nine children who have previously attended the preparation hours were publicly examined on the teaching of the Lord's Supper.

Today, after the first hymn and before the afternoon sermon, they were confirmed. Through this act, the dear Lord gave me a strong awakening and impression, not only through these children but also in the adults who were present, in particular those who in previous times openly established their baptismal covenant with their hearts, mouths, and hands, but did then backslide. This was evidenced by many tears that were shed during this ceremony. Among the children confirmed were the following: Johann Balthasar Metzger, Georg Rieser, Thomas Schweighofer, Anna Barbara Kiefer, Maria Margaretha Mengersdorf, Maria Anna Rheinländer, Eva Gephart, and Margaretha Schwartzwälder, whose parents, mothers and siblings all reside in our town. Johann Valentin Deppe, young Mrs. [Margaretha] Kieffer's brother from Orangeburg, has been admitted to the Lord's table for the first time after proper and public examination and previous instruction and proof of his worthiness. He was not confirmed with the other children, however, because he had previously taken the Lord's Supper at another place. We have called upon the Lord to maintain and multiply the spark of His grace which He has kindled in the hearts of these children through His word and to let it mature from blossoms to ripe fruit.

Saturday, the 24th of March. Yesterday our dear Lord so strength- ened young Mrs. [Margaretha] Kieffer that she could be delivered of a boy, who was publicly baptized after the afternoon sermon. This morning young Kieffer brought me the news that his wife [Margaretha] had become progressively weaker by evening and had finally died. He

---

[1] Cf. Psalms 34:9.

was able to testify that, especially after my last encouragement, she was ready to prepare for a blessed departure in a Christian manner so that he did not doubt for a moment that she had died in the wounds of the Lord Jesus, who died for her and has been resurrected.

Truly, when I visited her last, she showed clear signs of repentance which later, through the word as transmitted through the labor of the Holy Ghost, became ever more manifest. Therefore, she took great delight when she was told that Mrs. Piltz could say in praise of her late husband: "His pain, misery and sorrow came to a blessed end, he bore the yoke of Christ, died and yet liveth."[1] She then resolved through His grace to reach the same state and said that, with her end, her misery and sorrow would end as well.

Oh what mercy Jesus the Good Shepherd has shown to these lost sheep. In Carolina, before her marriage to this man, she was quite lost; even later on the plantation, when she was restless with the solitude there, she would have become further lost and fallen into eternal misfortune if the faithful Shepherd had not barred her way with thorns.[2] She came to us quite ignorant,[3] but along with other children she used the instruction in the preparation hour for several months and was faithful in attending divine worship. Since her marriage, she fell and stumbled quite often so that she was all the more ready to be seized and convinced of her most miserable and dangerous state.

Yesterday, I was told that Zettler and his wife have fallen into disorder and discord, which had happened before in the course of this week of the Lord's suffering. I went to their house yesterday even before the repetition hour so as to admonish them to reconcile themselves with their Lord and with each other. I found the man, who is being driven about by bad emotions, much better than I had feared. He blamed himself and said, among other things, that he had often promised himself to improve and thus deprive others of the occasion to judge him. However, his improvement did not go forward because he had not really started upon his true conversion and the change of his heart but had only wished to appear to others as on the road to betterment. But now he

---

[1] *Sein Jammer, Trübsal und Elend ist kommen zu einem seeligen End, er hat getragen Christi-Joch, ist gestorben und lebet noch.* From the hymn *Nun lasst uns den Leib begraben*, translated by Michael Weisse from the Latin hymn by Aurelius Prudentius.

[2] Cf. Hosea 2:8.

[3] Ignorant of Lutheran dogma and Pietist practice of repentance and conversion. She had been of the Reformed faith.

intended to truly convert through the Lord's grace, and he planned to come tomorrow to speak to me about some necessary things.

I showed my joy at having found them in a better state than expected, and therefore my intended sermon of blame turned into a beckoning to Jesus, who knows well how to turn around even grave offenders and men so that they may all the easier be convinced that a good-for-nothing resides in them. This morning I returned to the said couple and heard a fine testimony of the good that our merciful Lord had aroused in them yesterday during the sermon and the repetition hour. On these occasions much was preached to comfort and impress the heart of repentant sinners and those who wish to repent, but Zettler said that, while he had liked to hear these words, he was much too bad to accept them.

He knew from experience that, the more God had awakened him through His word and the stronger he had been in his desire to convert to Christ, the more obstacles he had encountered so that all turned as to water. In this he recognized the reach of the Enemy[1] of our eternal bliss, for he has in our own wicked heart a secret correspondent, traitor and helper. They both begged me to pray with them, and they were serious in trying to see the face of the Lord. We then prayed with notable effect upon our souls and they recognized my encouragement with heartfelt gratitude. Several weeks ago they had rent a deep wound in their consciences by an intentional deceit against me, and they felt this wound painfully both internally and externally, as they confessed with sadness.

The 25 and 26th of March. Sunday and Monday, on which days we celebrated the Easter holy day in love and peace. While the bad- natured Uchee Indians came to our place both on foot and on horseback, they did not disturb us. On Saturday it looked like rain, but it remained dry and the air was warm. The great friend of man, our Savior Jesus Christ, has during this week of His suffering from Sunday to the last hour of Saturday given us for our mutual edification many wise lessons from His word and from the highly esteemed little book: *Short History of the Passion Story for the Week of the Suffering of our Lord.*[2] He has shown Himself just as generous and benevolent on this day of Easter, for which His eternal love and mercy must be highly praised for all time and in eternity.

---

[1] The "enemy" (*Feind*) was a common term for the devil.

[2] See page 20, note 2.

Saturday toward evening the deceased Mrs. [Margaretha] Kieffer was buried, for which our dear Lord in His mercy gave us a good preparation for the coming holy day through singing and prayer and through His word, which was read and briefly summarized for the benefit of our hearts. I feel that the mourners were much impressed with this during this notable time of the year. For, in such circumstances, the souls who love the word of the Lord and their edification from it are awake and tender and their minds are all the more deeply impressed. Over the last year at the burial of our dead I have followed the custom of contemplating a hymn from the extract of the Freylinghausen hymnal,[1] in the order in which they are printed there, to provide for our mutual edification.

This time, we had the strong and edifying hymn *Christi Leben tröstet mich, mir ist ein erwünschtes Leben*, which must be counted among the strongest Easter hymns. When on Saturday prior to the burial I visited the tailor Christ, who is seriously ill, I read him this very song, and then the subsequent one, that is, *Christus der ist mein Leben, Sterben ist mein Gewinn*. This should be his burial text, if indeed, as it now seems, he should be the first in line to bid leave from this world. He thinks much of this song, and his weakness spoke with me of several matters which revealed the faithful hope of his heart. His large tumor comes ever closer to his heart, and he himself believes that he might come to his end quite suddenly.

He would have much liked to attend the confirmation of the children, for that has always given him much edification. But the severity of his illness has deprived him of this opportunity. He sought comfort in the two verses from the *Treasure Chest*,[2] "Say to the righteous, that it shall be well with him,"[3] "Remain pious and keep thyself righteous."[4] He lacks temporal goods for his support but is given sustenance from the gifts that our Christian friends in Europe send here, and he is being helped in many ways.

Tuesday, the 27th of March. In the morning a boat is being sent down to Savannah to carry two young women who are to be instructed by the Italian woman in silk-reeling and spinning. One of them, Ott's

---

[1] Johann Anastasius Freylinghausen, *Geistreiches Gesangbuch*. Halle 1704 ff.

[2] Carl Heinrich Bogatzky, *Güldenes Schatz-Kästlein der Kinder Gottes*. Halle, many printings. This very popular tract was imported to the Lutheran communities in North America throughout the 18th century, individual shipments running to several hundred copies at a time.

[3] Isaiah 3:10.

[4] Psalms 37:37. This verse does not appear in the King James version.

wife [Anna Magdalena], speaks English quite well and she, as well as the other girl, who is Thomas Bacher's youngest daughter, has both the skill and the enthusiasm required for this task. I visited both of them this afternoon and gave them and their families the necessary instructions in this matter and then prayed with them. In the course of this exchange, God's providence was revealed in many ways, so that we believe that this labor comes from the Lord and will benefit Ebenezer.

I also visited our miller and his wife and talked with him concerning the good gathered during the Easter holy day. We praised God for the great gift that is our mill, which has remained entirely without damage from the last heavy flood. The mill is constantly running both night and day, and he always has enough milling jobs, so that he has a good living from his work. For our people, it is a right useful gift to have a chance to grind their corn and wheat.[1] Wherever I went, I noted to my joy that the Lord has strongly roused all souls both before and after the Easter holy day and that it has in all been much blessed.

Wednesday, the 28th of March. I found Paul Müller's wife [Anna Maria] alone at home with their child of three weeks, and she told me much that pleased me of her health and other affairs. The man has much patience with her weakness and practices diligently both prayer and the word of the Lord with her. While we were talking, the husband came home, and I could tell him how much his wife's news had pleased me. I was particularly pleased to learn that the neighbors in this area gather in [Josef] Leitner's house for a repetition of the preached word and for prayer. They do this just at the time when we at the Jerusalem Church are holding a repetition and prayer hour, and our dear Theobald Kieffer was praised as a useful tool in his humble gift for contributing to the edification of others.

On the other side of the plantations, others gather for the same purpose. I hear quite often that the blessed Luther's extracts from the gospels and the sermons on the epistles, which were distributed among the congregation as a dear gift from Saalfeld,[2] are a right blessed means of edification. Likewise, the blessed Johann Arnd with his sermons upon the Passion and Easter,[3] which we also received in many copies several years ago as a precious gift from a godly person of rank and from which we have had much profit.

---

[1] By *Korn* Boltzius here means Indian maize.

[2] A German town with a strong Pietist community and an orphanage on the Halle model.

[3] Johann Arndt, *Passions-und Osterpredigten.*

A man told me that in all his life he had never had so blessed a martyr and Easter Week than this time, and he promised to apply everything to God. Another man said that, before and during the holy days, he had not read much in the aforementioned good books because he had heard enough for his spiritual digestion, which he repeated to himself and to his family. A woman in the town and one on the plantations each showed me a little written book in which were gathered the most important exordiums and other verses which had been repeated publicly with the children piece by piece, so that they could repeat them diligently for themselves and for their children.

One pious woman told me that her husband, when struck by sickness, had spoken to our dear God in prayer as if he were soon to take leave of her through a temporal death. Then she began to worry who would afterwards repeat the memorized Bible verses to her and her children. But God showed her by healing him that her worries about the future were unnecessary. I then let the little girl recite the little verse through which she had already unexpectedly edified and refreshed me. I can always comfort myself with it when need is at the greatest: "He is more than fatherly disposed toward me, His child."[1] Another Salzburger and his wife boasted that they are finding many beautiful things in the biography of the godly Luther, which had been sent to us from Halle; and they thanked God for saving them from the darkness of Popery.

Thursday, the 29th of March. After 12 o'clock last night the tailor Christ had me called to him to read him some words of comfort from God's word and to pray with him. He had great pain in his chest but was very patient, as I have clearly noted such patience in his entire sickness, although he formerly had a restless and impatient temperament. After I had prayed with him, Christian Riedelsperger came to him, and at day break he was relieved by the clockmaker [Friedrich Wilhelm] Müller and his wife, all of whom held watch and prayed with him and called out Bible verses to him.

When the last two people had barely reached home, he was suddenly freed from his pain and misery by temporal death. About this time is the anniversary of his conversion in the week before Easter,[2] concerning which benefaction he spoke with me just a few days ago. He said that he wished to have another opportunity to write to the pastor who had

---

[1] *Er ist gegen mich, sein Kind, mehr als väterlich gesinnt.* From the hymn *Sollt es gleich bisweilen scheinen,* by Christoph Tietze.

[2] He had been converted from Judaism.

instructed and baptized him and to others of his benefactors. He counted it among the greatest benefactions of God that soon after his baptism he was invited time and time again to a circle of good people, from whose words and good example he was strengthened in the recognized truth and was gradually led to the righteous nature that is in Christ.

Our good God had well seen that unknown masters and apprentices in his trade would hinder him in his Christianity and even become a cause of his falling into sin. Therefore He showed him the great mercy of tempting him out here and led him into this wilderness and spoke kindly to him.[1]

From the very beginning he has shown great love for God's word and the sacraments, therefore he did not easily miss an opportunity for edification. However, he had by nature a very restless and inconstant spirit, which caused much harm to his Christianity. Now at last he regrets painfully that in the orphanage, where he could have lived so calmly and contentedly, he let himself be ruled by so much wilfulness and obstinacy, for which he had to repent later on, for example in his marriage. Nevertheless, he put to good use the tribulations that he had largely brought upon himself in that way. He would gladly have moved back into the orphanage with his wife and children for the rest of his life if there had been space and means for it.

On the holy evening before Easter he received Holy Communion at his own request, and thus the Lord wished to prepare him through it for his important journey into the heavenly fatherland. He will be buried at noon today, and the beautiful hymn *Christus der ist mein Leben* will be his burial text, since his is the first death among us after that of Mrs. [Margaretha] Kieffer. Among other things in it are the lovely words "With joy I go from here to Christ, my Brother."

APRIL 1744

Sunday, the first of April. In the past month our dearest and most loving Savior has let us experience very many spiritual and physical blessings which we remembered today in our sermon and prayer hour humbly before His countenance. We considered ourselves entirely unworthy of these and praised Him communally for them.

---

[1] Allusion to Hosea 2:14.

On this first day of the month He has again shown His friendliness and loving-kindness not only by letting us gather three times together in the most desirable weather in great freedom and without the least fear and worry of being disturbed by the enemy (as the dear and timid souls were in today's gospel). Rather He edified us properly through His word and prayer. Just as in the gospel, He stepped right in among His timid and frightened little sheep and thus came very close to each and every one of them and brought His peace to all of them, so we too must acknowledge to His praise that He stepped right in amongst us today as Jesus and made true His word "For where two or three are gathered together in my name, there I am in the midst of them."[1]

Since many neighbors in the congregation come together on Sunday evenings for the repetition of the words they have heard and for communal prayer, the circumstance will doubtless have been very impressive for them since we have heard from the gospel that on Easter evening the dear disciples repeated those things that they had either seen or heard and that they conferred about them. This so well pleased the Lord that He stepped amidst them during such edifying conversation and revealed Himself to them entirely unexpectedly. On the other hand Thomas suffered great loss by having separated himself from the Lord's little flock.[2]

Tuesday, the 3rd of April. Hertzog, the sickly servant in the orphanage, came to me and told me that our dear God has been able to reach through to him better with His word than in previous times. However, he asked me to examine him according to God's word as to whether or not he was deceiving himself in this opinion. He said he was still in the period of grace and, through God's grace, he could still make up what he had previously missed. The explanation at the burial of the tailor Christ: *Christus Du mein Leben*, was used by the Lord as a means to effect much good in his soul.

He is the grave digger in town and therefore always has an opportunity to hear something good in the church yard. Also, the people in the orphanage are accustomed to attend the burials jointly. I presented to him the holy and good order of God in which one can assure himself of the grace of God in Christ, and I gave him such other admonitions that he especially needed because of his temperament. He went back home strengthened and with joy.

---

[1] Matthew 18:20.
[2] John 20:24-29.

Thursday, the 5th of April.   Old Kieffer has so far shown with undeniable proof that he has had nothing else but the salvation of his and his family's souls in mind by moving from Purysburg to our place.   He has great joy in God's word; he is not only a hearer but also a doer of the word.   He has been patient in all his suffering and tribulation and content with God's will.   On his plantation near Purysburg he has fallen into debt because of his Negroes, the cattle plague, and other things; and these debts have greatly increased through the excessive annual interest. Now he is seriously considering paying his debts; and, in order to be able do so, he is planning to sell his remaining Negroes and his large boat.

He formerly considered the boat, which has an interior five feet wide and thirty-three feet long, to be worth £21 8 sh., but now he will give it to the orphanage and congregation for £16 Sterling.   He did this to make good for the offense that the members of our congregation had taken against him.   Eight years ago he sold us for £18 a medium sized boat, which can carry scarcely a fourth as much bulk or weight.

Because it has been a communal boat and has become worn out in many ways, it is now almost entirely unusable and it is not safe to load anything heavy in it.   We have not rightly known how such boats are to be kept in a durable condition.   I see it as divine providence that Kieffer is inclined to let us have the new and easily operable boat at a right cheap price.   For we often have something that we must take to Savannah or to bring up from there which we cannot do with our own little boat.   And what would we do if Kieffer had sold the boat at some other place?

Since the orphanage has now rented the shoemaker Roeck's plantation and bought a piece of land near it (or rather the work done upon it), a large boat will be highly necessary for bringing back and forth cattle, hay, young calves, horses, and other things.   We will also be well able to use it in bringing oak and other hard wood.   Therefore I am planning, in God's name, to enter into this business and to buy the boat for the good of the orphanage and the congregation, because both Kieffer and we ourselves will be well served by that.

Without the boat we would have been unable to bring the large quantities of sawed lumber and boards here from Old Ebenezer or we would have lost much time and expense, yet at that time we had to pay 2 sh. Sterling for the boat, which amounted to a lot of money in fourteen days.   How much would it have cost the orphanage and the members of the congregation if they had had to rent such a boat often at such a price, which would not be regretted if Kieffer sold it elsewhere.

I well remember what trouble, inconvenience, and expenses we had in the past when we had to get a large boat from other places. If it must be, we would rather sell a horse or two from the orphanage than to let the boat get out of our hands, although I do not doubt that our heavenly Father will, in His time, know how to pay this debt that must be incurred in buying this necessary boat. The orphanage has already risked much for the sake of the congregation, and in this our dear God has never let us get stuck or brought us to shame.

Last year we bought a stallion for £9 Sterling, now everyone can see with his eyes what a great advantage the community has from it. In Purysburg, on the other hand, the people are in a bad way, for they have mares but no foals. Next year they will probably have none either because a single wealthy man has a stallion, but he will not let it be used unless everyone who wishes to use it pays 30 sh. Sterling, which is difficult for poor people.

Saturday, the 7th of April. This year the shoemaker Roeck is faring in his silk raising just as the orphanage did last year. He is now living in Ortmann's house. Because there are so many spiders, cockroaches, gnats, and other insects, the silk worms have perished; and, in place of forty pounds of silk[1] he will not get much more than six pounds. Every day he must throw out several hundred sick or dead worms.

In the orphanage Kalcher has adapted the orphan boys' dormitory for raising silk worms; and on both sides he has erected broad repositories and containers in which some eight or ten thousand worms are fed and can spin themselves in very conveniently. However, they cause very much effort for Kalcher and his helpers, who can do nothing but tend the worms in this last period when they need the most leaves and care. Meanwhile they must drop all other work. Two girls and two boys are also occupied there, also the three wives, Mrs. Kalcher, Mrs. Lackner, and Mrs. Kogler work there as best they can when they can get away from their other housework and chores with their children.

Kalcher told me that, since the Lord Trustees are giving only two shillings for a pound of raw silk,[2] the orphanage will have more loss than

---

[1] The year 1744 saw the first practical success in sericulture, both in terms of the raising of cocoons and the first efforts at reeling silk in Ebenezer instead of Savannah. Boltzius refers here to a harvest in cocoons, not spun silk.

[2] Again, Boltzius is referring to cocoons, for which they had formerly received a 4 shilling bounty per pound.

gain from silk manufacture; for every task they neglect in the fields during this busy season they must hire day laborers later on. In eight days three hired hands cost us £1 16 sh. Sterling, and that is how much we would receive for eighteen pounds of silk cocoons. If we add to that all the work during the six weeks with the silk worms and the fertilizing, pruning, and protecting of the mulberry trees from the cattle and deer, there would have to be many pounds of silk if the effort should be worth it and a little profit remain.

Meanwhile, I do not regret that silk is being made in the orphanage, for now the people there know from experience how one must treat the silk worms from the beginning to the spinning of the cocoons. It is not so advantageous to make silk in this country, where there are so few people and where clothing and other things, and especially hired hands, are so expensive. Perhaps the Lord Trustees will let themselves be moved to continue paying the beginners in silk manufacture, as in former years, 4 sh. Sterling for a pound of raw silk, or perhaps our two young women really will learn to reel the silk thoroughly, for then we will see whether any profit can be made from the reeled silk.

Several families among us are raising a good number of worms for making cocoons, and they would like to devote themselves to it seriously since their mulberry trees are forever getting larger, if only the work were rewarded. Last year the orphanage fenced in a large place and planted it with young mulberry trees; and, God willing, we plan to continue next winter because we do not yet have many young undamaged trees. In addition to the mulberry trees our people have planted many peach trees, which now again are full of fruit on every branch. Our people greatly desire stills, for they cannot use the peaches better than by distilling peach brandy, as they already did last year.

Monday, the 9th of April. This morning Sanftleben called me out of school and informed me that his wife had wished for me: she had become so weak last night that people assumed that would not survive until day. After school I rode to his plantation on Ebenezer Creek and found her in bed, somewhat strengthened again. I told her and her husband that I had noticed that our marvelous God had visited them from the very beginning of their marriage with much suffering and tribulation, especially that all her childbirths were accompanied by much suffering and miserable circumstances. Whether this suffering and tribulation were to be seen as a cross and fatherly chastisement of God or as a punishment for sin, I could not judge until they, after well examining the state of their souls, told me whether or not they find themselves in divine order, for only the penitent and believing have the glory to come into the community of the cross and the sufferings of Christ.

However, in the case of the others, who live according to the flesh but under the appearance of Christ's name, it would be a dangerous self-deception if they considered their suffering to be a salutary cross and wished for that reason to believe themselves the dear children of God. I did not ask her to answer my question right away, rather I wished to visit her again soon. Meanwhile she should ask God to reveal to her the state of her soul correctly. It does no harm, I said, if she learns that she is still in an unconverted and graceless condition, for it is already a great grace if the sinner is awakened and brought to a recognition of his sin and danger. What she lacks, she should request of Christ, who calls to Himself all those that labor and are heavy laden[1] and finds joy in saving them with His grace, as one sees in the case of the sinful woman, the publican, and the one thief on the cross and in many other examples.[2]

At the same time I explained to her and her husband what true conversion is and how it is revealed openly and clearly that, through the grace of God, a true change has been effected in the heart, which Holy Writ calls conversion. If she will let such a base of comfort be laid in her heart and if she becomes penitent and believing, then she will not lack comfort for all the comfort that stands in the entire Bible belongs to a penitent heart that thirsts for mercy. I learned from her husband that she had sighed all night very deeply on her bed and, when he asked her the reason, she said she had cause for it, for her case did not stand well with God and she did not know how soon she would have to go to eternity. At last we fell on our knees and ask for blessing of the words that had last been spoken to this sufferer.

In the afternoon I had time to visit some of the people on the plantations on the Mill River. I found only the wives and children at home, the men were at work. I had much edification at Mrs. [Gertraut] Kornberger's house, for she told me various things about the good guidance of the Lord that she had experienced in this pilgrimage for the salvation of her soul. The course of her life is briefly summed up in the verse "I will allure her, and bring her into the wilderness, and speak comfortably to her."[3]

---

[1] Matthew 11:28.

[2] The sinful woman (Luke 7:37-38), the publican (Luke 18:10-13), the thief on the cross (Luke 23:40).

[3] Hosea 2:14.

She can talk very edifyingly and with tears that she was very blind and ignorant in spiritual matters and yet considered herself a good Christian. She relied on having left Popery and on the praise of others; and her good public behavior was, she said, a great obstacle to her conversion.[1] At first she could find herself in very few statements about conversion and examination of the heart in the sermons, yet she attended all assemblies diligently and prayed privately, as well as she could, about what she had heard, and from that a great desire arose in her to understand the word of God correctly and to know what she should do to be converted righteously.

Since she was too timid to request private instruction, our dear God accorded her wish already in our church hut in that the expressions concerning conversion and examination of heart in church were clarified and became completely clear to her through the illumination of the Holy Spirit. After that our good Father richly blessed in her the private visitations of the ministers, and she knew how to cite the little verse, which brought her great blessing. She received the strength to control her emotions and could well detect that others had prayed for her. She boasts to the praise of God that she has now had a good year, such as she had never had before, and that the assemblies of believers in her neighborhood on Sunday evenings were most profitable to her. Yet she still has many worries and concern about future things because of which she wastes much strength unnecessarily and she is now taking instruction.

About her husband she was able to say that he is more diligent now than previously in the use of the means of salvation and that she hopes he will acquire a right essence of Christianity if he does not let himself become entangled with frivolous company. She did not like the fact that he prayed so little for the Holy Spirit. It was a great blessing for her that she already had three children in the Church Triumphant.

Tuesday, the 10th of April. The Englishman in Old Ebenezer who has recently been put in charge of the Lord Trustees' cattle does not act like a neighbor to us but has begun to do harm to our cattle. He acted as if he wished to help our people regain their runaway cattle, for which reason he asked me to send a couple of men on horseback with him and his people into the region of Abercorn, where many of our old and young cattle graze. Two of our men traveled with him but had to see that the said man caught, branded, and drove off to Old Ebenezer a

---

[1] The Pietists as Lutherans taught that trust in one's own merits was a snare of the devil.

young cow that had been among our cattle and was still unbranded, as well as two year-old calves.

I soon wrote to him and asked him not to treat us that way because it was unjust and against the orders of his superiors. However, as an answer he told me that he had orders to brand all young unbranded cattle with the Trustees brand. I asked the man to give me an opportunity to speak with him on this subject, and he promised to come here. However, I waited in vain last week and the present week. Because we now fear that he will continue to take our people's young cattle away, I was compelled to write a letter yesterday to the President [Stephens] of the Council in Savannah and his Assistants in which I announced that the Englishman in Old Ebenezer has done thus and thus with our cattle and had justified his deed by saying that he had orders for it from the authorities in Savannah.

I asked them courteously to remember that a year ago I had informed them that for the past ten years various old and young cows had run away into the region of Old Ebenezer, which we had not been able to recover even though we had often seen them. The Council, I said, had at that time judged that the cattle in that region should rightly be ours and that our people had the liberty to fetch them and brand them for themselves. They did not wish to give us the permission in writing because they assumed that it would be of consequence. To be sure, last year our people had tried to lead the young cattle along with the old out of the swampy region and to bring them here, but because of lack of strong horses and adequate experience they had accomplished little except for one old cow and two young heads.

Then I requested them to write an order for their man in Old Ebenezer to give up our property and to do us no more harm. I said that our people had lost many cattle to the cattle plague and that it would be difficult if they should lose still more because of a dishonest hand. This would make it impossible for them to make any progress in their agriculture because most of their land is poor and must be improved with manure. In closing I asked for those cows that the Lord Trustees had promised to give the people of the fourth transport. At the present time we have twenty families of the fourth transport. Six of them received their cows last year, and four families are waiting for theirs in the future if the authorities find it suitable to give them to them this spring. We hear, God be praised, no more about the cattle plague at our place.

Wednesday, the 11th of April. This morning I received a friendly letter from Col. Stephens in answer to my question as to whether or not

I and Mr. Gronau had any authority in our congregation to control disorder in a serious manner. The gentlemen of the Council state beyond doubt that we have and must have such authority in case our flock should go astray, and they promise not to give any hearing to those people who wish to complain against us. They also wish to make Bichler a constable so that we can have in him a man who can give us a hand in all matters. Also, even strangers will be afraid of a constable appointed by the authorities and will have all the less heart to commit disorders at our place.

This morning I dropped in on Mrs. Sanftleben and found her very lively in body and spirit. She said that her case was not yet standing well with God, her many sins were a trap for her, and because of them she was feeling much pain in her conscience. She said, however, that she had taken refuge in God in Christ in her prayer and that she hoped the Lord would have mercy on her. She said she intended from now on to work earnestly on her salvation. I presented her with the verse Isaiah 55:6, "Seek ye the Lord while he may be found, call ye upon him while he is near. Let the wicked, etc.," for there is much forgiveness in Him.

I admonished her to learn rightly to recognize and reject the worldly mind of the flesh, which is so deeply rooted, and to guard herself from using the means of salvation so blindly all day long. Rather she should resolve with God not to rest until she knows that she has the grace of God and has received the forgiveness of her sins. I told her two impressive examples of such people who have recognized and feared the quantity and graveness of their sins. I also experience that God always makes His word true in the case of penitent sinners and wishes to blot out our sins as a thick cloud,[1] for the sake of the full merit of Christ.

This afternoon the Kieffers, both father and son, delivered the large boat to our orphanage, for which I paid him £16 sterling cash. The sale was so made that the boat is now entirely ours; but, if they make another some time later and it pleases us, we can make a trade and give something in addition as deemed right. However, this will surely not be necessary, since this boat will be so useful for the orphanage and the congregation that we will not need to ask for a larger one. It is more convenient for us than a usual trading-boat or local merchant-boat, and we could no more do without it than without horses and wagons.

Kalcher and Kogler were present when old Kieffer and his son were paid. We implored God on our knees to bless the boat to our use and

---

[1] Cf. Isaiah 44:22.

the money to theirs and to let us use it further in good peace and Christian order. We reminded ourselves at the same time in humility and gratitude of the many spiritual and physical blessings that our loving God has shown us from our beginnings in this wilderness; and we begged Him for his continued merciful care for us, but especially that in His time He will make good the money that was borrowed for this boat as His good treasure.

There are now various heavy things for us and the orphanage and for some members of our congregation to be brought up from Savannah, and therefore the boat was sent down toward evening. My dear colleague traveled with it because he had some matters to arrange with the authorities and elsewhere. He took along a letter from me to Col. Stephens. May God accompany him with His blessing and let him return to us soon strengthened in body and soul.

Thursday, the 12th of April. With yesterday's boat some pounds of silk were sent from the congregation to Savannah, among which were thirty pounds from the orphanage. Kalcher brought the orphanage's silk to me first and we marveled at the large and beautiful cocoons. In six days the remaining silk worms will have surely spun their cocoons and brought their work to an end.

Until then not only the women but also the men of the orphanage have had much work with the silk. Roeck's wife told me that in Purysburg and in other places where silk is made not 16 but 12 ounces make a pound. In this way people had previously accepted and paid for the silk. If that were the case, then the orphanage would expect to be paid not for thirty but for forty pounds of silk. Still, we are satisfied with what is being paid. For the Lord can bless a modest sum as well.

For there are now many people in the orphanage who need food and clothing and, if they are ill, care. Most of them, as is customary in the orphanage, are not able to contribute to their sustenance, for they are young and thus need to go to school, nor can they work the land, from which their livelihood must come with the blessing of the Lord. Thus, we are content if we can use them for the many little domestic tasks in the orphanage which in fact is the case with the Lord's blessing. The orphanage also has many expenses on the outside in the congregation, for the poor and needy receive as much help as is within our ability, and we take great care that the whole congregation shall benefit from this care. This in fact is the case, if it were only recognized by everyone. Since Mrs. Kogler is about to deliver a child, and has hardly any bedding, linen and other necessaries, we must take care of her needs, in particular as her husband is a skilled worker and his labor is done in the interest of the orphanage. But since there is nothing in money or in goods that we could use for this purpose, we must take up credit in Savannah for these and similar necessities until the dear Lord in His mercy shall provide for us. The silk will yield something, which will help us in our present straights. The European grain in the fields of the orphanage looks right good, und when Kalcher led me around yesterday, I was much amazed and grateful at the Lord's mercy. May He let us have a blessed crop in these European grains and in the native fruit as well and thus put us and the orphanage in a position where we no longer must rely on the benefactions from Europe. But now we cannot yet live *de propriis*, and thus must live on the gifts of our dear benefactors which are sent here by the good hearts and hands of our European friends. The lack of servants for a just wage is one of the main reasons that we cannot bring the affairs of the orphanage into the desired state. The day laborers whom we must use often for construction, in the fields and for other tasks cost much but we cannot do without them. For one can get neither male nor female servants for everyone is able to start on their own, however difficult that may be. But the people here prefer to labor on their own rather than go into service. The cattle plague as well has harmed the orphanage, for it is our cattle that was affected most severely. For in such circumstance he who has most must lose most. We have heard for some time now nothing more about the cattle plague. May God make us grateful.

Friday, April 20, 1744.[1]   Since we sometimes mention our wild cattle in our diaries, I fear that our friends will not quite understand and approve of our letting our cattle run wild, for in Germany that is quite a different matter. There, a farmer may not have more cows and oxen than he can feed on his pasture in the summer and for which he has fodder during winter. Here, however, the whole forest is free and cows, oxen, and calves can find their pasture wherever they wish. Those who wish to graze their cattle on their own land must enclose it with a fence or suffer whole herds of cattle to graze there. During our first years, we tried to let all our cattle graze under the supervision of several herdsmen, both summer and winter, so that we had no wild but only tame cattle, except for those that had been brought here wild and untamed and ran away before we could tame them. This task caused us much trouble and was often also beset with danger. As our herd grew, however, it was not possible to graze it in one place, because both near

---

[1] The Halle copy at this point is headed "Extract from the Diaries", indicating that the previous material was sent as one parcel.

our town and later on the plantations there was insufficient pasture, especially in winter. Thus, many head became so bony and miserable that they would drop from weakness. This required our farmers to set up some cattle herdsmen far out in the woods, who drove the milk cows to pasture in the morning and back home at night. For this, a large space like a sheep pen was fenced off. But here too, the pasture eventually gave out, so that we had to resolve, *nolens volens*, to let the young cattle, which were not needed at home for their milk, to run free in the woods. These ran off, one by one, into low-lying and swampy areas, where there is much young sweet cane; the English call these areas swamps.[1]

Here, there was quite a stock of wild cattle belonging to Mrs. Musgrove[2] and the Lord Trustees, which had originally been kept in a pen or on a tether. In their company, our cattle too became quite wild and were sighted only occasionally; nobody was able to get them out of the canebrakes. In the spring, the cattle would come out to feed on the young grass in the oak forests, but our people had neither the horses nor the skill to bring them in or even to mark them on their ears or brand them with a branding iron. This stock of cattle has now multiplied in the woods for eight years and some for as much as ten years, and we and other people in the colony have been forbidden to consider these unbranded cattle as our own or to brand them with our mark.

Dishonorable people (as is the case in Purysburg and in all of Carolina) might well abuse the freedom to mark their wild cattle and, under the guise of their rights, take what is not theirs; but our people are caused much harm by this and they are deprived of their rights for fear of bad consequences. In Carolina, every well equipped plantation owner has many wild cattle running in the woods. In the spring, they send out Negroes and white men on horseback and mark as many cattle as they can drive together into a specially built enclosure with a cut in the ear and a branding. But in most instances these cattle are so wild that horses and men often suffer harm and even death.

The Trustees' cattle manager also uses this procedure, but so far the harm has been greater than the benefit. For the horses cost much money and the men who are needed over the course of the year cause much inconvenience and expense. In Carolina and at Old Ebenezer only a few cows are domesticated and are milked for use in their kitchens, but they

---

[1] Boltzius writes the word *Swambs*.

[2] Mary Musgrove was an interpreter of European and American Indian origin who became a woman of considerable influence in the early period of the colony.

make only little butter and cheese. Almost all butter comes through Charleston and into the colony from New York and Pennsylvania. The greatest use of the cattle lies in their meat and in the sale of large and small herds, but later the buyers (as has happened to our people) have much trouble taming them; for some heads, taming will not work and they run off soon and multiply in the woods.

In Carolina there also are many wild pigs, just as we had here for several years on several plantations in this colony. But these are not like the wild boar in Germany but are domestic swine that have been driven into the oakwoods and the swamps to breed and feed on the many wild potatoes and other roots.[1] Occasionally, they are hunted with big dogs, herded together, and shot. When a good number of these pigs run together, they can fend off wolves and bears as well as the beef cattle can. Our people do not keep more pigs than they can feed and therefore they keep their own at home; but they nonetheless lose many, for, when they run off too deeply into the woods or stay out overnight, they are devoured by wolves and bears. If the arrangements concerning the cattle running in the woods are not changed so that we are given the same right as the Trustees' manager to mark our young cattle to the best of our knowledge and conscience, I cannot advise anyone to come here. If the Lord Trustees were fully informed of the circumstances, they would never approve of the arrangements for the cattle made by the authorities here. Even the Englishman in Old Ebenezer is said to consider the present state of affairs quite inequitable.

Saturday, the 21st of April. Kalcher came back at noon from Savannah. The silk from the orphanage which he took down weighed 74 pounds, which in all brings a fine amount of money. This stands us in good stead in our present circumstances, as we need clothing for the summer and other necessaries, particularly in view of Mrs. Kalcher's imminent delivery. It is true that most of the people in the orphanage have had much trouble over the last two weeks in collecting mulberry leaves and caring for the worms and thus were forced to neglect other necessary business. But they could never have made as much in this short time as was brought in by our present crop of silk. This confirms me in my view that the silk manufacture will be one of the most profitable labors in Ebenezer, if only people will take seriously the culture of mulberry trees and if they are supported in their beginning and

---

[1] This was the origin of the razor back hog.

for the next couple of years by encouragement and by some aid on the part of the Lord Trustees.

I have caused some of our people to collect white mulberries and have even collected them myself around our house. Unfortunately, they are regarded as of little value and are eaten only by the birds. I intend to have Kalcher press the seed in a large bowl or bucket of water (for dry, the seed does not separate easily from the meat of the mulberries and sticks to the fingers) and plant them in a good piece of land so that we might increase our stands of young trees by autumn. Yes, I would like to plant the whole town if our people were to be served by this. We still have four hundred or more young white mulberry trees with large leaves in the orphanage garden, which are to be thinned out and planted this coming fall, but I would wish that other people among us would raise a good number of such useful trees and turn to silk making.

Both in Purysburg and in this colony people have lost their incentive for this labor. Because the Lord Trustees pay only two shillings for one pound and will not buy the silk made in Purysburg, none will take the trouble to sow and plant trees. If it were not for the quantity raised at the orphanage, we would not have young trees for those others in our town who might be seized by the desire to make silk. The trees easily grow from seed if only there is a piece of fresh ground where the crab grass has not taken over; also the seed and the new sprouts must be protected against the heat of the sun from ten to three in the afternoon. This year, cultivated mulberry trees are ripe even now and thus too early, because the trees started sprouting by mid-February and were not damaged by the subsequent frost. The wild mulberries are still small and green and will hardly be ripe for another month. The vines in my garden finished blooming a week ago and are standing quite strongly, although I lack a skilled man to take care of them.

Monday, the 23rd of April.   This morning the manager of the Trustees' cattle came to see me and tried to justify himself for his offence of marking some of our young cattle. He brought along five of his servants, who were to confirm his arguments. He claims to have orders to brand with the Lord Trustees's mark all young cattle above one year of age and no longer suckling, regardless of their owner. He denies that the young oxen he and his men drove away had been among our cattle and other such things, but they are nothing but sheer fabrication. I would not believe that the man does in fact have such orders from the authorities, but he can show it to me in writing and swears that he will stand for his word before the authorities.

I shall see what Colonel Stephens, who will arrive in Savannah today, will have to reply to my letter. May God turn all to the best. Since I fear that the authorities will not change their orders with regard to the young cattle and that our people will therefore suffer much damage, it may well become necessary to write directly to the Lord Trustees, although I know that other Englishmen in this country have complained often enough of the same matter and yet no relief has been had. For the gentlemen of the Council will find a more receptive ear, particularly with regard to matters that are to the Trustees' benefit, than will private people. We are foreigners and are thus obliged to be silent and bow our heads.

Other people in this country who have lost their cattle in this manner have made up for their losses, but our people will not and, in part, cannot follow their example. For, although they may find some head of cattle in the woods which their neighbors attest are their own, they are not sure enough of their cause and scruple to mark them as their own. This has been attested to by the previous cattle manager who is now discharged, to wit, Joseph Barker. And the new man has today learned the same lesson. He notified me that he had brought a cow which had run away from Sanftleben to Old Ebenezer with his own cattle. This cow was suckling an unmarked one-year calf, and he therefore considers the calf as the property of the owner of the cow, that is, Sanftleben. But Sanftleben had in fact kept his calf at home when the cow ran off, and thus she was suckling a strange calf which had become attached to her. Therefore Sanftleben will not claim it.

The Englishman is so impertinent as to claim five shillings Sterling for each of our cattle that he brings back, although he spent little work in driving them to Old Ebenezer together with the Trustees' cattle. But that our people cannot bring back their run-off cattle on their own is due to the fact that they have mainly breeding mares, which are of little use in searching for cattle in the woods. They also know little of how to ride about in the woods and search for cattle.

The orphanage and Riedelsperger do have horses that can be used for this task, but the few men who know how to ride them for rounding up cattle cannot leave their other work, particularly at this time in the spring when it comes time to look for the cattle. Even if they put their mind to it now and then, it is not enough, and they receive little or nothing for this hard and difficult task. Other people who live in Savannah, on the

Musgrove cowpen,[1] or in the forts such as Mount Pleasant and Fort Argyle, have both the horses and the time to ride about in the woods, and they profit from this.

In Savannah, special people are put in charge, who earn, in addition to their wages, four shillings for each cow and calf which they seek out and bring home for other people in the spring. I write so lengthily on this subject so that our friends may be aware of how matters stand. For cattle raising is a large part of our people's living.

Thursday, the 26th of April. The current text of 1 Chronicles 30 shows us many beautiful lessons on the willingness of David and his servants to contribute substantially to the building of the temple, and this reminds us duly to render humble praise to the Lord for all the good that we have experienced in Ebenezer from the beginning through His servants and children. These have clearly been most liberal and have contributed, of their own free will and from their full hearts, their share to our two new churches, our parsonages, the orphanage, the mill, and to many gifts of books, suits of clothing, linen, etc. This has been confirmed by our parishioners, who have witnessed this giving, and we ourselves have read it in the preface to the *Ebenezer Reports*. My dear colleague reminded me yesterday of the preface to the 8th Continuation,[2] from which, in my present fairly pressing circumstances, the dear Lord has given me much for my humiliation but also much for lifting me up and strengthening my faith.

We are now beginning to consider the glorious prayer of praise and gratitude of our dear David, and this will give us grace to join him in the praise of our great and loving Lord for all our previous spiritual and material blessings. For have we as much, if not more, reason for this praise than David, if we but consider with a still heart our previous time of pilgrimage and dwell on the blessings of the Lord in accordance with all three main articles of Christian faith. For our wise and miraculous Lord must have a good reason for keeping back from us the two crates from Halle and Augsburg: this gives us time to search our hearts as to how we have applied our previous gifts and blessings; and He intends for us to prepare well for the reception of the now awaited gifts of love. For it is a great and important matter that, during these miserable times,

---

[1] Mary Musgrove's plantation near Ebenezer.

[2] One of the Continuations of the original series of the *Ausführliche Nachrichten*, from which these *Detailed Reports* have been translated. These reports were modeled on those from the Pietist East Indian Mission in Tranquebar and served as a vehicle of communication between the Halle missions and their sponsors in Europe.

so much good flows from the blessing hand of the Lord from Germany for our Ebenezer and is sent on such a long voyage over land and water. May He open our eyes to recognize His blessings and may He give us grateful hearts.

Friday, the 27 of April.   In the hope of finding a safe opportunity to transmit letters to Frederica during the first days of the coming week, I wrote to Pastor Driesler and to Captain Horton this afternoon.   My reason for writing to the commander of the fort was a certain insulting letter which the evil fellow who has until now pretended to be a prince[1] has written to a German shoemaker in Savannah and which that man sent me from there.   In this letter, the insolent man attacks a highly placed minister impudently and insultingly and even claims that this gentleman is desirous of introducing the royal Catholic religion into the Duchy of Württemberg.   He claims that he will not succeed in this, for he has received letters from England and Germany and will return home this month.

He has not changed his claim of being a prince and speaks ill of those at the Württemberg court who claim that they do not know him. I have translated the aforesaid letter into English and sent it to the commanding officer so that the fellow's tongue may be stopped.   I do not doubt in the least that this would happen quickly and firmly if the General [Oglethorpe] were still here.   At his request I inquired in letters whether they know anything or not of this man at the Württemberg court.   To Pastor Driesler, I sent this evil fellow's letter in the original so that he could produce it when necessary to prevent the man from escaping by denying everything or claiming that it was not correctly translated.   We have heard nothing of Pastor Driesler since his departure from Ebenezer but that he had safely arrived in Frederica.

My dear colleague has recently written him from Savannah; I would have written earlier if I had not waited for news from him, as agreed. I hope that he is not ill.   He may have much business and be unaware when there is an opportunity for mail from Frederica to Savannah, which in fact is rarely the case.   I have assured him of our brotherly love for him and of our intercession and edifying memory of his stay.   I have offered to perform all matter of service for him, and I let him know that, since his departure from us, there has been no news from either Pastor Mühlenberg or from Europe.   Also, the crates from Halle and Augsburg have not yet arrived.

---

[1] An impostor who claimed to be Carl Rudolf, Prince of Württemberg.

The man who carried my letter to Savannah yesterday returned this morning as early as 10 o'clock and brought no other reply but that the Colonel [Stephens] will give me an answer personally when I come down next Monday, God willing. The man told me that it had rained heavily in the Savannah region and that the hail had been as thick as a man's thumb. Yesterday, a thunder cloud passed by on our horizon, and on several occasions it looked as if there would be a heavy rain, but only a few drops fell in the end. The European grain[1] is well ahead in our fields and our heavenly Father must have protected it in saving our crops from the hail. The barley is quite ready and stands full and high. It will be cut shortly. By and by, rye, wheat and oats will ripen.

Saturday, the 28th of April. This week, Kogler in the orphanage and Rottenberger have been busy making a new and strong wagon so that the heavy wood for construction and the pine logs can be carried from the woods. The old wagon is being repaired as well and will be used for lighter tasks in the community and the orphanage. The new orphanage which is being planned is still lacking flooring and other boards which I would have liked to have cut by the members of our congregation if only they had the time. I believe that it is not by coincidence that this intended construction has had to be postponed until now, partly due to the lack of boards and partly for other important business at the orphanage and the community.

I am quite resolved not to be too hasty in this matter but let God and His providence guide and instruct me. This so that we will not incur unnecessary debt and cause want and sorrow for ourselves and inconvenience to our dear Fathers[2] and friends. A few days ago someone brought me an old torn little book, without a title page, and asked whether it was still useful for something or might be given to the children for play. When I opened it, I found that it was a separate printing of the moral instructions of Sirach, and the first words upon which my eye came to rest were the following, from the 29th chapter: "The essentials for life are water and bread and clothing and a house to cover one's nakedness."[3] Under it stood this remarkable note "(Want). It is not necessary to borrow or lend, except for the necessities of life, for example, for display, for great construction or for purchases. That is to say, if one wishes to lend or to borrow, it should be from need, for

---

[1] See p.4, n.3.

[2] The Reverend Fathers in Europe. See p.7, n.2.

[3] Sirach 29:21. This book is in the Apocrypha.

else many people raise a big hue and cry and wish to show off and to do so through borrowing and burdening other people."

My mind has been much afraid and depressed throughout the week for a number of reasons which concern the orphanage. For things will not come together; and, since we have no servants, we have little income and the orphanage must be almost entirely supported with the gifts from Europe. And, since I already have some debts and must have incurred further debt for the very necessary purchase of the large boat, our planned construction has sat heavily on my mind and I have sighed to the Lord so that it may proceed or be left off according to His will.

The aforementioned words which so unexpectedly struck my eye gave me new reason for thought and warned me against being overly hasty so that our Fathers and friends in Europe, in particular Senior Urlsperger, should not be troubled and distressed on my account. Today I am beginning to see more clearly how things stand. For a dear friend in the congregation confirmed what I had heard in passing, that is, that the carpenter, Kogler, does not wish to stay in the orphanage but wishes to return to his plantation as soon as the new orphanage has been built. While I have not yet spoken to Kogler on this matter myself, being prevented for the moment for certain reasons of prudence, I do not doubt it any longer for it is well known in the congregation; he has kept it only from Kalcher and myself.

Kogler has a wife and two children, and their third is shortly to be born with God's help. My only reason in planning a new building is that the old orphanage is lacking room enough for the three families, that is, Kalcher, Lackner, and Kogler, to live together. But if Kogler wishes to leave, the two closely allied families can make do until God shows us how to proceed. The threshold and flooring, the beams and the posts which have already been cut and the boards we obtained from Old Ebenezer will serve some other useful purpose even if this building is not erected. We urgently need a school in our town. I also feel that, after our dear Lord has helped most of our congregation make a living on their own, they can well take care of their own poor, such as widows and orphans, if they can only have a little help in this. Therefore, we may no longer need a house for widows and orphans.

Some of the boys and girls who were reared in the orphanage are married and some are in service with members of our congregation; some are old enough to be used by the farmers in their households, particularly in the care of their small children. They cannot find any servants here and are therefore glad to have the services of one of the boys or girls. And they are sufficiently conscientious to send them to school for a couple of hours every day. We have suffered much from ignorant people both here and elsewhere who have made uncharitable judgments of the orphanage, in particular when we refused to take in their sick or disabled kin or children (for they need all healthy hands themselves and take them away the minute they are well and can be of some use) because the orphanage is not a lazaretto or hospital.

We have been unable to hire servant girls or older women for wages, and we cannot place this burden on the wives of our three orphanage workers, who have to care for their children and their households. Therefore, if Kogler returns to his plantation with his family, Kalcher and Lackner will remain together, and the remaining children can be taken in by other farmers and thus be of use to the entire community in many ways, as indeed has previously been the case. The manifold uses and benefits of the orphanage have served the entire town and congregation. Another reason for this change (which is not yet resolved but is being carefully considered) is the great damage which the orphanage has suffered from the cattle plague and is still suffering from the unreliable and devious manager of the Trustees' cattle in Old Ebenezer.

In previous years we have lost many a head of young cattle and we were always told that the wolves had devoured them, although we had our doubts. Now the man has orders to brand for the Trustees all young cattle no longer suckling and one year or older. Even if he were restrained in this by a new order to exempt our cattle, he is so hostile towards us that he would go out of his way to harm us by devious means. The cattle have been a large portion of the sustenance of our people in the orphanage. I sigh and say as always: "May the Lord's will be done."

This afternoon our good Lord graciously heard our poor prayer, which we offered again in today's prayer hour in my house, and sent us a long, beautiful, and penetrating rain. Several days ago our farmers on the plantations on the Mill River had a similar rain. The garden plants, such as lettuce, cucumbers, and other tender growths have suffered much from the long period of sunshine, but they will surely recover now. The planted Indian corn and the European crops have had enough moisture so far and look quite beautiful. The worms have not been a pest for some time now. A Salzburger told me of his great pleasure and joy at the marvelous and beneficial guidance the Lord has shown him and the Salzburgers of the first transport.

He thought that God's gifts would not please him so much and he would not esteem them as highly in humble prayers to the Lord if the Lord had not shown him many trials and sorrows during the first years. At the very beginning, when we were still in Abercorn,[1] I was hasty in listening to the unjust presentations of others and dealt harshly with this dear and honest man. Since I have seen his honest mind, I have much regretted my previous words. I now brought this matter up in our conversation and told him of my displeasure at my previous conduct, but he could not recall anything that I had done in excess. Another man might well have remembered my injustice so deeply that he would not have forgotten it until the day of his death.

Sunday, the 29th of April. Yesterday afternoon I received a most pleasant letter from Pastor Driesler in Frederica in which he reports at great length of his own person, his dear family, the conduct of his office, etc. He is still well and healthy and takes much trouble with his office as pastor and schoolmaster to adults and children. He has his troubles and sorrows with it. During the Easter holiday he was obliged by the English to read a few texts and hold a service in the absence of their minister Bosomworth (with whose offensive conduct he has had some trouble). His poor wife is often quite weak and her health may well have suffered from the summer's heat and a threefold shock during the passion week.

I will describe this in Pastor Driesler's own words:

> I should end this long letter now. But with your leave I must mention a matter that occurred here during Passion Week and which we shall not forget for the rest of our lives. For on Wednesday before Maundy Thursday, one of the palmetto huts caught fire, which jumped over to the adjacent powder magazine. Since there were several thousand large balls and bombs full of powder in this magazine, they too caught fire, and it sounded as if heaven and earth would come crashing down. Some twenty houses or more next to it went up in flames. We live just about sixty feet from there; and you can imagine what there was of fire, noise, and rain of bursting bombs. My wife was immediately led away by good friends, but I was in the fortress of the grace of God, and I remained with Him alone in my house and prayed.

---

[1] The first Salzburger transport had sojourned at Abercorn on their way to Ebenezer.

Although it took hours of thunder, fire, and explosions until
all the powder had been blown up and rained down everywhere,
my former living quarters, which served us as a school and a
church, remained unscathed.   Oh, what a God is our God!
Hallelujah.   On Good Friday, another house went up in flames,
and we thought that the strong wind would set the whole town
afire, and for that reason all our listeners ran away just as we
were giving the sermon on the Savior's death.   But the Lord was
again our help and we managed to come together again and
properly conduct ourselves on this day of the death and the burial
of Jesus Christ.

But now comes the most astonishing part:

On Easter Saturday, I was at my desk in the afternoon
reflecting on the sermon for the day of the resurrection of Jesus
Christ.   I was not expecting anything bad, but my poor soul was
delving deeply in the life of Christ, when suddenly a musket ball
passed through the window and over my head.   The window
shattered with a loud noise, pieces and splinters of the glass hit
my face, but the ball hit the wall only hand's breadth over my
head, making a hole big enough to place an egg in.   If I had
been standing before the desk I would have died instantly.   But,
since I was sitting, it passed a hand's breadth over my head.   I
do not really recall what happened when the shot went off, but
my family followed the noise to its origin and found that a
clumsy servant had set up a target in a garden opposite us to
shoot at and the ball went above the target and into my window.

Of the often mentioned pretended prince, Driesler reports the
following:

The so-called Prince Louis was brought here as prisoner a few
days ago for punishment because he was found asleep on guard
duty.   As he was about to run the gauntlet, he wrote a moving
letter to me which I received Wednesday after our morning
prayer meting.   As Mr. Holzendorff and an aide de camp named
Robinson were among my listeners, they took the letter to show
it to Captain Horton.   Although I had not said anything to this
effect, Captain Horton thought he was doing me a favor by

setting this useless fellow free at once and remitting his punishment. He ordered him to come to me to offer his gratitude.

When he had done that, he told me that Pastor Boltzius had sent him a most unpleasant letter. I confirmed this letter and told him of all his evil deeds to the extent that I knew them and assured him that I would never again in my life so much as utter a word on his behalf. I knew him for a liar and told him that if he did not anticipate the justice of the Lord by a true conversion, His heavy vials of wrath, which already were dripping down on him, would run over.[1] He finally asked me with tears in his eyes to prevent a further investigation or execution of punishment on the request of Counsellor Georgius.

Since coming to see me after his imprisonment, he has passed off a lot of stories on the people here, for instance, that a Mylord had sent him letters from London via Charleston (which he even showed to the innocent people) assuring him that a galley would be sent here and he would be put in command. I fear a heavy descent of the Lord's judgments on this man. One thing I do know, he had better not come to ask anything of me for the rest of his days.

Dear brother Driesler praises the good Lord for everything that he has experienced in and from the people in our poor Ebenezer and uses such fulsome expressions that we do not like to repeat them. He is full of love and good faith in us and assures us of his constant intercession and prayers. He asks the same of us and his office, for he lives at a place of which there are not many to be found in this world. Concerning the English schoolmaster in Frederica he writes that he is an offensive man who drinks so much every day that he has to be picked up in the streets and carried home. He continues:

Never in my life have I seen such people, such a place, and such manners of living. Captain Horton has told Mr. Holzendorff (a German surgeon) in confidence that he would prefer me not to be here but on his plantation, for I must be getting a terrible impression of Englishmen. Of General Oglethorpe, they say in Frederica that he is on the way with a battalion of soldiers. This is much desired by everyone, for the news continues that the

---

[1] Allusion to Revelations 16:1.

Spanish are preparing for an invasion with all their might. May
the Lord remain with us!

Monday, the 30th of April. This morning, I and several of our
people started on the journey to Savannah in our little boat; and we
arrived there in seven hours well and healthy, with enough time left to
take care of some business, particularly with Colonel Stephens. He
doesn't seem to have been annoyed at my last letter, and he places the
blame on one of his assistants for having put greater trust in the story of
the cattle manager in Old Ebenezer than in my letter. He told me to
come to the meeting of the Council tomorrow morning, so that our cattle
searches and related matters might be set aright. The Englishman from
Old Ebenezer has been summoned here for the same purpose.

Mr. Stephens has news from Frederica that in Russia a new and
lamentable conspiracy has been raised against the Empress [Elisabeth]
and her consort, to which the French and other ministers to the Russian
Court who incline to the French party are said to have joined themselves.
General Oglethorpe is truly reported to be en route here with 400
soldiers and is said to be bringing with him several galleys and other
vessels for the protection of this colony. In Savannah a company of
soldiers will be quartered, and this will please some here because they
hope for better commerce and an opportunity for sales. Some Negroes
have been brought from Fort Argyle to Savannah, but then they were
sent on to Frederica as prisoners, since the people there did not wish to
give the captain the reward he expected.[1] In the evening several of our
German people came together at my lodgings to whom I read some of
Mr. Driesler's reports and then prayed with them.

MAY 1744

Tuesday, the 8th of May. A woman who came to see me in order
to register for Holy Communion praised the great mercy of the Lord,
who had opened her eyes so that she might recognize her folly,
stubbornness, and other bad characteristics as a sin. On Sunday she had
learned from the gospels that even people who consider themselves
servants of the Lord can be too blind to recognize either the Father or
the Son and that this spiritual blindness is not only by itself a grave sin

---

[1] These were apparently runaways from South Carolina on their way to Florida,
where the Spaniards had promised asylum.

but the mother of many other sins. This she had learned from her own experience. She admitted that she had taken offence when her husband on his sickbed had bared his whole heart from the fear of his conscience. This had caused her much unrest, in particular since the disorderly start of her married life had been revealed in the course of this. I had told her at the time that she should not be upset, for she could not understand how necessary it is to recognize and confess one's sins, and she had thought that she understood things better than her husband and her minister.

At another time, Mr. Gronau had asked her whether she was content with the will of God, who had taken her child from her through temporal death. She had not replied, for she could not understand the question. Thereupon another pious woman had said of her that she was most ignorant if she could not see the reason for such questions. She needed instruction. These words had so much hurt her old Adam that she never could forget them or forgive the woman as long as she lived. But now her recalcitrant behavior caused her much grief, and she would much like to ask the woman's pardon if only she were still alive. God has wrought much in this woman, as those know who have known her before. He keeps her under the rod of material sorrow, which she considers a great gift and a useful means of salvation to prepare all the more eagerly for her departure from this world and for blessed eternity.

Wednesday, the 9th of May. Glaner and his wife are without family here, and they have suffered much from various sicknesses during the first year since their arrival. But, as they fear God and work industriously and keep their affairs with wise counsel, they have established themselves well on their plantation and make a good living. I was much pleased when I saw their beautiful crops in the fields and their cattle and other things belonging to their household and heard them praise the Lord for His bounty. They much praise Him for humbling them, for this has been for their best. In particular, Mrs. Glaner will never forget that she spent some months in the orphanage because of a serious injury to her hand. This made her lose much external work,[1] but it was for the greater benefit of her soul.

During her stay here, she has started to read; and, as she continues practicing it, her delight is like that of a child that she can now read God's word for herself and look up words read in church and repeat them with her husband. God reveals to them more and more of their

---

[1] In Pietist usage "external" work meant attending to unimportant matters such as making a living, which were secondary to the task of achieving salvation.

perdition, which causes them much beneficial grief so that they are driven to Christ, the Physician and Savior. It is most edifying to hear them comfort themselves with God's word and use it for proper direction, which is truly a good work of the Holy Ghost in them. She has borrowed a Bible from Mrs. Zant, a neighbor, and asked me to give her one as a gift when our crates arrive, which I will gladly do.

Their present solitude gives them much pleasure, and they use it for prayer and for discourse with and before the Lord. She only complained that the black birds in the fields often disturb her, for in this she sees the source of evil and unrest, that is, her rotten heart. He has learned that a Salzburger woman with a little child for whom he stood as godfather in Memmingen has returned from Prussia[1] in very poor circumstances and, since he knows the duty of this relationship, he would much like for the woman and her little child to come here so that he could take her in, for they are without children of their own. He wishes to write to her and regrets not having done it a year ago. I often hear that our Salzburgers hope and wish that their families could soon follow them into this pleasant wilderness. Both spouses said that the words have been fulfilled in them: "I will allure her and bring her into the wilderness and speak comfortably to her."[2]

Thursday, the 10th of May. I hear that several head of cattle have showed the same signs of illness as last year, when the cattle plague started here. Until now, things were quite calm and we all thought that the plague had entirely ceased. Therefore, the people from the fourth transport have requested, upon my asking, that I might help them obtain the cows and calves which the Lord Trustees promised them. They will shortly receive fourteen cows and as many calves from Old Ebenezer; and, upon my request, the widow Kurtz and her children will also get one, making a total of fifteen. Some of the people of the 4th transport received six cows and as many calves last year, making a total of twenty cows and twenty calves for the entire transport.

This is indeed a great benefaction, and I only wish with many sighs that none will sin in connection with it but instead thank the Lord for this large and undeserved gift of the Trustees. For this great Lord, of whom much glorious praise is said for our comfort in our current text, the story in 1 Chronicles 29:11[3] can easily lift the plague entirely from our

---

[1] Most of the Salzburger exiles had found homes in East Prussia and Lithuania. See most recently Mack Walker, *The Salzburg Transaction*. Cornell University Press, 1992.

[2] Hosea 2:16.

[3] Boltzius cites 1 Chonicles 30:11. This book is now numbered 1 Chronicles 29.

shoulders and keep alive both old and new cattle. And this gives me cause for worry, for I know that many among us have sinned with regard to these cattle, by discontent, envy, and quarrels, if not in public then privately. May He not deal with us according to our sins and merit, but according to His great mercy. He knows well what kind of creature we are, and how our people need their cattle for their nourishment. Yesterday evening some of our men brought in a few head of cattle, some branded and some without marking. The latter they branded and then set free. The branded cattle were brought to their owners. I shall immediately inform the authorities of this, for their cattle manager in Old Ebenezer is quite hostile to us and likes to slander and accuse us falsely. The Lord Trustees shall not incur the slightest loss because of us, and we are full of confidence that they will not let our property be damaged or seized by their people here, who seek their own advantage under the cloak of responsibility. Bichler takes good care of these unfortunate matters, which formerly were almost entirely on my shoulders, and he renders me good service.

Today, I gave Bichler a commission with regard to the cattle intended for the 4th transport, since I fear that a certain man, if I refuse his undeserving request, will be embittered not only against me but against my office and thus do himself and his family more harm than all the cattle on earth are worth. This man has been much displeased on his voyage here and has in particular brought many written and verbal complaints to me concerning Mr. Vigera; and, although he praised Mr. von Müllern[1] highly, I see in a letter which his wife brought me yesterday that this gentleman also failed to please everyone, for the husband wrote in this letter: "I do not write this without cause, for she (his wife, whom he married here) has often said that she always had the same bad luck. In London, it was always the others who were given skirts, shirts, caps, and shoes." If I ask her why she did not receive any gifts, she said that nobody had taken care of her and therefore it was incumbent upon me to do so now.

This man was among the six families who received their cows last year, when he had already been married to this woman. But he still insists that she was owed a cow since other unmarried men, widows, and widowers, as well as Walburga Krell and Apollonia Kreder were to receive one together. Of himself, Bichler admitted to his shame and humiliation that in previous times he had been bitter not only against my

---

[1] The commissary who brought the fourth Salzburger transport as far as London.

person but also against my office; and another man had sorrowfully admitted to the same. I had not expected the gentlemen in Savannah to grant my petition and allow twenty cows and as many calves to the fourth transport, and this should serve to turn us to the Lord in humble gratitude. And still there are people who are envious of His very bounty, and that is enough to spoil our pleasure.

Friday, the 11th of May. Today before the edification hour on the plantations I again spoke to the man mentioned in yesterday's diary; and I again sought to convince him that neither he nor his wife were being treated unjustly. He seemed content, which in part may be due to the fact that he has just recovered, without any bother on his part, one of his escaped cows, together with a fat calf. I am sure that the cow which he received, which ran off a while ago, will also be found, and I will help him to bear the cost of finding and returning it. In the Zion Church we sang with reverence the last part of the beautiful song, *O meine Seel erhebe Dich*, in particular the cherished words "Thou art a generous Lord who giveth good abundantly. Let me be content with that which is Thy blessed will. Also grant that I await only from Thee and the abundance of Thy goodness."[1] Here, I only wish that the aforementioned man might learn a lesson from these words, as indeed, we all should.

The clockmaker, [Friedrich Wilhelm] Müller, and his wife wish to go to the Lord's Table this time, and I took this occasion to pray and talk with them. Both have often sinned through gross judgments of my person and have angered and worried both their children and other people through their loose talk, although my conscience is witness that I have never hurt them on purpose but instead have done everything in my power to be of use to them and their children in both spiritual and material ways. Since none of the children were home, I remonstrated with them because of their offenses, which neither was able to deny; nonetheless, they still held to the belief that they had reason for their conduct, until a recounting of the circumstances and the context which they believed justified their complaints and judgments convinced them of the very injustice and offensiveness of their conduct.

They feel that they have asked God to forgive them for ill judging me several years ago with regard to the distribution of provisions, and thereby doing me an injustice and causing themselves great damage. To the contrary, I showed them that such prayers will not be heard if one

---

[1] *Du bist ein milder Herr dabey, der reichlich gutes gibet. Lass mich mit dem zufrieden seyn, was ist dem Seeligen Willen, gib auch, dass ich von Dir allein und Deiner Güte Fülle erwarte alles in allem.*

does not relinquish one's evil ways, but insists on repeating the same sin, as was true of them. They asked me for my pardon and promised to behave properly towards me and to question me directly concerning what they felt they could not accept. Since they offended their children with their hasty judgments of me, I admonished them to admit to them that they had acted badly and had sinned, and henceforth to lead them by their good example. Both these people have had much to complain about the orphanage and to blame it for matters for which they themselves were the cause.

On May 13 and 14, we celebrated the feast of Whitsuntide. My dear colleague Gronau is still quite weak and very hoarse, so that he could not deliver any sermons during these holy days, despite his earnest longings. It is, however, the Father's will that he should be quiet and I alone should speak and carry out the tasks of the office; and in this He gave me much strength, both last Sunday and on this Holy weekend. On Whitsuntide Monday we went to the Lord's Table with seventy-five persons, and here my dear colleague helped to the best of his poor health, which gave me much relief and support. Since he cannot fulfill the duties of the ministry, he prays all the more warmly for me, and in this he is joined by many of the honest prayers in the congregation, and that is why God has done great things for my humble person, to my own wonderment and that of many others.

I trust Him right simply in Christ that He will also bless my poor service to the souls during the last days. He has filled my poor heart from the contemplation of the gospels and has given me so much that is sweet and wholesome from His love and mercy that I can testify to the assistance of the Holy Ghost not only on my behalf but of that of other members of the congregation. On the first holy day, we treated the regular gospel dealing with several points of the rich store of goodness, mercy, and love of the Lord, using Psalms 36:8-10 as an exordium: "How excellent is thy loving kindness."[1] The next day we discussed the same subject with regard to two specific points from the gospel of John 3:16 ff., which deal with the bounty of divine mercy and love and with the requirements that must be fulfilled to obtain it. The exordium was from Titus 2:11-12: "For the grace of God that bringeth salvation hath appeared to all men."

On the second holy day, after the sermon, we called the young children who will, from now on, be prepared for the Lord's table. I

---

[1] Psalms 36:7.

admonished them briefly and recommended their desire to the prayer of the congregation. I have not yet been able to hold preparation hours because the parents have needed their children for the work in the fields and I have had to teach school and conduct other business. Therefore, I have been willing to postpone preparation until now, for both children and adults have enough instruction to prepare for the Lord's Supper and blessed eternity. If only they had as much faith as opportunity for edification, they would all stand in a state of salvation. The Lord be praised, humbly and from our hearts, for all He has done for me and my listeners in both our spirits and bodies. May He let us recover a blessed fruit in eternity from the celebration of this Holy Day of Pentecost.

Tuesday, the 15th of May. This morning several of our men and I had to travel to Old Ebenezer to receive the cows and calves intended by the Lord Trustees for the 4th transport. I would rather have stayed here and taught school, but the superintendent and cattle manager did not want to deliver the cattle in my absence. We think the cows are young and in good health and may well not be as troublesome to tame as formerly. The following families have received a cow by lot: 1. Mr. [Ludwig] Mayer, 2. the widow Bacher, 3. Mrs. Piltz, 4. Mrs. Theobald Kieffer, the former widow Mayer,[1] 5. the widow Kurtz, 6. Eigel, 7. Eischberger, 8. Kohleisen, 9. Scheffler, 10. Schrempff, 11. Glaner, 12. Graniwitter, 13. Klocker's children, 14. Waldpurga Krell and Apollonia Kreder shared one, 15. Lackner.

A year ago the following families received their cows: 1. Köcher, 2. Haberer, 3. Scheraus, 4. Balthasar Bacher, 5. Lechner, 6. young [Johann Georg] Mayer. The man who only recently was ill-pleased that his wife was not to receive a cow has today received, among the cattle returned from Old Ebenezer, the cow he had received last year, and with it a beautiful calf. The cow had run off a good while ago. Now his cattle have been returned to him and he has lost nothing from the cattle plague, and I can only hope that he will be grateful for this turn of events. This afternoon, I wrote Col. Stephens and thanked him and the Lord Trustees, in the name of the people from the 4th transport, for this new and great gift of the cattle. At the same time, I wrote him concerning the herdsman, [Michael] Schneider, who with threats and insistence on his rights is holding back his son from service in the

---

[1] Her husband drowned in the Rhine on the way.

community.[1] If the council agrees that he should be free and no longer bound to serve, the congregation will assent to this decision, for they only wish what is right.

The sick old Mrs. Rieser asked for me in order to talk about the state of her soul and to pray with me. She had hoped to go to church and to the Lord's Table on Pentecost, and her health seemed to have taken a turn for the better, but then she suffered a reverse, and a quartan fever attack has further afflicted her. Although she thus was unable to hear the word of the Lord, He has not left her without grace. Through His Holy Spirit, He has reminded her of many beautiful words that she had heard from pious people back in her homeland, and has also sent her a little girl who on the Holy Day recited for her the cherished evening prayer: "Everyone that thirsteth," Isaiah 55:1-3. She was much touched that our wise and benevolent Lord will and can use little children to awaken and comfort the old, and she told me of another example from her own experience. Once, during the summer, she had been dejected and sorrowful during the harvest and could not stop her tears.

At the time, she had been rearing Grimmiger's child in the mother's stead, and the child had seen her sadness and tears, leaned on her lap and said: "Mother, it is said: 'Commit thy way unto the Lord; trust also in Him and he shall bring it to pass.'"[2] These words had offered her much comfort and had stayed in her soul until now. In her continuing bodily weakness, this woman is very concerned for her soul. She also works faithfully in admonishing and chastising her own family, and she feels it as a heavy cross that her words do not always find a full response in her husband and children. The man soon joined us, and I instructed him as to his and his children's duty with regard to their sick mother and her admonishments. Yesterday, this man was much touched by the word of the gospel, and he confessed this to me and his wife with tears, repeating several points that had touched his heart. May God render him and us all faithful and obedient through His Holy Spirit.

Wednesday, the 16th of May. This morning, Mrs. Rieser received the Lord's Supper in her house, for which she had yearned for a long time. She would have preferred taking it with the rest of the congrega-

---

[1] The Trustees had recently freed all minor male indentured servants so that they might help their parents, knowing that this would cause them to do more work. (*Col. Rec. Ga.*, 2:406, 5:653, 30:262.) The right to the labor of children and others in the Ebenezer orphanage was one of the issues dividing the community from its pastors during this period.

[2] Psalms 37:5.

tion, if she had only had the strength for it. But, since her improvement is still far off and the next public Holy Communion is another five or six weeks off, she has prepared for it today. She asked all her family to be with her so that they might share in the edification. We humbly benefited from the beautiful pithy old hymn: *Jesus Christus unser Heyland, der von uns Gottes Zorn*; we prayed with each other and used our time in an edifying manner and for the salvation of our souls, in which the Lord supported us noticeably.

Old Mrs. Rieser often thinks of the charitable city of Augsburg and in particular of its blessed poorhouse,[1] in which she and her family received much good in days of sickness and health. In return for this, she will call God's blessing upon her benefactors in return until her breath shall expire. She is quite content with her cross, which she has now borne for some time, and she cannot work, or only very little. She prays all the more industriously for herself and her family, and she considers it a great blessing of the Lord that she has both strength and the Lord's help for this. Some days ago, her last young cow died, and most of her cows were lost in the cattle plague last year. It is not without reason that she considers this a just punishment and a discipline of the Lord that has befallen her house, and she does not hesitate to refer her family to specific and special misdeeds in this respect. They, in turn, tend to think that she is too harsh in this.

I found a couple in poor spirits, and they had even been quite angry that they had come here from Germany. They testified that they liked living in Ebenezer but that certain sufferings made their life here quite difficult and caused them much regret. I asked whether they had not consulted God's will in Germany when they resolved to travel here, or had asked some tried and true Christians for their advice. For, if they had come here according to the Lord's will and His divine providence, they were in sin for regretting having accepted His call because of a few gnat bites (for such is the size their sufferings), for what else were they regretting but having done God's will.[2]

They should rather recognize that such sufferings are also a gift of the Lord and that, without His will and permission, neither this nor any other untoward thing can happen to them: He had, rather, a final goal in

---

[1] The Evangelical Poorhouse in Augsburg was used for housing exiles from Salzburg.

[2] Those who have attended the Salzburgers' Labor Day celebrations will sympathize with these people.

humbling them for their previous sins and thus carrying them away from all things to Christ. He would not find it difficult to change their condition, as He would certainly do if they persevered in His trials. And above all, this was in the order of the salvation: "We must go through much tribulation to enter into the kingdom of God."[1]

The better to remember this lesson, I told them of a certain pleasant story which had happened to the late Professor [August Hermann] Francke. Through God's blessing this couple recovered their spirit, and they very quite happy at having revealed the state of their mind to me. We occasionally witness people behaving much as in the story of the old ungrateful Israelites who regretted their exodus from Egypt because of a few subsequent trials. But some of our congregation will accept instruction; and, when they consider their situation well, they find much cause to praise the Lord for their exodus from their homeland.

When and if people in Ebenezer convert truly to the Lord and seek His kingdom as a first and only thing, they will certainly not regret their departure and arrival here, for they now have a better understanding than previously of the obstacles they had to face on their way to the Lord. Still, the people among us remain mouth-Christians. They have brought with them their worldly intentions; and therefore every little wind will frighten them and they feel that in this wilderness they meet obstacle upon obstacle, so that, as they say, they cannot become pious Christians. This wicked attitude even leads some to proclaim that they never met as many bad people as in Ebenezer. But this makes me think of the words of the Lord Jesus: "And why beholdest thou the mote that is in thy brother's eye, but considerest not the beam that is in thine own eye?"[2]

Thursday, the 17th of May. Some of our people have plowed a few pieces of land during the winter and planted them in the spring with Indian corn. By using a plow to work the land, they hoped to suppress the crab grass or at least prevent it from spreading too profusely. But now they have learned the opposite, for the land which was plowed under has had more of the aforesaid spreading crabgrass than seen elsewhere, and it came up earlier. For the terrible thing about this weed is that, unless it is uprooted during very hot and continued dry weather, it will soon reappear, for each little blade has its own root.

The orphanage has plowed under about four acres of old land for planting, and now we have all manner of work to eradicate the abovesaid

---

[1] Acts 14:22.
[2] Matthew 7:3.

grass and preserve the corn from yellowing and drying out. This weed does more damage than other weeds and is most difficult to remove by hoeing, for this has to be done during the worst heat, and the weed has long roots and grows back immediately. It is true though that it is excellent fodder grass and we would have no trouble feeding our cattle if we could let whole fields go into hay as cattle pasture. It does not grow in the woods where there are trees, but only on good soil that has been worked for a few years and yielded several harvests. It will come back in the next year.

It is indeed a great shame that our people do not have enough land, for if they had as much as others in this colony and in Carolina, they could let the old weed-choked fields go to hay and prepare new land for Indian corn and peas. For it is easier to clear a piece of ground of trees and bushes than to clean out the old fields choked with this grass weed and preserve the harvest. And they would much like to do this if there were only enough good land. For apart from a few plantations, the good land on this side of the Mill River has now been used for several years and needs to lie fallow; but on the other side of the river, little work has been done because the water has flooded the fields three years in a row. No doubt, the mill dam is partly to blame for this.

If they had enough cattle and calves, they could use the old fields for European grains, which do not let the crab grass take over. In turn, new fields could be cleared in the pine woods for planting local crops. There are many among us who believe in the great God, of Whom we were told in yesterday's evening prayer hour from 1 Chronicles 30:12:[1] "Thine is the wealth and glory, thou rulest over all: in thy hand stands strength and power, in thy hand it lies to make everyone great and strong." For He has wrought many great things among us, and if we only have and keep faith, we shall see more of His glory.

The young couples among us who have little babes in arms are much distracted from their field and housework and urgently require maidservants, who cannot be had in this country, however. But, since there are some little girls in the orphanage who would be well suited for this type of service, several of the men have asked me for them and I cannot in good faith refuse their request, since the orphanage is intended for the benefit of the entire congregation. The children in the orphanage have agreed to go into service; Sanftleben will have Elisabetha Schrempf and Zant will take Christ's girl Margaretha, for which the mother, being a widow, will get some ten shilling's worth of compensation. Mr.

---

[1] See note 3, p.52.

[Ludwig] Mayer, who also has no servant, may well take in the widow Kurtz' youngest daughter, or else she will be useful to Mrs. Kalcher and Lackner with their small children. But Mr. Mayer shall have first choice, and the mother is content with this.

Some good people feel that Paul Klocker will be better provided for in a Christian single family than among the many children and adults in the orphanage, who do not all come from the same place. Much effort has been spent on this frail child, who came to the orphanage after his parents' death; and it has caused Mr. and Mrs. Kalcher much work both day and night. Since we wish nothing for him but the benefit of a Christian education, we will leave it to the Lord to decide about the provisioning of this child. Before Whitsunday, I went to speak to Glaner and his wife; and, against my previous intention, God directed me strongly to speak about said Paul to these two honest Israelites. I then heard that Mrs. Glaner, who herself is without child, loves not only all small children but in particular this boy, so much so that she will take him as her child.

I thereupon asked these two if they wished to care for and bring up this Paul Klocker; and, while they did not agree immediately, they promised to consult with the Lord in their prayer and ask Him for His will. This morning, the man came to me and told me that he and his wife had made up their mind in God to accept this child as their own and to rear it in accordance with the will and the intent of the Lord as He would direct them. They do not need to give Him any children, for he is well supplied with them,[1] and God will provide for the rest. Glaner will get the cow and the calf which have been awarded by lot to the children of the late Klocker.

The two girls will each receive a cow from among those owned by their parents and which have not been affected by the cattle plague. Glaner has his plantation close to the town; and therefore the child, once it has become bigger and stronger, can easily be made to attend school and church. Also, they have good neighbors, so that, wherever he goes, he will see and hear nothing but profitable examples. His oldest sister, who is quite disobedient, will be taken into service by Bichler, who with God's help will do all he can to give her a Christian education and instruct her in the use of the means of salvation and in useful work. The

---

[1] *Sie dürfen ihm keine Kinder geben, denn damit ist er schon versorgt.* This clearly written but enigmatic sentence may mean that they cannot give the Lord any children to sing His praises, as good Christians should. This was apparently Georg Glaner, aged forty, husband of Gertraut Lemmenhoffer.

smallest sister is with Hans Flerl, where she conducts herself well and is well provided for.

Saturday, May 19. This week our people have been busy harvesting and bringing in their wheat, and the weather has been as good as can be hoped for. We had several rains earlier this week, which were needed in the fields, but after that and until this afternoon, when we again had a small shower, the weather has been warm and dry. I have been told that several stands of wheat have been spoiled by rust, and in some cases worse than last year. The rye, however, is quite beautiful and is beginning to ripen. The water in the river is quite low; and, if it should continue to fall, this would stop the mill, which has until now always been usable whenever there was grain for grinding. This would be much to the detriment of our people, since they like to grind their wheat and corn as quickly as possible for it does not keep well in the hot summer and is wont to be infested and eaten through by little worms.

Some years are better than others for protecting wheat and corn from these infestations, and our people have gained some experience in preserving the seed corn from worm damage. But this is not possible for the wheat and rye which is to be ground for flour. I hope they may eventually find means to preserve the European grain from one harvest to the next. The flour can be kept well enough if it has been dried sufficiently and packed tightly into barrels. Grains such as wheat, barley, rye, oats and even peas are easier planted in fields worked with the plow than Indian corn and peas: the seeds are put in during the winter and spring, and once it is in the ground the fields need no further work; by contrast, Indian corn requires much labor during the worst summer heat if it is to bear well.

Also, the European grain does not need as much guarding at night as do Indian corn and peas, since these are much sought after by raccoons and wild cats[1] and also bears and deer. So far, no one among them has followed General Oglethorpe's advice to plant wheat and rye as early as the end of August or the beginning of September, for in hot countries this grain needs two summers to ripen well. Lacking plow and horses, our people have until now spent until Christmas to prepare their fields; but if they could seed the grain three or four months earlier, the grain would ripen before the heat turns oppressive, and thus they might prevent the rust. We have seen that this affliction is promoted by strong thundershowers and rains followed by hot and humid weather.

---

[1] Wild cats do not, of course, eat corn and beans. Boltzius often says wild cats when he means raccoons.

Our people have much trouble getting started and established in this foreign country, where everything is quite dear and clothing and other necessities must be brought from England. Therefore our benefactors in Europe who have until now sent our congregation so many generous gifts for their support will find a rich reward in heaven for their generous and voluntary contribution to the settlement of the Salzburgers in this country. Oh, may the Lord never let us, nor our descendants, forget what spiritual and material benefits we have received in this wilderness through Christian hearts and hands.

Sunday, May 20, 1744.[1] An English merchant in Port Royal who had business in Purysburg yesterday sent a letter from the Reverend Mühlenberg through a special pilot.[2] He let me know that he had received this letter, which is addressed to me, from a captain from Philadelphia whose ship was wrecked a few weeks ago near Port Royal, off the island of St. Helens, while he was on his way to Frederica. Mr. Mühlenberg's letter was dated the 15th of March, and he does not mention my letters of 9 and 30 January and the first of March, but informs me that he had received only this March a letter from a friend in Savannah dated from last September. Therefore I hope that he may eventually receive my mail, even if later than expected.

In it I wrote on several important points which are of great importance to our dear brother as instructed by, and in the name of, our dear Court Chaplain Ziegenhagen. I would heartily wish for the prompt delivery of these points for they will give him some *soulagement* and comfort and relief in his current and still persisting difficult circumstances. He also makes no mention of the letters which Pastor Driesler brought for him from Europe and sent to him from Frederica via Charleston. But my hope is that the Divine providence that has protected his current letter to me in the manner recounted above will strengthen him further and that he will finally receive these urgent letters in good time. None among those which he wrote to us have so far been lost, which the dear Lord may well have arranged for us to assist him with

---

[1] The entry for May 20 is one of the few edited entries for 1744. Some deletions were made for brevity; some material is now illegible. The changes and deletions may have been made in preparation for printing in the *Pennsylvanische Nachrichten*, but the main text was not changed. A clean copy of this entry is found at the end of the manuscript comprising the 1744 diaries (Missionsarchiv der Franckeschen Stiftungen, Series 5D9, fols. 100-103).

[2] As for the entry for February 29, the letter by Mühlenberg was lost and is preserved only in this excerpt. See Introduction, p.viii, note 2.

our poor prayer and intercessions, for that is all we can do. He is deeply in need and is much burdened by the building of the church and the school. Despite his large congregation, he cannot even get the help of a decent schoolmaster.

Mr. Vigera is still with him and keeps school in the country. Whatever he builds up in one congregation is as good as destroyed and ruined in the fortnight or three weeks during which he must be gone from that congregation. Since he has not received a single letter from his Fathers in Europe so far, he is suspected of turning the European collections to his own use, which is of great detriment to his office. The Herrnhuters are not sitting still during all this. His congregation in Philadelphia consists almost entirely of old people, poor day laborers, servants, and widows and orphans who cannot contribute anything to his support. He thus is forced to subsist and work entirely without a stipend. But the Lord does not deprive him of all blessing, in particular in regard to the congregation in Germantown, as set forth in the following:

> For, while this Germantown congregation was entirely rotten and terribly divided, it has now recovered a little bit and is showing some buds promising flowers and fruit. But you will well imagine, my dear brother, how I feel. If one wishes to serve, and is quite alone in such an extensive calling, one is hard put to carry one's head in joy. If a green bud breaks open in one place and one must be off again for another parish for a fortnight or as much as three weeks, caterpillars and other vermin will eat it up. One would rather be dead than alive. I have often thought I would rather stay in one place and leave the other parish to itself as I have no help nor am I promised any, but I cannot do that in good conscience. The best would be Isaiah 30:15. "In returning and rest shall ye be saved."
>
> I cannot write much of special blessings, since I am like a plowman who has accepted a piece of overgrown land from which to make a plantation. I must first fell trees, root up stumps, build fences and pick up the boulders. More harm can be caused in thirty years than can be made up for in a year.[1]

---

[1] Mühlenberg is referring to the long period when the Pennsylvania communities were lacking a steady supply of ordained Lutheran ministers. See Charles H. Glatfelter: *Pastors and People: German Lutheran and Reformed Churches in the Pennsylvania Field, 1717-1793.* Kutztown Publishers, 1980.

Those who follow me may plow, sow, and harvest. One can see here how much God's word can do on its own, for we are without any human help and also without any support from the secular authorities. People show their hunger for God's word, but there is also no lack of terrible mockers and of those who attack the Lord and His word in the most frightful manner. A few of the simple minds have confidence and will say to the wicked, I shall complain of you with our parson. But here the most subtle answer will be: What do I care about the preacher, this is a free country. But elsewhere I see that the Lord does assist us. Our winter school in Philadelphia can be continued, thank God.

If we but had a learned pious schoolmaster, he would accomplish more than three preachers. Mr. Vigera looks after the necessities and, out of the love of his heart, has gone to New Hanover and there assists in teaching the young. I consider this a great comfort. We cannot, it is true, offer him much in the way of expensive hospitality, but he makes do.

Of the congregation in Philadelphia, he writes as follows:

Our merciful Lord has helped me over the harsh winter and kept me in halfway decent bodily health and spirit. The Philadelphia congregation is still together and edifies itself without interference in our new church. This is indeed a great blessing. The congregation consists mostly of poor old people. Those who want to pretend to status have partly turned to the Anglican Church and partly to the sects, and a few remain neutral. But we will have to see if this state of affairs will persist. I cannot say much on this topic, because prior to my arrival things were indeed strange and there was much discord and disorder. But people are quite hungry for the word of the Lord, and it is a great shame that I can preach to each congregation only every third Sunday, in particular in Philadelphia, where there are many churches and meetings where people go when I am not in town. I rely more and more on the verse: "Pray ye the Lord of the harvest that He will send forth labourers into His harvest."[1]

---

[1] Matthew 9:38.

The two country congregations in New Hanover and Providence are growing fast and I have established with them several articles pursuant to the laws of this province, and I have obligated the members in such a way that a preacher who does his work in these two congregations will have enough for his subsistence. In town, however, the congregation is not yet well off and thus cannot establish a proper salary. Every time I celebrate Holy Communion in that church, we have two hundred or more communicants, but they are all poor sheep, mostly day laborers, servants, widows, and orphans. For Philadelphia is the first place of refuge for our Germans after their arrival.

Those who cannot pay for their passage or who have been orphaned or widowed on their way over are bound to stay close to the city after their arrival. For this reason, I have not yet demanded any salary from them and have kept the Germantown congregation so that one pastor may serve both congregations in town. If only the dear Lord would send us a preacher to help out, I would gladly leave him the choice of those congregations which are in reasonably good order. One cannot force matters here but must proceed gradually, in particular as Count Zinzendorff and his preachers have offered their services without pay. But with a little patience, and if one is concerned with the Kingdom of the Lord above all else, the rest will follow on its own, in particular once we have some relief from the heavy burden that the building of the church has imposed on us.

Tuesday, the 22nd of May. An honest Salzburger came and bore witness of his own grief and that of other people at the story that our orphanage is no longer to continue as before. Only recently, he and his friends had taken comfort from the verse: "I will plant them in this land assuredly with my whole heart and with my whole soul."[1] But he did not think that it bode well for our congregation and its future if the orphanage were to be abolished. I gave him my explanation, that is that the ingratitude of many adults and children had been strong and they had considered this salutary institution more like a workhouse than like a benefit.

By these and similar judgments they had sinned heavily against the orphanage and above all against the Lord, and therefore it was little

---

[1] Jeremiah 32:41.

wonder if God had withheld the bounty which had until recently flown to us on its behalf.

I was unable go further than be guided by the Lord through conviction and His providence. I had no business to incur debts, and now even less desire to do so since so many took offence at the orphanage and considered it a superfluous institution. And it now seemed to me that it was no longer necessary to continue it, for there was no need for widows and orphans to live in the orphanage, nor did they show any desire to this effect, and the children were far enough along to serve for several years with other Christian people in the community who need someone to stay with their little children, for they would always have enough supervision by these people.

Some were dissatisfied with the orphanage because some children who could go into service are kept in it and used for labor. From the very beginning the orphanage was not to be harmful to the community but useful, and it may be useful that the children should go into service with the people here. In this way they can be maintained much more easily with clothes and food than in the orphanage. For, because Kalcher has no other workers but Lackner and the sickly Hertzog and because no servants are to be had, it is not possible to raise enough food as is consumed in this household.

Linen and all sorts of clothing cost a lot of money all through the year. Not to mention white flour, sugar, tea, lard, etc. The cattle plague did a lot of harm to the orphanage; and from now on, if they had to feed a lot of people, they would have to buy meat, for which there is no money.

With his aforementioned helpers, Kalcher has a great deal to do from morning until late at night. Mrs. Kalcher now has four small children of her own. Mrs. Lackner is also nursing one. Therefore they have no time to look after the orphans or to instruct the little girls in sewing and other womanly chores, and otherwise there are no competent persons to be had for instructing the children.

Kalcher well sees the lack of supervision and the harm the children suffer from it. He worries because he cannot help because of his many tasks for the good of the orphanage and the community; and he is becoming weak and sickly from his heavy work and troubled mind. European and local crops are planted every year at the orphanage and a kitchen garden must be maintained, for which many hired hands must be employed all year. The same holds of sewing and laundering, which cause many expenditures. I can be spared these if I let the children go into service with Christian people. By this there will be not the least harm to the children but a great alleviation for me and the honest Kalcher, and a blessing for the members of the community. May I never have to dismiss the upright manager and let him go out empty-handed after he has in the last seven years used his time and strength in the service of the orphanage and at the same time has rendered good service to the congregation and as well to me and my dear colleague. We could not do well without him, for we always need someone who can lend a hand with the public works, but these are matters of which I cannot provide any detail at this time.

Therefore my thoughts are as follows: Kalcher and his close friend, Lackner, will stay in the orphanage and keep in service a few of the girls and one or two boys, as well as the sick servant, Hertzog. I intend to keep in food and clothing him and one of the boys. Kalcher in turn will take care of the others who help him in his work and also help his and Lackner's wife and their children. He has had a good harvest of European grain and hopes for rich yields of Indian corn, beans, and pumpkins, which will amply provide food for him and his people.

I intend to make up for the expenses incurred now and in harvesting the crops, using whatever means will be at my discretion. Should Kalcher be in need unexpectedly, I shall gladly try to help him. And thus he will use the buildings of the orphanage for his household and be the supervisor for the few cattle, horses and other possessions of the orphanage, until God may indicate what should be done. I much hope that this institution will remain a place of care and provision for widows and orphans under the blessing of the Lord, although we shall not now need it (and may God give that we shall not need it for a long time), although I am not free to express myself in detail on this matter. In the meanwhile, I intend to contribute enough from my own means, and from that which God may send our way, that these institutions can be maintained in their buildings, that agriculture, silk culture and other profitable things may be improved. In this we can make good use of the land on the other side of the Savannah River, which I have partly bought and partly leased for three years from the shoemaker, Roeck. If by chance a pious widow, or a woman who may be widowed, or a little orphan or a sick man or woman shall ask to be taken in because of honest need, we shall gladly provide for such people to the extent that God will enable us. But such gifts shall not be forced on anyone, and shall be denied to those who are openly lacking gratitude and in whom the purpose of such an institution cannot be realized in any event.

I hope that the Lord may by and by enable us to pay the current debts of the orphanage, which are not half as large now as several years ago. Once we have paid off our obligations by so curtailing our affairs, we shall be careful not to take up new ones and use the present blessings to further a good cause. My dear colleague [Gronau] is quite fragile and I fear that I am a stranger and a guest before the Lord, as are all our Fathers. Thus it would not be prudent and Christian conduct to leave a burden of debt on the orphanage manager and others who come after us. This is all the more urgent in that we can arrange matters differently without offending the honor of the Lord and the charity of our neighbors.

If our heavenly Father should desire further gifts from Europe to flow to our orphanage and we had no widows and orphans to care for, we should see to it that such charitable gifts of love were well used in our congregation. The Zion Church remains to be finished. Repairs and changes in the design of the mill will also require expenditures, as will many other matters designed for the common good which have in part been sustained by the orphanage and in part from other gifts. Last month, the cattle plague recurred on the plantations, and it seems as if many a housefather would lose all his cows and thus a large portion of his physical support.

I would dearly love to put such people who are punished by the hand of the Lord in a way of returning some cattle to them if only the heavenly Father, in whose hand lies the power and the glory, would let something flow though my hands for this purpose. It will go as it goes. My Father on High provides counsel and help in all matters.

From now on, I shall no longer have any expenditures for the orphanage and shall only see to it that the debts are paid off. It is difficult to manage a house for orphans and widows in America which must be largely maintained from gifts coming from Germany, for we have received few donations from England. One hundred German Imperial florins[1] are about equivalent to eleven pounds sterling, and this amount is quickly spent in the management of such an institution, although it is a big amount by German standards. Servants cannot be had and, if the fields are to be worked by day laborers, the expense will far exceed the income.

---

[1] Boltzius and his correspondents in Germany were well aware of the various exchange rates of German monies in England and North America. For the period at issued, see McCusker, John J., *Money and Exchange in Europe and America, 1600-1775*. 1978, University of North Carolina Press.

There is no longer any real need for a house for widows and orphans in Ebenezer, as we can now see clearly: for all children are lodged according to their will and the farmers are glad to have them to help with their work, in particular with their little children. If in the future God should direct to us widows and orphans and the sick who are in need and desirous to join our congregation and live in the orphanage, we will gladly oblige them if this is God's will. Once our debts are paid off (toward which we shall sell some of the horses), we shall use any donations from Europe which the Lord may provide in His generosity to finish the Zion church sooner rather than later and start a new and necessary addition to the mill and undertake other useful tasks for the building of our Plantation City.

In particular, we would much like to give a sum of money to the dear people who lost most of their cattle this summer and last year so that they might be assisted in purchasing new animals. And the poor and sick shall not be forgotten. Here too, it is said: 2 Corinthians 9:8, "God is able to make all grace abound toward you; that ye, always having all sufficiency in all things, may abound to every good work."

Wednesday, the 23rd of May. Our dear Pastor Mühlenberg is well beloved in our congregation and, as he knows that our listeners like to hear news of him, I have read to them the letter we received and instructed them to use his news to good advantage. His many trials and harsh circumstances serve us for Christian intercession, and the good which the Lord works in him and through him gives us cause to praise the Lord. We have again learned how both large and small among us have many advantages in body and soul over those who live in Pennsylvania, and none among us has reason for discontent. May we instead use everything that the Lord gives us in such a way that His purpose is reached in everyone, for else it is an easy matter for Him to withdraw His excellent grace from us. We have instructed our listeners with much seriousness in this lesson, for we all tend to become accustomed to the easy life and thus think little of our gifts; but, when new trials beset us, everyone acts as if we had been in dire need all along.

As we can see from his letter, in Pennsylvania too there are poor people by the hundreds who cannot start their own household and must seek to earn their bread as well as they can. They can hear their preacher only once every three weeks. When he performs his office in the other congregations and they want to hear some of the Lord's words on a Sunday, they are attracted to the meetings of other people and thus they do damage to their souls. Children and adults who keep to the preaching of God's words must witness the most terrible offenses and hear frightful calumnies against the Lord, Christianity, His words, and the office of the minister. In short, the liberties granted there are being abused to insult and seduce one's neighbor.

The authorities do not interfere in religious quarrels. Who would feel safe and content in a country in which God is so much despised and abused? No doubt, one day the courts will wake up to these offenses and their long arm will reach those as well as the people who live close to the Spanish border.

The winters are excessively cold and cause much inconvenience in church and school and during work. Since it is only the poor who hold on to their church there and use Mr. Mühlenberg's office, it is only the children of the poor who come to school and that only during the winter, as is the case in Germany in the spring in poor villages. Until the fall, they are needed for work and forget during this period what they have learned in the winter. How much discord and error rule there in matters of religion. We see this in all places where they lack ministers and schoolmasters. The authorities offer no assistance whatever to the churches. And if the teacher does not look out, the most dissolute fellow can bring a complaint against him and cause him trouble and unrest.

The frequent news from Europe also offers us much comfort, and poor Mr. Mühlenberg has been forced to do without it. God truly makes a gift to us of that which he and his listeners are forced to go without: That which burdens and tortures him and others, we are being spared; we have easy access to His word, for not only can we hear Him each day, but we also sing and read because we have Bibles and hymnals and other goods books in every house and cottage. And he sees to our daily needs. If we only seek the kingdom of the Lord and His justice with an earnest heart, we shall continue to be given all. True, there is no lack of chastisement among us, but this will work to our best because of God's great mercy.

Thursday, the 24th of May. Today my dear colleague began holding the catechism lesson in the school, so I had time to visit some people on the plantations. Last year the two neighbors Brandner and Steiner suffered much from the cattle plague, and this summer one head after the other is being taken from them, and no external means can help against it. In all that they see the hand of God and turn this chastisement to their humiliation; and they thank Him for treating them so mercifully, since they deserved far harsher punishment. Now they must do without milk, which falls rather hard on their small children. Now they will also lack manure, which they need very much to improve their exhausted land. God has granted both of them very beautiful German crops. Thus, to be sure, our marvelous God takes with one hand but gives back again with the other; and we have heard Him being praised from 1 Chronicles 30. In His hand are strength and power, in His hand it stands to make everyone great and strong. It says earlier in this same verse : "Thine is the wealth and glory before thee, the dominium over all things." From Him, indeed, we have and enjoy everything that we have in this foreign land (where we are surely guests and strangers in a very special sense like the Patriarchs). Therefore, to test us He can take back everything that is His, and no one may think that it is happening without reason or is happening unjustly. However, since He rules over all things, He has in His hands the hearts of rich people in Europe and all places and can so guide them now or at some other time to our needs that our wants have been filled and we will be refreshed again after our tribulation. In our conversation we were guided to the beautiful story in Tobit 13:24, and in the prayer of Sara we found many pleasant matters and expressions which were well made to strengthen us in our faith and encourage our prayers.

It is written very expressively in v. 14: "When thou art wrathful thou showeth mercy and goodness, and in troubles thou forgiveth the sins of them who call upon thee." Likewise, v. 21, "Thy counsel standeth not in human power, I know that, but verily, he who serves God will be comforted after the judgment and redeemed from troubles; and after chastisement he will find mercy. For thou hast no pleasure in our perdition."[1] I know that for true and do not let it leave my mind. Christ's cross has its limits, and must finally end. When the winter has finished its shouting, beautiful summer enters, thus after the pain (if one can await it) we shall again rejoice.[2]

Saturday, the 26th of May. With the noticeable help of the Highest, the complicated and expensive economy of the orphanage has been

---

[1] This passage, which suggests Psalm 76 and Tobit 3, is unidentified: *Wenn Du zürnest, zeigest Du Gnade und Güte, und in der Trübsahl vergiebst Du Sünde denen, die Dich anrufen, IT, v. 21 Dein Rat stehet nicht in Menschen Gewalt, das weis ich, aber fürwahr, wer Gott dienet, der wird nach der Aufrichtung getröstet, und aus der Trübsahl erlöset und nach der Züchtigung findet er Gnade. Denn Du hast nicht Lust an unserem Verderben. Das weiss ich fürwahr, und lasse mirs nicht aus dem Sinne gehen. Christi Kreutz hat s. Masse, und muss endlich stille stehen.*

[2] *Wenn der Winter ausgeschreyet, tritt der schöne Sommer ein, also wird auch nach der Pein (wers erwarten kann).* From the tenth strophe of the hymn *Solt' ich meinem Gott nicht singen?*, by Paul Gerhardt.

settled. The manager Kalcher is happy about this and with me has thanked God. With me he will wait with faith and patience to see what He plans to do with this institution that was established in His name. There remain in the orphanage Kalcher, his wife, and their four children. Joined with him is Lackner, who has a wife and a tender little baby. Kalcher wishes to move back to his plantation again. He has a wife and three children.

Kalcher and Lackner have taken into service the two largest girls, namely, Susanna Haberfehner and Catharina Holtzer,[1] who have been in the orphanage from the beginning and give them annually a certain fair wage. Both of them were free to move out or to remain there, but they preferred to remain there, which was the best thing for them. Herzog, a sickly servant, and an eleven year old boy, Johannes Schneider, are being retained by me as servants to help and lighten the work for Kalcher, who does a lot of tasks for me and my dear colleague as well as for the whole community.

Kalcher is now beginning his own household and will use the orphan house, its land and horses until God reveals what is to be done further. No reasonable person will envy him, for so far he has applied his time and efforts for the best of the orphanage and has therefore been unable to begin his own household. From now on I shall have no more expenditures because of the orphanage but I will see to it that the debts are paid.

It is difficult to maintain a house for widows and orphans in America that must be supported largely from charitable gifts from Germany, for little has come from England for that purpose. A hundred Imperial guilders make approximately eleven pounds Sterling, which are quickly spent in such institutions. That is a large sum according to German money. Servants are not to be had; and, if the fields are to be cultivated by day laborers, the expenditures far surpass the income. There is also no more need to have an orphanage in Ebenezer, as one now clearly sees, since all the children have found shelter as they wished. The householders are happy that they can get children for their chores, especially with their little children.

Monday, the 28th of May. This morning my dear colleague Mr. Gronau journeyed to Savannah on horseback and received a Ranger as

---

[1] Susanna Haberfehner was the daughter of Franz Haberfehner, an Austrian who came with the third Salzburger transport and died soon afterwards. Catharina Holtzer was the daughter of Susanna Holtzer, an Austrian who also came with the third transport and died soon after.

a guide. Our friends in the orphanage in Savannah [Bethesda] have long since offered to receive him in love and to accommodate him as best they can if he should come to them because of ill health or to have a change of air.[1] Now Mr. Thilo has advised him to do so, and circumstances have come together so neatly that we have been able to recognize in them the good and pleasing will of God in this matter.

His physical and mental strength has increased right noticeably with his previous use of the well proved Halle medicines and with continued exercise. However, his speech has not yet entirely returned, yet his speaking is now getting easier than formerly. He took his own horse with him in order to exercise with it often, that being a very necessary part of his present treatment. It goes very gently, and on it he will go very comfortably from Savannah to the orphanage and to the German people in Vernonburg and to the surrounding plantations of Col. Stephens and Mr. Parker (a councilman in Savannah) for exercise and recreation. We continue to pray for him and hope with certainty that the Lord will bless this change for his health. For this we will praise Him heartily and humbly. He took with him a letter from me to Pastor Driesler to forward with the opportunity that will go today from Savannah to Frederica.

Tuesday, the 29th of May.   The man who accompanied my colleague to Savannah returned this noon and brought word that he arrived there safely yesterday at three o'clock and that the trip was neither very exhausting nor difficult. The doctor there assumed that he had a little fever toward evening, which, however, will probably have already ceased. Our friends there received him in a very friendly way and wish to supply him with everything possible for his recovery. Mr. Habersham, the manager of the orphanage there, wrote to me and attested his great joy at our dear brother's arrival. He also requested that his wife come down there and spend a while with him at Bethesda. However, her physical and domestic circumstances probably will not permit it. Like the people in my house, she is nowhere calmer than in Ebenezer on the green pasture, on which our good Shepherd leadeth us daily and truly restores our soul.

Two other letters were forwarded to me that Pastor Driesler sent in great confidence to a German butcher in Savannah. In them were very dreadful reports of the Spaniards' great military preparations in Havana and of their threatened attack on Frederica, which a great patron had

---

[1] Bethesda, being surrounded by salt water, was not afflicted by malaria, which was attributed to "miasmic vapors" coming from the fresh water swamps and marshes.

revealed to him. He wished to have his wife and grandchild at Ebenezer and a couple of chests with his best things in Philadelphia. In my last letter, which went along to Savannah yesterday, I asked our dear brother Driesler to be cautious in writing this and that grave matter to the Reformed man (by the name of Alther, a Swiss) because the confidential revelation of this and that secret thing or the expressions and indications used by other people can be evilly applied and accompanied by many harmful remarks.

I wrote a bit about that to my dear colleague saying that, when the letter was given him to read, he should not be afraid of the Spanish shadow men and their arms. It is true they wish to do us harm, but first we must have Immanuel's consent for it. I believe we would be sinning greatly if we were afraid, since two years ago we saw the strong hand of God so clearly for our salvation. Tomorrow, God willing, I plan to write a letter to Pastor Driesler, since I have to write another letter anyway to Capt. Horton, the commanding officer at Frederica. Our Rangers will bring these letters on the first of June to Old Ebenezer and from there to Frederica via Ft. Argyle.

Wednesday, the 30th of May. I believe that our merciful God has awakened many married people through His word right mightily and has sought to draw them into the order of faith repentance. But the Enemy[1] soon sows the tares of disunity so that their spirits bump into each other and sin through many useless and sinful words, and through this all blessing of God's word falls away as if it were mown down. For they often begin again to consider their sin and danger, make good resolutions, and promise much good. However, because they do not both attack the work with earnest prayer, imploring, and waking, then one of them becomes the other's obstacle again.

Today I was with such a family, where disunity had arisen because of stepchildren. I tried by the means God gave me to put them aright from God's word, but it remains to be see how much success my encouragement has had. In such activities much comes out that was previously hidden so that we know what sort of people we have. The disunity between married people is a very common sin that is accompanied by many other sins. When the wrath and anger are past and they are content with each other again, many of them never think of the former sin again. Rather they think that everything is all right with God

---

[1] See p. 23, n. 1.

because it is all right between them again. It is written, however, "Whatsoever a man soweth, that shall he also reap."[1]

Thursday, the 31st of May. A couple of Rangers had ridden around to find out who might have shot the horse that my dear colleague's guide found shot to death with a bullet beside the fence of the old orphanage's cowpen three miles from Abercorn on his trip back from Savannah. It belonged to our carpenter Kogler. At Abercorn they found some Indians, of whom the inhabitants there said that they had left at the same time that the horse was shot and were presumably the culprits. It is their bad habit, when they want the bells from a horse or from cows to shoot them down without any qualms. They do the same thing with the oxen on which they see beautiful horns, which they use as powder horns.

Today I wrote to Capt. Horton, the commanding officer at Frederica, the circumstances of the shot horse and what clues our rangers have found that it might have been the Indians who did it with the request that he talk with Mrs. Musgrove so that the culprit can be found. But now the same Indians are in Abercorn who have constantly stayed at her plantation or right near it. This woman is now at Frederica. I am also asking said commanding officer to compensate the man to whom this great damage occurred as much as the general [Oglethorpe] or the Lord Trustees allow in this case, for they will surely not leave their subjects alone in such trouble. This case is a warning to our people to search for a long time for their horses rather than to put bells on their throats.

It is already a blessing for us that the Indians seldom come to our place. They come quite often to Old Ebenezer and Abercorn, and horses and children go that far. Today a man who has spiritual and physical concerns said that he remembered the words of David: "I must suffer it. The right hand of the Highest can prevent everything."[2] I believe that too with regard to the many kinds of hardships that our inhabitants have to take on in this pilgrimage. If the Lord should grant enemies, then some good arrangement will have to be made for the Indians. So far they have become entirely lawless and unbridled, and the authorities have no power in their hands to restrict them the least bit in their wickedness and excesses. We hear great complaints about the Indians in the country, yet no help can be provided. While we have been at this place much damage has been caused. A couple of years ago they robbed our gardens, fields, and huts; a short time ago they shot a beautiful calf belonging to Dresler along with the cow and ate the meat at Musgrove's

---

[1] Galatians 6:7.
[2] Psalms 77:10.

cowpen and boasted of their evil deed. A few weeks ago they took a large draft horse belonging to the tailor, Metzger, and drove it to Old Ebenezer, took the bells and the foot straps which had been used to tether it in the pasture. They would have driven it to Carolina if an Englishman at Old Ebenezer had not taken it from them, together with his own foal. Rottenberger recently lost a foal that had been with his mare and nobody knows if it was eaten by the wolves or taken by the Indians. As mentioned, they will shoot a horse or other domestic animal for a trifle. Our people have not received any compensation for their losses, although I have written to General Oglethorpe and the magistrate in Savannah and requested something to make good for the losses suffered. And we have fared as badly with requests and petitions in other matters. But the right hand of the Lord can and shall change everything. Such accidents do not happen for nothing and we must consider them in part as a well-deserved chastisement and in part as a trial which shall serve for our best if we can only remain in the order of the Lord and become ever more faithful in His grace.

JUNE 1744

Friday, the 1st of June. I visited a converted woman who had before her the open volume of *True Christianity* by the blessed Arndt. She said that the two consecutive chapters[1] let her see clearly who she was in nature, and who she could become through the unspeakable grace of the Lord in Christ. Therefore, she was deeply bowed by her immeasurable sins, yet nonetheless rejoiced that even she could be helped. Our bountiful Lord assured her of this through His comfort, the gospel. She had attended the prayer hour in a certain household and had received much spiritual benefit from what the head of the house had repeated publicly from our sermons and from their joint prayer.[2] She confirmed what I had heard from several people, namely, that the repetition hour in the public prayer meeting and on each Sunday had given her much benefit because she had a much clearer and lasting impression of what had been preached and said. She had sinned deeply against the second commandment a number of years ago.[3] This she

---

[1] The two chapters are not identified.

[2] This is one of the rare references to edification hours conducted without pastoral supervision.

[3] The third commandment according to the King James version. See p. 10, n.3.

remembers clearly and often, and it makes her all the more careful in her use of material things.

Jacob Kieffer asked me concerning some points on the articles relating to the choice by which grace is bestowed[1] in order to be sure that he had received a sound understanding of this matter through the Lord's word. Recently he was in Savannah and was quickly challenged by the preacher of the orphanage there, Mr. Barber, and by Mr. Habersham, who is the orphanage manager there and who also runs a store in Savannah.[2] However, he answered them well from the Lord's word concerning the great and general love of the Lord for the fallen sinner and Christ's great merit and His reconciliation.

It is typical of these two men, who propagate, wherever they can, the dangerous and bleak teaching of the bestowal of grace through the *absoluto decreto*;[3] in fact, there is no way to escape this matter in speaking with them. However, they no longer try to challenge me on these grounds. When I was last in Savannah, Mr. Barber told me that their family had increased because the schoolmaster's wife had been delivered of a child. I answered that I was pleased at the successful birth but had to admit that my joy would be all the greater if they baptized their children.

He asked how they would be improved by this act. Response: They are reborn by baptism and made into children of the Lord and become the flesh of Christ. Yet he denied all this and said that, if that were true, then all who had received baptism would be reborn and stand in the grace of the Lord through the faith in Christ. This was because one who had faith and was reborn could not again lose this state. This he confirmed with the example of David, who had fallen into the sin of adultery and manslaughter. He even showed me from John 6:37, for these people are usually content to argue on the basis of v. 44. Then they brag that God does not wish to save all sinners but only those whom He, as a free sovereign Lord, has chosen for all eternity. Only those, and no others, are drawn to Christ, and He will deliver them to Him and

---

[1] The German is *Gnadenwahl*.

[2] Habersham was an Anglican, but he had acquired a belief in predestination, following the current teachings of his master, George Whitefield. Because Barber and Habersham so annoyed the Anglican minister in Savannah with their promotion of this doctrine, they had to spend a night in jail. Whitefield in fact was brought to trial in absentia by the Commissioner of the Bishop of London in Charleston, the Rev. Gardiner.

[3] The belief in grace by predestination.

abandon all others to their perdition. I curtly refused to listen any further to his arguments.

Mr. Habersham said afterwards that they were waiting for Mr. Whitefield, for once he came they would all have their children baptized and also use Holy Communion, of which they had all deprived themselves for as long as Mr. Whitefield has been gone. In other matters I find these people to be good and honest, but when I think of their *principia* and of their great desire to convert others to them, my heart aches and a good part of my confidence in them falls away.

Saturday, the 2nd of June. Mr. Habersham wrote me a friendly letter under the date of 31 May in which he reported that Mr. Gronau had traveled earlier from Savannah to their orphanage and that he was well. He had seen him again since then and was also intending to travel back again shortly after writing this letter in order to deliver my letter and a packet of medications. Dr. Hunter feels that if he recovers in S[avannah], it is to be attributed, more than to anything else, to the fact that he has had a change of air and has been able to relieve his mind of serious business. The sea air in the vicinity of the Bethesda orphanage is very healthy and they have very few sick people there. Mr. Habersham added in confidence that their doctor suspected that Mr. Gronau had a damaged lung and that it would be the sign of special divine providence if he could be cured. He will not likely undergo a special cure there and will therefore use our own medicines and those that Mr. Thilo has sent him. May the Lord bless all this in Christ and hear our poor sighs and prayers on his behalf.

This Mr. Habersham is much surprised that there is no news from Europe and that there are no letters from General Oglethorpe or from Mr. [Thomas] Jones or Mr. Whitefield. He recently returned from Charleston without news. Therefore, there can be nothing to the rumor that Mr. Driesler heard in Frederica that the General was being expected every day. Captain Horton has not written me in this respect, although he does not usually hesitate to forward good news from the General because he knows that we consider him our great benefactor and are eager for good news of him.

Since the new moon, we have had a thunderstorm every day. But a few times this was but a weak storm with little or no rain. Today toward evening there was a heavy rain, but it was not too much for the parched high ground. The hail that fell Wednesday night did considerable damage to peaches and grapes, for the wind drove it with great force onto the fruit. Although still green and due to ripen in several weeks, the fruit is now beginning to rot. Although the thunderstorms in this country tend to be quite strong and do much damage to the trees, the Lord has protected us with His hand so far, and we have not incurred any damage. Pastor Driesler writes that the heat in Frederica is oppressive but that they have many thunderstorms and sufficient rain.

Tuesday, the 5th of June. Carpenter Kogler has set up the new sifting or flour box in the mill and brought the news that the little stream had eaten into some of the earthwork of the mill dam and left a hole. This may well increase rapidly and cause much trouble to repair if we do not take care of it in a timely fashion. We have very little in the mill fund at this time. That which remains and the money we borrowed for the purchase of the big boat I will shortly need to pay for the work already done on the mill. I told the people assembled for today's edification hour about the damage to the mill and impressed upon them that we need about eight men among those who still owed a few day's labor from last year's common work to prepare the fascines and close the hole in the dam. God would provide a reward for this by and by so that I would no longer have to burden them with voluntary labor for the mill, although this installation is only for their own profit. Instead, I assured everyone who wishes to work there of a reasonable wage. Those who still owe labor were willing to commence the work on their own tomorrow morning, even though they are knee deep in work on their own fields, which are now bearing beans, corn, sweet potatoes, and rice.

Some of their wives are ill, some are pregnant, or they have little children and much housework so that they cannot offer much help in the fields. Thus there are a good few who use up their strength before their time in cultivating their fields, particularly those on the old plots where the crabgrass is as good as ineradicable. It is a great pity that our people cannot get any servants or day laborers for a reasonable wage. I cannnot be blamed therefore if I do not ask them to perform public works as if it were mandatory labor,[1] even though the works themselves are in their own best interest and to the benefit of the whole community. They need a steady income in this country, where any kind of goods are excessively dear; and they would gladly take on day labor if the work on their own land permitted it. If they have time to work on the church, the mill, etc., we pay them gladly and trust that the Lord, who knows our needs, will help us.

---

[1] Boltzius in quoting his parishioners uses the word *Frohn-Dienst* (corvée), the labor exacted of the peasantry by the landlords.

Wednesday, the 6th of June.   Old Mrs. Rieser, who has had a lame
hip for several months now, is not getting any better. She is in constant
pain, very tired, and prevented from even the most necessary daily tasks.
When I wished to visit her last night, she cooed like a dove in her
prayers and laid her needs before the Lord. I admonished her to the
constant exercise of trusting and faithful prayer which would yield her
more benefit in blessed eternity than all this daily work. She should
fight against the anxiety and fear caused by the needs of her daily living,
because these are sins and prevent us from the good. God, Who has
provided for her until now, will continue to take care of her and her
family. She said that she had just presented to the Lord in her prayers
how He had led her and her kin from Salzburg and had provided for all
their needs on their journey, in Augsburg, and here as well; He would
surely continue to do so. I offered again to employ her husband and her
three sons in fencing our church yard in the town so that they might
make a good bit of money conveniently and without detriment to their
work in the fields. Since they have lost all their cattle during the cattle
plague and must now spend much in her protracted illness, this is sorely
needed. She much appreciated this offer.

Our boat has just returned from Savannah and has brought a message
from Mr. Habersham that, just as our boat was about to depart, he had
returned to Savannah from Bethesda and could tell me that Mr. Gronau
is much improved. You could tell it by his appearance, he added. He
does not say whether his speech has improved as well, but he hoped that
he himself would write me a few lines on his return to Savannah. "I and
other friends in Bethesda are much pleased," he added, "that we had
occasion to prove our love to Mr. Gronau and are grateful from the
bottom of our hearts that our Lord in His mercy is beginning to restore
his health. What we can do for him we do with much joy; and I believe
that, since Bethesda agrees so well with him, he should stay until he has
fully regained his health. This he can do all the better since God has
strengthened you (and here he is speaking about my humble self) to carry
on the burden of your office. I quickly seize this opportunity to write of
Mr. Gronau since I believe this news will please both you and Mrs.
Gronau."

Friday, the 8th of June in Ebenezer 1744.[1]   Having read the points
that apply to our settlers, I much like Jethro Tull's[2] proposal to till the
soil in a new and very advantageous way. Everything he states from his
own experience is easy to grasp, and it is clear that it is not only
practicable but very advantageous; in particular, people will tend to make
tillage harder for themselves than is necessary if they do not know how
to use plows and horses. He shows one thing by many examples which
I like because of our settlers: even the worst soil can be made to bear by
being worked several times by the plow, and a good harvest of wheat can
be raised without any manure. And if even wheat can be raised without
manure, then this applies all the more to other crops.

I am sure that if our wheat, particularly in newly planted fields,
yielded only small grains, this was due not so much to the heat or the
quality of the soil but to insufficient working of the ground with the plow
and late planting. Also, if rot, rust, and mildew are observed, they are
probably due to the same causes. The wheat has in fact improved under
the plow compared with the previous use of the hand-held hoe, and this
although the fields have been plowed only once and then planted.
Nonetheless, this much improved the yield, and how much better would
it have been if each plot could have been plowed several times. For this,
however, we have had neither plows or horses, nor time.[3]

Jethro Tull does not use a hoe in his fields, whether the crop be
wheat, turnips, or another crop; but he has some kind of horse-drawn
plow with which he works wheat and other crops, weeds out the grass,
and loosens the soil, so that the dew can penetrate to the roots. Instead
of sowing by hand, which causes the seed to fall either too thickly or too
thinly and without order, he uses a certain instrument which he calls a
drill. A boy draws this implement across the field in a straight line,
where it makes holes, distributes the seed in an orderly fashion, and

---

[1] The Halle copy at this point is headed "Extract from the Diary". See p. 37,
n. 1.

[2] Jethro Tull, English agronomist, author of *The Horse-Hoeing Husbandry*,
London 1733.

[3] In 1744 and 1745, the discussion with Europe centered repeatedly on the
virtues of Jethro Tull's New Husbandry, whose method was designed for poor soils by
means of heavy and multiple tillage. Boltzius promoted Tull's horse-drawn drill and the
plow as labor-saving approaches to permit use of the pine barrens. Although Tull's drill
may have been imported, greater emphasis was placed on 24 plowshares and tackle
provided through Court Chaplain Ziegenhagen in London; and funds were made available
for the purchase of several draft teams by v. Münch in Augsburg. See also the diaries
for March and April of 1745, in this volume.

covers it with earth (all in one go). In this way, he economizes on the seeds, and the grain sprouts evenly and in orderly rows, which can easily be worked with his newly invented plow. He considers this to be a great advantage and he gives many good examples of this.

I cannot really understand how these tools are constructed, although they are shown in his treatise. Perhaps we can find someone here who has seen them or can imitate them. Our pine woods are not to be despised. If they could only be worked according to his proposals, they would surely make good wheat fields and we would not have half the trouble with this as with other so-called rich land which is thickly wooded and where the roots will grow back for several years. By contrast, the pine stumps do not grow back and they rot within several years or they can be burned off because they contain much turpentine.

Our people hesitate to experiment or try new things, for they are poor, and the poor cannot afford much risk. If only I had, as I have often wished, my own honest servant and if God were to give me the wherewithal to maintain him, which is expensive in this country, I would love to make some experiments to provide an example, and I would expect no loss but much profit. I much prefer the pine woods over the so-called rich bottom land; and, once our people have set up their plantations here, they will find it much easier to provide for their nourishment than on the rich land, where they are plagued by insects and vermin day and night. The mosquitoes are a great bother, and these are not to be found in the pine woods. Nor do bears, squirrels, and racoons have their abode there, which do much damage to the corn. The old land that is full of crabgrass would also be good for planting if we were to follow the proposals of this Mr. Tull and get rid of the grass by means of the plow and encourage it for new growth by repeated plowing but without manure. For he does not think it necessary to let the ground lie fallow for one or several years as long as one is willing to put in the work required. If the author of these proposals has managed to work his wheat and turnip fields with the plow as described, to loosen the soil, and to eradicate the weeds, it will be profitable for other workers to work their Indian corn in this manner and eradicate weeds and grass by planting in a straight line while leaving enough room between the long furrows for one or two horses, walking behind each other and not next to each other, to draw the plow.

Planting their Indian corn and beans in this manner would be a great relief to them, for they will not be able for long to withstand the rigors of working it with a hoe and by hand during the hottest summer, as previously. After today's edification meeting in the Zion Church, I gave them a few examples from this man's work, to show them how they could earn their bread with less trouble, with the blessing of the Lord. They understood most of it readily and were glad of the Lord's providence in this matter. We will discuss this matter further. A man told me that he felt the Lord would prevent the Devil[1] from driving us from here, because He sent us this good advice for our farming. His remark pleased me greatly.

Tuesday, the 12th of June. Dear Pastor Driesler sent me a letter to Savannah which was brought here by a man on horseback. It seems that Colonel Stephens[2] thought that the letter came from the commander of Frederica [Horton] and was therefore an important matter. It is a shame that there is no mail in this country; thus, one must often wait for an opportunity to receive or send mail, or else hire an express messenger to travel by land or water if the mail is urgent. This letter was very dear to me, for he wrote it from the bottom of his heart. On my request, and as is necessary, he has omitted all the fancy terms with which he praised us and our listeners in his last letter. He writes that news has come to Frederica that General Oglethorpe has been promoted by the King and been given the high command of all troops and fortresses in America, as well as full powers to conduct the defense in the new war with France. Thus we now learn that there is open warfare between England and France. May God let us soon hear about peace, as we start the history of the peaceful kingdom of Solomon from 1 Kings 1.

Yesterday, we considered the last part of 1 Chronicles 30.[3] Mr. Driesler is still well despite his work and the hot climate, which seem much worse this summer there than here. His dear wife, too, is better. He requests twelve catechisms in a single edition. However, I cannot meet his request because we have only nine left. I shall give him my poor and humble judgment how, in the absence of a catechism, he can use the new testament with the children for reading and spelling, once they have laid the right ground with their ABC. We have both Testaments and ABC books in abundance. Hallelujah. He has given me some matters to relate to Mr. Verelst, but I cannot take care of these because I lack an understanding of his business and also have no real occasion to write to Mr. Verelst. He writes as follows: "Should you write to Mr.

---

[1] See p. 23, n. 1.
[2] William Stephens, the Trustees' secretary in Georgia.
[3] 1 Chronicles 29. See p. 52, n. 3.

Verelst, please inform him that his warm desires are fulfilled and that during our recent service I have Englishmen almost every day."

Both the Commander of Frederica [Horton] and Mr. Driesler wrote recently regarding the wicked fellow who still pretends to be the Prince of Württemberg. He has spread the most terrible lies and grossly insulted one of the captains there and has been brought to Frederica as a prisoner. In this letter, Mr. Driesler writes as follows:

> Past Tuesday, this Louis (whom others call Rudolph) has been charged in my presence and was presented with all his lying and devilish writings, of which Captain Horton will let you know the details. But the wicked man was not to be induced to make a confession in front of the officers present, and he so confused them that they no longer knew what to say. Finally, they all left and it was up to me to speak to him in private. The Lord gave me His grace, and he confessed to everything and contradicted everything and asked for grace on his knees. May our gracious Savior protect him from eternal perdition.

So far Mr. Driesler. We here have known this young man as one full of wiles and ready for all sorts of intrigues which he is a master at hiding from others. That is why I am worried about him as often as I hear of another invasion by the Spaniards into this colony. For, should he be able to run over to the Spaniards, he would surely love to avenge himself on this colony and Ebenezer, for it is from Ebenezer that his lies and pretenses were laid bare. For as a matter of conscience we have had to inform the Commander of Frederica of the information in Senior Urlsperger's letter which he received from the Counsellor in Württemberg in response to the request of General Oglethorpe through our humble offices. But it is our comfort that Jesus is the Lord of the Earth and, in a manner of speaking, holds His and our enemies on a leash and puts a bar before their wickedness and guiles. He is more than Joseph, without whose permission none may move hand or foot.[1] Who is it then who could harm us, or our successors?

In yesterday's prayer hour and today in Zion Church we heard that Solomon sat on the throne of the Lord and that all of Israel, from the highest to the lowest, paid obedience to him and thus all was well and no enemy so much as stirred. If only all our listeners were obedient to the

---

[1] Allusion to Genesis 41:44.

true Solomon,[1] our dearest Savior, from the bottom of their hearts, He would doubtless let us win peace and its sweet fruits both materially and spiritually. For it is written: "Oh that my people had hearkened unto me, and Israel had walked in my ways!"[2], likewise, "If ye be willing and obedient, ye shall eat the good of the land: But if ye refuse and rebel, ye shall be devoured with the sword: for the mouth of the Lord hath spoken it."[3]

Wednesday, the 13th of June. Mrs. Schweiger had some business with Mr. Mayer because of her small son, and she paid me a visit to talk about the condition of her soul. I hardly expected her to tell me this tale, for usually she comes with this or that discontented complaint about this or that external matter, or that there is discord between her and her husband, or between her and her sister. Today, however, she told me with bowed spirit and in tears that a week ago, during the edification hour in the Zion Church, God had implanted deeply in her mind these words: "For as many as are led by the spirit of God, they are the sons of God."[4]

This had caused her much unrest and sadness in her spirit, and during prayer when she heard the words: "I know, my Lord, that Thou triest our hearts."[5] These had multiplied so greatly she could not keep from crying. She had never been touched that way by her sins; and she felt that God had begun to give her the gift of repentance which He had previously offered to her many times and last year on her sickbed, but which she had never used faithfully.

She considers her heart wicked, vain, and full of deceit, and she begs the Lord to relieve her of these horrors and grant her faith and constancy. I repeated for her the words: They return, but not to the Most High,[6] and thus it had gone with her sister, Mrs. Bischoff, and herself, and thus she would have to put all her strength into her prayers to lay a solid foundation and reach Christ, yeah, to penetrate into Him, so that she might obtain forgiveness of her sins, life, and blessedness. If God would give her in response to her constant prayer an honest heart

---

[1] Jesus, as the Prince of Peace. Solomon means peaceable.
[2] Psalms 81:13.
[3] Isaiah 1:19-20.
[4] Romans 8:14.
[5] *Ich weiss, mein Gott, dass Du das Hertz prüfest.* Allusion to Psalms 7:9 or Proverbs 17:3.
[6] Hosea 7:16.

she would soon become a useful help for her husband, whose soul is in a poor state.

That her son was turning lame she considers a just punishment for herself and her husband because they had often fought over this child and sinned against the Lord. This was ordained at the end of the 10th Commandment, where it is stated that the sins of the father shall be visited into the third or fourth generation. The future will tell whether her present behavior is truthful, for she and her two sisters have often started well but are now again in a miserable state despite all external use of the means of salvation. Few resolve to make an honest denial of their selves, which self is their dearest joy and coddling sin; and thus they remain bound as if by a silken thread if their hearts only hang onto as much as one favorite sin.

I was told that Steiner had his little son of three months before him and had asked him, in all simplicity, what will happen to me and you my dear child if the heavenly Father permits the Spaniards to drive us away, whereupon the child laughed heartily; this was the first laugh of his life, since it has been sad and unsmiling since its birth. This dear man uses everything in his Christian way, and therefore our present condition, for his instruction. Oh that we might all turn around and become like children and like them receive the kingdom of the Lord, how comforted would we not be! No hair on our head would be harmed.

Saturday, June 16. During today's prayer meeting in our house, the Lord gave us much instruction through His word and prayer and we undertook together from this moment on to practice through the spirit of His mercy and through prayer that which our Savior has ordered us in Luke 13:1. The parents should take their children to prayer, for He has created a power through the mouth of young children and babes to destroy His enemy and those who seek revenge. We asked the Lord for grace to accept His son as the highest present of grace, for then we shall be able to apply to ourselves in these dangerous times what is said in Romans 8, "If God be with us, who can be against us? He that spared not his own Son, but delivered him up for us all, how shall he not with him freely give us all things?"

Our two Rangers, who went to Savannah because of my letters and who returned yesterday, told me that in the area of our cowpen they had met three men in the woods, an Englishman, a Swiss and an Indian, who had slaughtered two young oxen and were about to steal away on their horses, carrying the meat. The skins had neither brands nor earmarks, and therefore we assume that they came from our unbranded young cattle. Recently, several cows were slaughtered and carried away in this area and only several days ago Eichberger's large fat calf was shot and mortally wounded. It would seem that these unauthorized butchers were responsible. Today I have reported these unpleasant events to Colonel Stephens and his assistants, and hope to have an early opportunity to send this letter to Savannah.

I also answered the letter from the preacher, Mr. Barber, and translated the major part of Mr. Driesler's letter to him. Quite against my expectations, this caused me much work and yielded a long letter. I also had to answer Mr. Habersham, whose fine letter dealt with the danger of these times. I had no time to write to my dear colleague, but I will do so before we have an opportunity to send the post. I do not like to send a special messenger to Savannah on this Monday, because I have decided, with God's help, to hold a public day of atonement and prayer, which shall be held on Tuesday with the entire congregation. *Quod Deus bene vertat.*[1]

Sunday, the 17th of June. Today we remembered the many acts of charity which we have received over the last two years since the Spanish invasion. The occasion for this act of remembrance, in which we duly praise the Lord, was today's gospel for the fourth Sunday after Trinity, in which our dear Lord Jesus tries to tempt us through the beautiful example of the Heavenly Father to love and charity toward our neighbor. But, since we have also seen many sins which have provoked anew God's anger at us, we have good reason to humiliate ourselves before Him, to confess with Daniel all our sins and those of the country, and to make this day a day of penance and prayer which will also be a day of thanksgiving. This will take place coming Tuesday, God willing. Our listeners, who came in good numbers to hear our sermon, have been asked to join with their families and neighbors today and tomorrow morning to prepare for this important day in humility and sincere prayer. They shall also instruct the children in the purpose of this holy exercise; and I shall do the same in the morning school hours, God willing.

The children constitute a goodly part of the congregation and therefore they shall pray with us and help us praise the Lord. I am always much impressed that many children are brought to church who are still minors and even babes in arms. The Holy Ghost who dwells in them will not tarry to perform that which is said in Psalms 8, and from which I gain much comfort at this time: "Out of the mouth of babes and

---

[1] "May God let it turn out well."

sucklings hast thou ordained strength because of thine enemies, that thou mightest still the enemy and the avenger."

We have much edification and enjoyment from the confession according to the scriptures for our baptized infants. This joy is lacking to those in their churches who see in baptism only an outward sign but not a means of grace by which they are reborn, transposed to the Kingdom of the Lord, and made one with Christ. Pastor Driesler either does not know or has not remembered that the children in the orphanage at Savannah are not baptized for the reasons stated above, however poorly grounded in scripture.[1] For, when the preacher in the orphanage there, Mr. Barber, wrote to him, as he did to me, that his wife had been delivered of a child and thus their family had been enlarged, he wrote him in a letter the following well-intended words: Kiss your little well-grafted branch on my behalf; we shall strengthen and shade it with our prayer, so that it might grow inseparably into the tree of life that is the Lord Jesus Christ and make heaven and earth rejoice with the fruits of its blessedness.

Monday, June 18. In School this morning, I sang with the children, *Erwach, O Mensch, erwache*. When I had prayed with them, I told them of the meaning of tomorrow's day of penance, prayer, and thanksgiving. We all, large and small, have much cause to celebrate this day with a repentant and humble heart in the honor of the Lord and for our own salvation. I told them that sins will bring about the wrath of the Lord and all types of judgment, and I mentioned in this connection several particular judgments which the Lord could easily have imposed upon us through the hostile Spaniards who were right close to us as little as two years ago. We can not deliver ourselves from these judgments, I said, but must fall to the feet of the old and the young Lord, confess our sins, and begin a new life through His mercy.

In this connection, I told them from the prophet Jonah the important and noteworthy tale of the Ninivites who were close to perdition with their children and their cattle, in city and country; but, since they repented within the prescribed time upon hearing the jeremiad of the prophet Jonah, the Lord gladly forgave them their just punishment. For He is merciful and His mercy is as great as He Himself. I then encouraged the children, whom the Lord had made quiet and attentive, to pray with me on our knees and confess our sins. My heart turned tender at the thought of the Mercy of the Lord. In closing, we sang:

---

[1] Boltzius is referring to Whitefield's orphanage and to the doctrine of predestination preached there. See entry for June 1, above.

Gleich wie fein ein Vögelein. I dismissed them and charged them to return home and to continue praying with their families so as to prepare for tomorrow's Holy Day. Some of these children came to the prayer hour in my house between 1 and 2 in the afternoon, when we sang a song of repentance, read the beautiful 2nd chapter of the book of Sirach, applied it briefly to our situation, and finally prayed on our knees. We also had some people from the closer plantations among us. After the prayer meeting, a woman remained behind and told me in sadness that she would like to be sure of her state of grace but could not obtain this certainty; therefore she was full of fear and doubt. I pointed out to her the holy order of divine salvation as fully suited for us poor sinners and advised her to remain constant. If she had converted honestly to the Lord, but still found her road to Christendom full of error and defects, she should not be deterred but come to Christ in prayer and with heartfelt entreaty, for He would accept all sinners, wash them in His blood and would never become tired nor disdainful of her. But truth had to be in her heart.

Tuesday, the 19th of June. On this day (as previously noted) we celebrated in Ebenezer a public day of penance, prayer and thanksgiving for which we have tried since Sunday to prepare with singing, praying, reading of the Lord's word and Christian conversation. In last night's prayer meeting I set aside the normal discussion of the order of the gospel and chose instead for a pertinent and thoughtful preparation for today the very edifying and blessed letter of our dear Professor [Gotthilf August] Francke. He wrote this tender, loving, and fatherly letter to our whole congregation when he learned of our glorious delivery from the hands of our enemies and the terrible invasion by the Spaniards two years ago.[1]

The text from which this entire beautiful letter flows is Psalms 68:2-4. "Let God arise."[2] He clearly presents the condition of our congregation in which there are both friends and enemies of the Lord, as well as the salutary purpose which the Lord had sought to effect through the attack of the Spaniards. No wonder that this attack is now threatening us again, since His purpose was not fully obtained. Professor [G. A.] Francke movingly admonished us:

> Let you yourselves be awakened to examine yourselves whether there are not still many among you who have gone through

---

[1] Battle of Bloody Marsh.
[2] The King James Bible differs greatly.

many good trials and have made many good resolutions but have stopped there and still treat lightly many a sin which they do not wish to abnegate fully. For then there are still enemies of the Lord among you, some in the secret of their hearts and some quite openly. For whosoever loves a single sin which offends the Lord, he is the enemy of the Lord. So seek out if there are not some among you who have learned much but have gone to sleep again, and you shall see that in those who do not have a true aversion to all sin. May everyone among you examine himself, and those whose conscience shall be touched should realize that the Lord has averted the danger of the Spaniards so that all among you who are still asleep might be awakened.

Think further that the Lord has shown for this reason to His and your enemies that which all His heavenly enemies who shall remain unrepentant will have to undergo, if not in this time then surely in the time to come. For He has rendered His help in this time of need so that you might be fully convinced that He is a good Lord who wishes to be your protection and refuge in all adversity if only you will honestly abjure all sins and surrender yourselves full to Him. But those among you who belong to the just and who in the order of repentance, that is through faith, have been delivered from all their sins, they shall rejoice and be glad in the Lord, yeah, they shall rejoice from the bottom of their heart and offer to the Lord a happy offering of gratitude for all His great mercy which He has shown you from the time of your exile from popery.

We sang the most edifying songs at both morning and afternoon services, prayed, and considered the Lord's word with humble hearts. Today's text of repentance was taken from 2 Chronicles 33:1-13, which shows us the condition of the King, Manasseh, both before and after his conversion. We briefly explained the historical circumstances, and for each point a proper application was made to our congregation and our present lamentable circumstances. My sermon went as follows:

This lamentable story is included in the book of the Bible also for our sake. For that which has happened in earlier times has been written down as a lesson for us, and it is our duty to derive from it lessons, instruction, warning, and comfort to the extent it applies particularly to our present circumstances, for it is not without reason that we are being instructed in this important text of penance. The main sin that drew the wrath of the Lord upon Manasseh and his subjects is described in v. 10, and this disobedience of the Lord's word has at all times, in both the Old and the New Testament, been the ruin of man. We gave examples from both scriptures.

And the Lord now gives us this inestimable gift that He will talk to us and convey to us His will. He works on us not only close by but across the seas through His servants, of which we have the testimony of many (very) beautiful letters. But how many will take note of this and consider it a benefit that we are the recipients of His word? If Manasseh and his people had been obedient, we would not read of the terrible events that occurred in vv. 11 ff. And therefore the Lord let them be vanquished by the princes of the army of the King of Assyria at Hiskia.

In these historical times the army of the Assyrians was much weakened when the Angel of the Lord killed 185,000 of their best men before Jerusalem, and they were defeated and humiliated. Manasseh may well not have believed that they would be the tools of his punishment. Now, although the Spaniards were forced to withdraw ignominiously and at great cost two years ago and have lost much territory elsewhere, the Lord has no difficulty in arraying them once more against us and this land for our sins. For it says here: The Lord lets the Assyrians come, and neither they nor the Jews will have thought that this was the work of the Lord. But the repentant and the faithful gain much comfort that their enemies are not free to do as they wish but must observe the order of the Lord. We sang: *Die Feind sind all in Deiner Hand...* Compare Isaiah 54:15-17, Romans 8:31.

Just as a child need not fear the dog in his father's house, thus need the faithful not fear the enemies on the chain of the Lord. So that they attacked Manasseh, and he was not protected by either his men or his fortresses. They captured him under the thorns and the thickets (after the Hebrew). He was not helped by flight or hiding, for who can flee the hand of the Lord? Oh how the sinners and enemies of the Lord are damned: They disdain the lap and the wings of grace of the Lord, and in times of need must seek refuge in the bushes or other mean places.

But, if one is in Jesus as in a fortress, we can say: "I will not be afraid of ten thousands of people."[1] "God knows His own and well

---

[1] Psalms 3:6.

knows through judgments how to find among the multitude those who are sinners and godless."[1] There is no mercy and no hiding, for misfortune will persecute the sinner. Therefore it is better to do penance here in Ebenezer than in the bushes, or even in jail, as it is said of Manasseh.

And who knows whether the sinners who test God's mercy with their impudence and risk the utmost will get of this easily? For have not many died in their sins at the time of judgment? Manasseh was not treated as a King but as a miscreant, they put him in chains and he was treated without mercy in Babylon. He let Satan chain him with the chains of darkness, and now he is being carried off in chains of iron. He treated others without mercy and caused much offence and damage. He disdained the service and the word of the Lord, and now he has learned the justice of God's revenge.

In his solitude, he had time for reflection and felt great fear, not only for his body but above all in his conscience. Truly, he thought himself the greatest sinner and he may have thought that God had not only ejected him from His kingdom but also from His presence, and that there was no mercy left for him. That will cause much fear. And in this fear he will have prayed and implored the Lord eagerly day and night, as the Holy Ghost has ordered, vv. 12,13,18,19, and even rebuked His own son and successor, v.23, that He had failed to pray.

But that He has now done honest penance is shown by the fruits of this penance, and it is a great comfort for heavy sinners that there is indeed mercy for sinners if they will only flee into the mercy of the Lord in Christ, which is as large and great as He Himself. And therefore, if penance out of fear of punishment is dishonest in the beginning, our merciful Lord will not reject it on that ground alone. How will not Manasseh have praised the Lord for the rough paths on which He has led him for his salvation, for during good days and in plenty he would have repented as little as we know of the lost son. But now the minds of his enemies considered him with gentleness and compassion and became willing to let him return to his kingdom in honor. Oh how wonderful, merciful and all powerful is our Lord, whom Manasseh now recognized as a living force in his own tribulations. For Manasseh learned to honor the Lord God as the Lord.

At the end of the afternoon, our listeners were told that God loved their souls as dearly as Manasseh's soul, and He wished for their salvation, for which other servants and children of the Lord prayed as

---

[1]   *Gott kennet die seinigen und weiss unter dem Hauffen durch Gerichte diejenigen wohl zu finden, die Sünder und Gottlose sind.*

well. But, if they would not let themselves be won over in Ebenezer, then God would force them to walk the stony road with them, as is shown by Manasseh's fate and that of others. And the many horrible reports that reach us here have the same purpose; Jeremiah 18:7-8. At the beginning we heard the words from Psalms 90:11, "Who knoweth the power of thine anger? even according to thy fear, so is thy wrath." May the Lord bless all this in us.

Wednesday, the 20th of June. In today's class I repeated for the children the meat of yesterday's sermon and on the text. When I returned home, I looked in the repository of my dear colleague Gronau for a certain book so as to reread a passage, but my hand fell first on the Report by Captain von Wreech [1] on the Swedish prisoners in Siberia. I had not thought of this for a long time and thus not today. Since this strange story fits marvelously with yesterday's text of penance it impressed itself on my mind with great force. I could not but give witness of this in our prayer meeting, after I had recalled the events in question from this edifying work.

Since God was unable to bring our brothers in religion -- the Swedes, among whom were many Germans, to a recognition of their sins, errors, and false justification during their goods days, he led them onto stony roads and let them become prisoners of the Russians, where they led a pitiful existence for many years. But the end was worth it, in that God had in all this a salutary purpose which was reached by and by in the conversion of many souls.[2] The children as well were served well by this story, and they thanked the Lord for this sharp rod of discipline which, in a manner of speaking, He tied onto their backs not for their death but for their lives. After I had told my listeners a summary of this story of the Swedish prisoners and showed how much mercy the Lord had shown them in body and soul at the time of these trials, I read them something from a letter which these pious souls had written to the late Professor [August Hermann] Francke as an armor ordained by the Lord. In this letter, they testify how the eternal love of the Lord had run after

---

[1] Boltzius here refers to the report on officers and soldiers of the Swedish army defeated by Peter I at Poltava in 1709 and living as prisoners of war in Tobolsk. A conversion movement was fostered among them by Pietist preachers supported through Halle. It is described by Curt Friedrich von Wreech in his *Wahrhaffte und umständliche Historie von denen schwedischen Gefangenen in Russland und Siberien*...published in Sorau, 1725, and circulated among the Pietist communities in Europe and abroad.

[2] In fact, von Wreech's narrative relates mainly to the officers at Tobolsk. The enlisted men were forced to labor in the mines and in construction.

them unto the place of their imprisonment and how He used first His holy word, but as well several strange coincidences to awaken them, bring them to reflection and conversion, and to lead them onto His path.

We implored our listeners urgently to use the lessons they heard yesterday and to become obedient to the Lord throughout their life, for else He will use the same rough means for their salvation as we have seen for Manasseh and these Swedish prisoners. But frivolous people always say: "Who knoweth the power of thine anger? Even according to thy fear, so is thy wrath."[1]

Saturday, the 23rd of June. Before I could leave for the preparation hour on the plantations, some letters from Savannah were brought to me. One was from Mr. Habersham, and the other from my dear colleague Gronau. He again wrote that he was well taken care of in Bethesda in both body and soul and that he was not worthy of all this attention. God's word, as it comes to him in reading, listening, and meditation, is much blessed in him and in his soul as he prepares for eternity. He is still weak in both body and spirit, although he sleeps well and his appetite is good. He himself does not know when he can return to Ebenezer, for, just as the Lord determined for him the travel to Bethesda, so he will wait for a sign of His will to return to Ebenezer.

He dearly longs to see us here again and, as much as I would like to have this dear brother back with us, I cannot ask for his return because I would rather have him stay there and get well. If this delays his return, it is better than to have him resume his work here and relapse into illness. I would not want to bear this burden of guilt. The Lord will convince him of His will as to staying or returning, for I know that this His servant has no other concern than to serve Him though his deeds, his patience, and his suffering. Neither he nor Mr. Habersham gives news of the rumors of war. The latter wrote as follows in his note:

> I opened your letter to dear Mr. Barber, it much refreshed me and drew tears from my Eyes. May the Lord strengthen you and us in Himself, and then we shall not fear, though a host encamp around us. We hear nothing further about the enemy as yet.

The preacher in the orphanage at Bethesda, Mr. Barber, had not only noted in his last letter that God was doing great things for the body and

---

[1] Psalms 90:11.

the soul of my dear colleague Mr. Gronau, but he also asked me to give him some news of the kingdom of the Lord in Ebenezer. I then told him in my reply that I had heard and read with much pleasure, joy, and praise of the Lord that the Father of all mercy had shown much of this mercy to my dear colleague in soul and body during his stay at Bethesda, in that He edified him from his word, and had miraculously returned him to health. In this the Lord had also shown much mercy to me and my congregation.

I let it be known that, as the merciful Lord was with him in Bethesda, so His presence edified us here, in that I can feel His blessing and help in many tasks I perform in the absence of my faithful colleague. The grievous news of the approaching judgment of the Lord helped us in our congregation to draw the people to greater attention to the word, to go into themselves and recognize their sordid and dangerous state. This again leads them to look eagerly for Christ as the only help in their spiritual and material needs, as we can see in many daily examples. The faithful among us are again driven to pray the Lord to spare us and our children for some time and give us an occasion to prepare for eternity. I knew, I added, that there were some in Bethesda who are the apple of His eye; and His friends, who join us through the spirit of grace and through the prayer that lives in them to call upon the Lord in heaven to preserve this colony and extend His kingdom in this and other places. We can and will base our prayer on the dear words in Romans 8. "If God be for us, who can be against us? He that spared not his own son, etc. How should he not with him also give us freely all things?" I also told him that in the current situation the words from Proverbs 10:24 had an impressive effect on me: "The fear of the wicked, it shall come upon him; but the desire of the righteous shall be granted." Now that the Lord is ready to seize our souls, there are two things that impede the Lord's work and sadden me: 1) that good souls prefer to stay within the Law instead of penetrating into the gospel of the Lord Jesus Christ.[1] They feel their sins and hate them, but because they do not feel the full measure of repentance and sorrow as strongly as they would like, they consider themselves to be hard and spiteful and do not wish to seize upon the true mercy of the Friend of sinners, Jesus Christ. 2) I have noted that the Enemy sows a dangerous seed among neighbors and acquaintances through trivial suspicions, harsh words, wrong interpretations of each

---

[1] Boltzius is again contrasting the law of the Old Testament and the grace of the New Testament.

other's speech, etc. This has caused much damage, in particular among fearful and weak minds. May the Lord protect us against these and other weaknesses that beset our Ebenezer-Zion, may He trample Satan beneath our feet, and may His arm be victorious.

About 89 persons had announced their wish to take Communion, which, if the Lord so wishes, will be administered tomorrow. As I have learned today, 10 of these wish to abstain, as well as several married couples who have been disturbed in their minds and therefore fear to come forward. Some of these I myself was forced to advise to step back from the Lord's table, and with these I will gladly use my services next week to remove the obstacles in their path. Oh how busy is the Devil to prevent the good even among husband and wife. The only encouragement in these matters is that some who are in bad shape as regards their union and reconciliation let me know about this and desire instruction. Others, however, as is shown by the example of [Johann] Michael Rieser, cannot be brought to any confession of their misdeeds but know how to extricate themselves in front of others. If we were truly to reject these, they would close off their minds against my office once and for all and thus would be deprived from all instruction through the word and all church discipline, as this Rieser has done previously.

Ebenezer, June 26, 1744.[1] Jacob Kieffer has been asked to pilot and steer a Purysburg merchant's boat to Charleston and has just returned. He told us of the defenses being thrown up in great haste around Charleston. In Savannah, people are thinking of flight and are beginning to take out their most valuable possessions; for this, they have asked for the service of our large boat and our people. Mr. Driesler wrote me that his German listeners had resolved to flee to Ebenezer if the danger should increase. He himself does not know what to do with his many belongings brought from Germany, which are valued at £300 Sterling. He wishes he had left them behind. He has asked my advice on this. May the dear Lord Himself give him advice and teach him to do His will also in regard to the material goods brought here. I also ask Him to instruct me what to write this our dear brother.

As befits Christians, we will also seek to profit in our souls from all sorrowful news. For this reason, I do not try to keep from our listeners the news we learn from credible people by word of mouth or in print. I am much impressed that Pastor Driesler had set a day of penitence and prayer that very Wednesday, while we spent the preceding Tuesday as

---

[1] The Halle copy at this point is headed "Extract from the Diaries". See p. 37, n. 1.

a solemn day of mortification before the Lord. In today's edification meeting at the Zion Church we repeated what we had learned during the day of penitence and in preparation for Holy Communion from the impressive Bible stories. For our listeners' instruction we also added some news of the heavy judgments of the Lord on this earth, such as I have learned from the Charleston newspapers and from other sources. Here our heavenly Father has acted as one would with a naughty child: He did not proceed to punishment right away but shows them switch and cane, swishes these on the table or against the door and then puts them away if the children turn to obedience. The two verses: "Prepare to meet thy God, O Israel," and "if God be with us, who can be against us"[1] please our hearts right well. Since the Enemy[2] mixes the chaff of misunderstanding, secret insult, and dislike against one's neighbor among the wheat that the Lord is now sowing into our hearts during these sad times, we showed both the offenders and those whom they have offended their duty from the words of the Lord Jesus: "Agree with thine adversary quickly, while thou art in the way with him" and "If thou bring thy gift to the altar."[3] We drew some lessons as to the goal of life from 1 Kings 2, of which goal many of our faithful listeners deprive themselves by excessive work in the fields (which is an unrecognized offence against the second commandment).[4] I therefore repeated our suggestions for an easier way of working the fields and added a few explanations.

Reasonable people agree with me that, by using a plow in the manner suggested, they can plant 10 acres with native crops with a third as much effort as they must now expend on 4, even if both man and wife work most diligently. This spring, when the Indian corn was planted on plowed land, I heard them say that now that the ground had been worked over, the crabgrass was growing in with much greater strength, and therefore plowing was not a good way to till the ground. Now, however, no one will repeat this, for the crabgrass was easily pulled from the loosened soil, while on other fields it had to be cut down three times and the growth in Indian corn on these fields does not compare with that on plowed land. Indian corn must be planted from 4 to 5 feet apart; and, if they work the ground along a straight line they can weed out the grass with their plow, which has no wheels.

---

[1] Amos 4:12, Romans 8:36.

[2] See p. 23, n. 1.

[3] Matthew 5:25,23

[4] Following Lutheran and Roman Catholic numbering, Boltzius numbers the commandment on keeping holy the Sabbath as number three. See p. 10, n. 3.

The long furrow, five feet wide, has been loosened with the hoe-plow[1] around Michaelmas, when harvesting of the local crops has past. For their wheat crop, the long furrows where the Indian corn stood now are used to work the wheat and other European grains with the hoe-plow[2] and eradicate the grass. Their old fields, which are now full of grass and yield hardly any crop if worked in the old manner, can be left fallow according to this new method, as long as they plow the ground and eradicate the grass during the fallow period. Everyone now would like to have a plow, for they are all convinced that these proposals are practical and advantageous.

Thursday, June 28.   Our boat came back from Savannah on Wednesday full of flour and other items for our manager, for our houses[3] and for some people in the community. Mr. Habersham wrote that he had learned that flour, sugar, wine, tea, and coffee were sure to go up in price and some items might become unavailable altogether; he therefore had wished to make sure that our houses had enough in the way of provisions. The merchants in Savannah had cleared their stores and sent off their goods, and others were thinking of doing the same as soon as the danger of invasion appeared imminent. This is why I have been asked to lend out the orphanage's big boat. But we had no further news of the enemy than that reported last week.

Our dear brother Gronau went from Bethesda to Savannah on horseback on the very Tuesday when our boat docked there. He writes that my news and that of the congregation have pleased him much. His health is changing often: sometimes he is very weak, on other days he feels a bit stronger. He gets exercise and fresh air by travel on both land and water, and this makes him feel much better. He is longing to come home, but he does not wish to make his own choice but defers to the will of the Lord and our advice and well considered counsel. If the Lord will strengthen him, he will preach to the Germans in Vernonburg next Sunday. We too wish to see our dear brother, and we will beg the Lord to advise us on the counsel which we should extend to him regarding his return. Colonel Stephens has kindly accepted my package of letters and, not yet having sent off his own mail, will include it on the next occasion for safe delivery.

Friday, June 29.   After our edification meeting, Gabriel Maurer asked me to visit him, for he was dangerously ill. When I arrived, I

---

[1] *Hack(?)-Pflug.*

[2] This seems to be Boltzius' rendering of an implement suggested by Jethro Tull.

[3] Boltzius means the two parsonages.

learned that before the edification meeting his horse had thrown him onto
a sharp stump and that he had been unable to breathe or speak for some
time afterward. His wound is in his side at a dangerous spot, and Mr.
[Ludwig] Mayer, who was called in for help, has tried to alleviate his
severe pain with compresses and potions and seems to have succeeded
with the Lord's help. He and his wife had looked forward and prepared
for the edification meeting, and little thought that such an untoward
incident would prevent them from attending. Last night he had a
dangerous and terrifying dream, which has awakened him and led him
to himself. He recognized that he and his wife were not yet quite ready
to please the Lord with their state of mind, and he considers this incident
as a special and possibly the last occasion for repentance before the Lord
should call him into His kingdom.

I talked to him according to his circumstances, instructed him briefly
in the order of salvation, and warned him of faithlessness in the face of
the Lord's mercy which He has shown him for the last six years. He
cried and wept with us before the Lord as much as his weakness would
permit. When I left, he implored me to come back as soon as I could,
which I shall do tomorrow with God's grace, although this will mean
turning school over to the schoolmaster. In the afternoon, I have a
prayer meeting at my house and must prepare for Sunday. Mrs. Kocher
next to the Maurers has fallen ill again, and I intend to see her on this
occasion, but this will require additional time.

Saturday, June 30. Our Rangers, or reconnaissance scouts, have
learned that shoemaker [Peter] Kohleisen drank himself into a stupor on
rum or sugar cane brandy during his stay in Savannah and on the way
back. Because he had two inexperienced boys bring him back in the
little boat and could not show them the way, they lost their way and
drifted about close to three days. Ordinarily, the trip back past Abercorn
requires less than a day. Yesterday afternoon, I had him called into
town and discussed his case before Bichler and the three Rangers. I
reminded him that I had visited him shortly before our day of penitence
and had pleaded with him to watch over himself so that he might not fall
back into his accustomed sin of drunkenness, for this would be a much
more serious transgression right after our day of penitence. He took my
advice with gratitude, and he and his wife bent their knees with me
before the Lord. Nonetheless, he now has caused much offense and
grief, as he had recently done in Purysburg. What, I asked, would be
the end of this? He was under the wrath and the judgment of the Lord,
and his heart was empty of remorse and would finally deprive him of the

salvation of his life and his soul, as has happened with shoemaker Arnsdorff.[1] I had almost exhausted all forms of punishment but to no avail. Thus, he forced me to proceed as the Lord Jesus has prescribed to His church and its servants in Math. 18, and this will take place coming Sunday. On the occasion of his marriage, I paid on his and his Swiss wife's behalf a debt of 17 shillings Sterling, on the condition that he would have to repay this money if he continued in the vice of drunkenness. I had warned him of this obligation on several occasions, and this would now be his material punishment. He also would have to pay the three Rangers for the trouble they had to take with him, for a total of 3 s. May God have mercy on this poor slave of his vices and of Satan.

JULY 1744

Friday, the 6th of July. Other demands on my time prevented me from my intended visit to Gabriel Maurer. Therefore I was all the more pleased to see him in the meeting at the Zion Church. He has been quite close to death but the Lord has helped restore him and has blessed the internal and external remedies used on the instructions of Mr. [Ludwig] Mayer. When I visited him last, I saw that the Lord has begun to show his soul much mercy; he felt his sins to be strong and sought his only salvation in Christ. I told him something about the King Hizkiah, who had been close to death like him, but God had added a few years to his life when he had prayed humbly to Him. Hizkiah also had resolved to avoid for the remainder of his life those matters that had troubled his soul. But the Book showed the extent of his subsequent frivolity and arrogance, and Maurer should use this example not only to make good resolutions but to pray and watch over his intent so that it might not turn into water, as many times before.

I called out to him: "Behold! you have been restored to health (so far, and I hope for good), do not continue in your sins so that you might avoid a worse fate." I reminded him that so far God had graded his punishments. At first, he had fallen ill like many in Old and New Ebenezer. More recently, a worm had crawled into his ear and he had been in danger of losing his hearing. Soon afterwards, his face and eye had swollen shut and he had been in much pain. And finally, he had

---

[1] The shoemaker Andreas Lorentz Arnsdorf had drowned while returning drunk from Purysburg.

suffered his fall from his horse. Therefore I called to him, "Sin no more, lest a worse thing come unto thee."[1] My admonishments were dear to him and he publicly asked me to continue them.

Saturday, July 7. Since we have received word of the fears of a Spanish invasion, the cattle plague here has come to a stop. This I am sure has been brought about by God's mercy, for the fear of danger and deprivation has driven many of our faithful into renewed and urgent prayer. This in turn has helped them to tear their hearts away from all tangible things by means of His grace, and they have thrown themselves and all their families into the merciful hands of the Lord. Simon Reuter has lost almost all his cattle this year, and he thanked the Lord for this chastisement from his heart and with many tears. For, he said, he had not believed that his heart had indeed been so attached to the things of this world until God tested him by the loss of his cattle. This recognition has been very useful to him, and he has humbled himself all the more before Him in the name of Jesus Christ and has had all the more reason to seek His grace. This has caused him to humble himself fully before the name of Jesus and to seek His mercy. He in fact has shown him mercy and he now felt much better.

The plague has spared the cattle of the faithful and honest [Ruprecht] Zimmerebner, and all his cattle have come through alive and well, although many losses occurred in his neighborhood. As a sign of gratitude, he gave a tame milk cow to one of the poor in the congregation. Another faithful man, who has had to bury one after the other of his cattle this year, was now quite calm and resigned, but he told me that he was not sure if this should be called resignation or if his heart had lost the power to feel pain. For he recognized that his sins had earned him much punishment but he could not be as sad as he thought he should be. A woman told me that she often thought of the words: "Punishment and pain must follow upon sin," etc. She often feels both weakness and pain in her body and she was nonetheless content for she knew how much she had sinned in previous years and during her marriage before she had come here. And yet the Lord had mercy on her. In the afternoon, a woman from the plantations came by to let me know that the Lord had continued the work of mercy in her heart. He also took care of all obstacles and difficulties that were barring her path, and He had given her the power to understand His word much better than previously.

---

[1] John 5:14.

JULY 1744   103

Sunday, July 8. Our merciful Lord has given us great joy today by enabling both of us to preach His word. We thus could resume the repetition hour from three to six in the afternoon, which had been turned into a prayer hour during my colleague's absence. He has testified several times that, even at the orphanage in Savannah, he could feel the prayers said in Ebenezer on his behalf, and this had been the Lord's special sign of grace in his circumstances. Today, he praised the Lord before the entire audience for the mercy that He had shown him both in Bethesda and in Ebenezer. We recited Psalm 126:[3], "The Lord hath done great things," etc. The dear brother is still weak in body and spirit, and therefore a full sermon is a hard burden on him, involving as it does the effort to tax his mind with meditation. But this time he himself had wanted to preach, although I was more than ready to repeat the morning sermon in the afternoon as I have done during his absence. The merciful Lord still gives me enough strength. In the morning, we used as exordium for the gospel for the 7th Sunday after Trinity the beautiful words: Sirach 34:20, "The Lord is," etc.

Monday, the 9th of July. Today court is being held in Savannah, and the two men who encountered the unauthorized cattle butchers in the vicinity of our cow pen travelled down, as they were asked to testify by the Savannah authorities. I have again offered the Germans of our confession to preach during the week on any day of their choice, and to celebrate Holy Communion with those who are hungry in the spirit. I still cannot absent myself from Ebenezer on Sundays because of my dear colleague's feeble health. A week ago, Mr. Gronau preached to them in Vernonburg on the words: "Draw us after thee"[1] and the Lord supported him in body and spirit despite his weakness. He had held close to the words: "They that wait upon the Lord, they shall inherit the earth."[2] During his sermon, he could see that many among his listeners were touched in their hearts.

Mr. Habersham, the Bethesda manager, had advanced me some money for urgent expenses, and has sent flour and other necessities from his stores. This enabled me, despite the current severe lack of funds, to pay off some of those who were owed for their services to the orphanage. But I no longer could defer repaying this dear friend in these meager times, and I also needed some more funds, and thus have been

---

[1] *Zeuch uns nach dir.* Unidentified hymn.
[2] Psalms 37:9.

forced to write him a draft on Mr. Tillard.[1] This draft had been written last week together with our letters of avis but is dated as of today, and I have sent it down with the two men who have gone to court. Since I did not have express permission for this draft, I added to the letters of avis one to court chaplain Ziegenhagen with two copies and informed him duly of why we were forced to write this draft. The last letters we have received from Europe were dated from November and December; since then, nothing has come in. We have heard that the Spanish had seized a boat destined to our coast, and it may well be that this carried our crates and letters. This we must suffer gladly, for our sins have merited not only this but more severe punishment.

Tuesday, the 10th of July. Young Mrs. [Magdalena] Mayer sent word on Sunday that she was ill and would like to speak with me. When I saw her yesterday on her plantation, she was weak in body but had gotten up and her illness had abated somewhat. She told me that the Lord had richly rewarded her for our day of repentance, which for her had indeed been a day of penitence; and, when she went to the Lord's table soon afterwards, He had shown her mercy, so that she now surely felt her sins had been forgiven. In her illness, from the night of Saturday to Sunday, all her sins, including those that she had not regarded as such in her previous life, had been presented to her mind vividly and quite awfully, and she felt as if Satan had touched her and pulled her away from Jesus. She remembered that God had pursued her while she was under the Popish yoke and had shown her great mercy not only in leading her out of the Pope's dominion but shown her the truth, while many of her countrymen were left to be guided by the gospels in a valley of fear and death.

She now much regretted her lack of gratitude and of faith before the wisdom revealed to her, and she regretted that she had often hidden what the Lord had given her in His words. But she now had resolved with all her heart to yield to the Lord Jesus even if she should find it hard to believe that He would receive and pardon a sinner like her, full of ingratitude and lacking faith. I told her that this was a merciful testing of her spirit, for God gave her now, as she had begged Him on many occasions, the opportunity to recognize and feel her sins. And this was

---

[1] William Tillard was a London merchant. He acted as one of the Trustees for the Society for Promoting Christian Knowledge in administering a fund from which the Ebenezer ministers were paid. See Archives of the Society for Promoting Christian Knowledge, London, Series A1, 2 and 3, in particular "An Account of the Contributions toward the Relief of the Protestant Exiles from Salzburg..."

many thousand times better than leaving her in her blindness and false comfort until she would be forced to recognize her sins before His chair of judgment.

The Lord's intent in this her trials was to draw her to Christ, of Whom it is said: "This is a faithful saying, and worthy of all acceptation, that Christ Jesus came into the world to save sinners."[1] While we talked, we thought of several hymns, and I partly sang and partly read one to her: *Wo ist mein Schäfflein das ich liebe,* since neither she nor her husband knew the melody. Mrs. Lackner[2] also was present and joined in this awakening, and all begged me to return soon and enrich their edification through the word of the Lord. I have great pleasure in visiting such souls whom the Holy Spirit has made hungry for the word of the Lord, for it is easy and rewarding to my soul to talk to them.

I was told that the low water under the mill dam had dug holes into the dam and would cause further damage unless we could devise a way to stop it. The channel through which the water is to run is now above water level; and, since the water must seek its course, it has run partly under the channel and partly under the ditch which was built to lead the water to the wheel. When I returned home from the Zion church, I asked Kogler and Rottenberger (two skilled carpenters) to ride out to the mill with me and consult on how to control the damage. They now recognize that they did not really know enough about mill construction to build a durable installation, and we fear that their work will not withstand the test of time because too much has been missed in the beginning.

If there is no real improvement, the mill will not last long, and it will not be possible to use it all year. Our people need the mill now, when the wheat, rye and barley has been brought in, but the water has fallen so low that not a drop reaches the mill wheel, and this causes much damage to their interests. But these mills, as everyone knows, are a major benefit to our people, since they are thereby encouraged to take up seriously German agriculture, which is less demanding on their strength. Therefore, I have not ceased planning for the improvement of the mills this summer. But our carpenters could not be convinced because a new construction project would require much in the way of funds and labor.

---

[1] 1 Timothy 1:15.

[2] Boltzius writes the name Lochner, Lachner, and Lackner, mostly the latter. See p. 11, n. 3.

Now, while we stood together and contemplated the damage, they told me how they would improve the mills for long-term and efficient use. The water would no longer dig any holes into the dam, and the mill would run even at low water; also, a rice stamping mill and a much needed lumber mill would be constructed. They have learned much from their previous experience and their plans are quite reasonable. If I can provide the funds, they will regain their spirit; for our poor congregation, which is still in their difficult beginnings, cannot contribute to this project. Also, we cannot expect people to contribute as much free labor as previously. For the sake of the Lord and our community, the mills must be returned to a useful and permanent condition, and we thus trust in His almighty power and prudence to provide the means for us to start and finish this project, for which the faithful among us pray to Him with all their heart. We are considering all this in the fear of the Lord and shall continue in His name.

Wednesday, the 11th of July. Young Lackner no longer wishes to stay in the orphanage and work jointly with Kalcher. Instead, he has received a large tract of land from Rottenberger on which he will build and start his own household. His wife is said to be the cause for his wish to leave Kalcher, with whom he had worked both in the fields and the house. She understands little of how farmers manage their household and has contributed little or nothing to their work. Kalcher will have little loss from this new arrangement, but time will tell whether they can make do on their own land, since she can do little to help him in the house. Their new plantation is next to the bridge and thus close to the town. It is a beautiful piece of land and one of the best locations in this area. They will receive provisions of corn, rice, and meat and other necessities from the orphanage, for they would have a hard time making ends meet otherwise. It is an equitable arrangement, since he had helped Kogler and Kalcher work the fields and in planting. I hope they will keep on good terms with Kalcher and his family. It will profit him in his work if he can continue to use the plows and other equipment of the orphanage.

It is not clear yet where Kogler and his family will end up. Lackner did not wish to stay close to him because of his wife. I would wish for Kogler to stay with Kalcher and continue in their fieldwork as well as serving the community as a much needed carpenter. This would be profitable for himself and his family. Since her confinement, his wife has been quite weak and would rather stay at the orphanage than move out to a plantation. She feels the pull of the Father to the Son quite strongly and keeps close to Mrs. Kalcher, so that it would be a shame if she were to remove herself from this opportunity to work for her own good. I trust the Lord will settle all for the best.

I had given the three families the two oldest girls for servants, that is Catharina Holtzer and Susanna Haberfehner; but, since there is now this change regarding the Lackners, and Mrs. Kogler prefers doing all the heavy work herself, the Haberfehner girl has been given into the care of Brandner, a move which has pleased her well. I myself am pleased by this change for the girl's sake, since she will be well taken care of and supervised in his house. Catharina Heinrich will work with Mrs. Kalcher in taking care of the children and the house, in return for room and board. She will take care of her own clothing because most of her time is spent in working for herself and other people.

Sunday, the 15th of July. There was much rain yesterday, and since it lasted well into the night, we were prevented from our ordinary prayer meeting in which we had planned to finish the story of David. All that remains is to consider the circumstances of his death and burial from 1 Kings 21 and 1 Chronicles 30. We were much edified recently in contemplating from 1 Kings 2 how dear David, who during his time served the will of the Lord with a grateful heart, went into blessed eternity. For during his lifetime he had not only been grateful to the honest Ben-hadad and his clan but before his death had ordered his son, Solomon, to show mercy to the children of his old benefactor as they had shown him love and generosity when he had to flee Absalom.

We used this occasion to recall the story of the Salzburgers' expulsion and flight and all the good that they had received in body and spirit from strangers in Germany. They were eagerly awaited in the towns and received as dear guests, as I myself saw in Halle and as is well known from the newspapers and other pamphlets; I used the opportunity to make some specific mention of this in the assemblies at both churches, Zion and Jerusalem. And how much have we, who belong to the Salzburger community of emigrants in Ebenezer, benefitted from the goodwill of the Honorable Trustees, the Honorable Society, and other dear but quite unknown benefactors in Germany and Scotland whose spiritual and material benefactions continue to flow upon us to this day. In particular, their ministers and schoolmasters receive annual salaries from the Honorable Society, and there is a constant stream of love and benefaction that flows towards us across the deep and wide oceans from Europe.

Whenever our church bell is sounded, we are reminded of the gifts that came to our church and its construction with this bell and we are encouraged to thank our benefactors in our prayers and sighs. And these great matters we as elders, as was done by David, must communicate to our children and thus encourage them to give thanks not only with their mouths but also with their deeds. Above all, this should consist in reaching the goal which our benefactors and the Lord have set us, which is that we should surrender ourselves to the Lord as an eternal sacrifice of gratitude in body and soul and carry witness to our benefactors by our open and full piety. In this we shall render the greatest benefit to ourselves and our children, for it is said: "Whosoever offereth praise glorifieth me,"[1] but whosoever does not offer praise and does not let the Lord reach this goal in Him, according to Romans 12:12, then he will dishonor, and that is the way on which we shall lose our salvation and our benefactions. See also Revelations 11:5.

Monday, the 16th of July. The Savannah authorities have ruled that the two children of Michael Schneider (our former cowherd) should be freed from their indenture.[2] He had taken back the oldest son last fall, but yesterday he fetched the youngest, who had been reared in the orphanage from his 6th year. I had informed the authorities that this younger son, who came to us in a feeble and sickly state, had not been able to serve our congregation, but we had instead served him by taking him into the orphanage and providing for his body and soul for now well over five years. Therefore, his father was acting in an inequitable and ungrateful manner by taking back the child now; moreover, this would only redound to the boy's disadvantage, since he is still too weak to resist the evil temptations to which his wicked and blind parents will expose him. But the gentlemen of the council paid no heed to my argument and simply wrote that both boys should be free. On top of that, they informed the father before they wrote me, and this has done further damage.

I sent word to him on Saturday of the decision made in Savannah, but he was quite uppish about it and used coarse and disrespectful terms about me, saying that he had known of their decision before I did. He refused to take his words back today, although I surely did not deserve this conduct in view of what I have done for him and his children. Today he fetched his eleven year old boy from the orphanage and gave

---

[1] Psalms 50:23.

[2] Having been donated to the Salzburgers, Schneider and his family had not previously enjoyed the emancipation granted to the Trustees' servants.

not the slightest sign of recognition that his son had been raised here for the sake of charity. This is not much different from other parents whose children have been reared in the orphanage; and, since the goal of the many expenses in the orphanage has not been achieved in either children or parents, I have had ample reason to close the orphanage down until the Lord shall indicate His will to me.[1]

Recently, the beautiful example of David's and his children's gratitude for the benefactions they received led us to the verse: "Whosoever offereth praise," etc., and so we must say *vi oppositi*, those who do not make a sacrifice of gratitude dishonor the Lord, and that is the path on which He will withdraw His blessing from us. And therefore I had to tell my listeners that the Lord has taken from us some valuable gifts because of our monstrous ingratitude, among which I listed 1) the health of my dear colleague, who yesterday was still not able to preach a single word, 2) the mills, which we have been unable to use for almost the entire summer, 3) the orphanage, which only future times may recognize as a benefaction of great importance for our community unless our people throw off the shackles of their blindness; 4) the two crates from Augsburg and Halle which probably have been seized by the Spanish; 5) the loss of much cattle through the cattle plague.

How easy it would have been for the Lord to deprive us of peace, yeah, to seize our land and houses, if some of the faithful among us had not stood like a wall and stepped before the breach. May the Lord reward them for this! Quite recently, Margaretha Haberfehner went into service with Brandner and there is now only one girl in the orphanage, that is Catharina Holtzer, a sickly thing of about eighteen. I hear that she too wishes to move away from Kalcher and take service with others in the community. For young people like change, and many among the older ones secretly give them poor advice. Lackner and his wife and child will shortly move to their own plantation, and I do not yet know if Kogler and his wife and two little girls will stay and continue working with Kalcher. Young Hertzog, a sickly Salzburger, will probably remain with Kalcher, and I will provide for him, as I would have for Michael Schneider's son. But Kalcher has little use for him, for he is often sick in mind and body, and one has to humor his moods if he is to remain calm.

---

[1] As throughout these unpublished diaries, Boltzius is seeking to justify the imminent closing of the orphanage, which would have put the charitable donations to Ebenezer in jeopardy.

One of the main reasons why the orphanage cannot be maintained without imposing a heavy burden on the benefactors in Europe is the great difficulty that faces us in raising our cattle, which are the major source of income. But since the Trustees' manager in Old Ebenezer is entitled to brand all young unbranded cattle running in the woods, we have lost a number of head of cattle and on top of it had much annoyance with this man and the authorities in Savannah. We would rather give up the lost cattle than harm our good standing with the Trustees and other benefactors connected with them. Although I have been specifically asked to provide them with information and have been promised help, I have yet to receive an answer to my lengthy letters and specifications of the number of our old and newborn cattle that has run off into the woods and cannot be returned.

Tuesday, the 24th of July.   This morning, the Surveyor General, Captain Avery, came to see us and we and others who know him were much pleased to receive him. Around noon we went out to inspect our mill with the carpenters and he told me of his surprise at the excellent work our people had done. But since they had no engineer to instruct them and are not familiar with the type of construction customary here,[1] they could only go as far as they did. I showed him this year's wheat, which has as many kernels and is as heavy and yields as much flour as the English type does. He was very pleased with the flour which the miller took from the sieving box for his inspection. It is in no way inferior to English flour. He was much surprised to hear that the miller had ground several bushels of Indian corn and thirty bushels of wheat from Sunday night to Tuesday morning, that is, in two nights and three days. He can see better than during his last visit how far Ebenezer has come with God's blessing and how little justice there is in the accusations of those in Savannah who slander us and wish to do us an evil trick under the guise of good advice. He knows full well the intentions that the Savannah crowd harbors against me and my people, and they are no better than Thomas Stephens, who had several lies printed about Ebenezer.[2]

---

[1] Boltzius' reporting on the merits of each stage of mill construction changed considerably over time. The design by Avery that is published in this volume should provide the basis for a more objective assessment.

[2] For Thomas Stephens and the Georgia Malcontents, see Trevor R. Reese, ed., *The Clamorous Malcontents: Criticisms and Defenses of the Colony of Georgia, 1741-1743.* Beehive Press, Savannah, 1973.

Mr. Avery advised me earnestly to ask General Oglethorpe or the Lord Trustees to reign in those who wish to extend their power to Ebenezer and cause grief and damage under the guise of justice. I do not like to enter this controversy, but will let the Lord guide my mind in accordance with His wishes. But I do know from many occasions that our success in Ebenezer is a thorn in their side; and, since the Lord Trustees use this success as an argument to fight against plans to import Negroes into this colony, they would be much pleased if they could sow discord. But the Lord shall stop them in their tracks.[1]

Captain Avery told us why the canon was sounded yesterday between three and four in the afternoon, namely, to make public the declaration of war against France, with the citizens standing at arms. I was much impressed with the parallel of this news of war and today's Bible lesson, for the wisdom of the Lord has arranged it that we should start upon the impressive and useful story of Solomon from 1 Kings 2, both last night in the Jerusalem church and today at Zion church. If this Solomon reigned in peace over his subjects despite the wiles of his enemies, what can we not expect from our great Lord and King of Peace, without whom none can move hand or foot, and who said: "All power is given unto me in heaven and in earth ... I am with you always."[2]

So why should we fear the anger of the Spanish and the French. For the faith of a true subject of Solomon says: "I will not be afraid of ten thousands of people,"[3] Just as Solomon sat on the throne of his father David and his kingdom grew in peace, thus Jesus, once He conquered the nature of man, sits on the throne of the Father and rules over a constant and peaceful Kingdom, until all His enemies shall lie prostrate at His feet. He has given great hope to His subjects, who have followed Him in battle and victory, in these words from Revelations 2, "He that overcometh..."[4] And since this Prince of Peace has promised us this larger gift, how should and could He not give us the less important gift of material peace in the face of all our enemies.

---

[1] Boltzius' rationale against introducing slavery in Georgia was in part based on the need to provide labor for the Christian working man, a view he shared with the social reformers among the Georgia Trustees. His letter on this question was one of the few excerpts from the diaries for 1744-1746 which Samuel Urlsperger saw fit to print in 1747 (13th Continuation, Part I, 30-46). His views conflicted sharply with those of George Whitefield, who used slaves to support his orphanage in Bethesda (letter to Boltzius in Colonial Records of Georgia, 24, pp. 434-444).

[2] Matthew 28:18, 20.

[3] Psalms 3:6.

[4] Revelations 2:26.

Thursday, the 26th of July.   Some of the people who wish to work for wages will soon be able to find employment, for Captain Avery spent all day yesterday to find out the circumstances and location of our mill and has made several good proposals to restore the mill to a more lasting condition at little cost.   He also proposes to add a rice stamp and a board mill, which would be very advantageous and of great help for our feeble newcomers in making a living.   There is enough water for everything and all will be well arranged once we have shored up the dam in a permanent manner.   This skillful man, who is very well disposed toward me, is not only instructing our carpenters in the details of the new design, which he has put on paper in considerable detail, but he will return to supervise construction once the wooden parts have been built and the present high water level has gone down.   He will arrange everything for the best of our community.   All his proposals and suggestions are quite solid, and Kogler and other men are entirely convinced that with God's blessing they will ensure a solid and durable design.

Monday, the 30th of July.   Zant came to my house this afternoon and brought me his Bible so that I might underline in red ink, for his easier recall, the exordia that we have examined this year.   Retracing these strong and beautiful verses from the Old and New Testaments has also worked for my own edification.   He as well as others rejoices that there are plans not only to repair our grist mill but to add a rice stamp and sawmill.   Many of our people need threshing floors for their European grain, for which they need heavy boards.   But if these must be cut by hand, as has been done until now, this runs into money.   The same is true for the boards they need for their floors and attics, and many have been forced to make do without wooden floors, which is deleterious to their health.

My intention with this mill is to obtain cut boards not only for our people but also for sale here in this area.   This in turn might yield something in support of the rice and grist mill, to which our people cannot contribute anything except the customary milling fee which goes to the miller.   Thus, I never have anything left over for upkeep and repair of the mills.   This is what I hope will come from the lumber or board mills, with God's help.   I also heard that the people in the congregation are looking forward to having a rice stamp, for stamping and polishing white rice is one of the most demanding tasks.   Just as they lost all incentive to grow rice for want of milling equipment, they now will resume planting in view of our plans. The land beyond the river is very well suited for rice culture. May God bless our plans and designs.

Tuesday, the 31st of July. The surveyor will be finished today with his work on the plantations and return home tomorrow, God willing. The German people of our confession in Savannah wish to go to the Lord's Table this week, since it cannot be done on a Sunday because of my colleague's continuing illness. I will use this opportunity to go to Savannah. The travel bears hard on my health these days; but, since it must be I hope that the Lord will mercifully preserve me and bless my work. Captain Avery has made detailed drawings for the impending mill construction so that everyone can have a clear impression its the design. As soon as Kogler's injured foot is no longer quite the obstacle it is now, he and several selected men (for many are more of a hindrance than help in this kind of work) will prepare long posts which will be the first thing required for repair of the mill dam.

All wooden parts are being prepared according to the design of this surveyor and engineer, and Kogler prefers following his instructions rather than his own head, since he is convinced of Mr. Avery's skill, experience and honesty. Once the wooden parts are ready and the water has come down, the surveyor will return to direct the construction. He is much concerned not only to ensure a permanent structure but to do it in an economical manner. Until now, the mill has run day and night, which has been of great benefit for our people in processing their European grain. I hope the water will remain high enough for this for some time to come. We see the value of this mill as soon as it is out of operation for a few weeks. The surveyor assured me that, if he knew of a mill location like ours in or around Savannah, he would build a saw mill on his own account. He has built five mills in Scotland but has never seen such a good flow of water.

AUGUST 1744

Thursday, the 2nd of August. We arrived in Savannah last night at around six in the evening, and I heard that many of the German people had assembled this morning to listen to the Lord's word, since they assumed I would arrive in Savannah Tuesday night and preach and offer the Lord's supper on Wednesday. Some had remained into the evening, and they and some other Germans attended a prayer hour and listened with much profit to the gospel from Jeremiah 33:24, which I had selected prior to my departure. This morning, I used verses 14-16 from this text in my service, and as an exordium I read Acts 16:30, "Dear Lord, what shall I do so that... "[1]

God strengthened me in body and soul both during the prayer hour and the sermon, and He helped me pronounce His word with joy and, as I found during and after the service, with considerable blessing. Some souls gave me much pleasure in their hunger and thirst for the word, and they may thus turn from darkness to light; others are growing in grace.

One man had much to suffer from his wife, but God has begun to rein her in and he showed great joy at this. He said to me that if she would continue on the path of goodness, he would not take the whole world in return, and that he would be content in all his poverty, even if it were to become worse. A man and a widower whom I visited in the afternoon after the edification hour, in which I had read the life of a forgiven sinner, testified that money was not as dear to them as the good which the Lord had given them from His word today. But they cried and lamented bitterly when they described their misery and the great grief which reigned in Savannah. True, there is much confusion among the high and the lowly, and clearly the sins of Sodom are being committed and this offends honest souls.

If we had good land in Ebenezer on which people could find a living, many would seek our solitude and calm, both in our town and on the plantations. Some of the people want to send their children to our school, but I cannot agree that they should do this now when my dear colleague Mr. Gronau is still ill and cannot keep school. I can only spend four hours per week in the school, and during the rest of the time the children are with schoolmaster Ortmann. For some of the people of our confession, we dispensed the Holy Communion, having taken confession after the sermon. It was very hot, but I had much strength for my office both in the morning and the afternoon.

Thursday, the 9th of August. A pious woman told me with much emotion how the Lord had blessed His word in her, both on Saturday at Zion Church and Sunday at Jerusalem Church. She wanted to repeat for herself a certain point and profit from it again, and she asked me to lend her a certain book for that purpose. Solitude and her secret discourse with God give her much profit in her Christianity. She knows of no better friend than Jesus, she told me, for He had never failed her. Her maidservant does not share her state of mind and prefers to go to those

---

[1] This is not Acts 16:30.

among the neighbors who speak of worldly matters, where she reveals her crass spirit.

Another woman came to ask my advice in some matter and this led us to speak about her marriage and her household. Her husband is still governed by the spirit of this world, and therefore he charges as much for his work as he can get and asks her to do likewise, although this is an injustice.[1] If she does not follow his example, she must suffer because of her conscience and even because of his recriminations. She feels much sadness; her heart aches and she wishes to cry when she thinks of women whose husbands are converted and who are joined to their wives in heart and soul, while she lacks this kind of blessed marriage.

Her husband is old, listens carefully and often to the Lord's word, and many times he is touched right closely by it and makes many good resolutions. Nonetheless, she thinks with horror of his end, which now might not be far off. I told her to continue in her prayers for him and be patient in her suffering and continue to give him a good example even if he treats her harshly. For this kind of Christian demeanor would burn in his heart and one day would let him feel his sins. She in turn complained of her sloth[2] and other things in which her Christian faith falls short, and she would much have liked me to speak to her of the law. The gospel did penetrate her heart so deeply that she was overcome by her tears and could hardly speak.[3]

Saturday, the 11th of August. In our reading of the story of Solomon, we reached the part which shows his respect for his mother, Bathsheba, in the 3rd Chapter of Sirach;[4] I had recommended this part to be read by adults and children. Solomon's example confirms the treasure which obedient children gather to themselves, while the opposite is shown by the example of Adonijah. Whenever the Bible gives us a topic relating to the 3rd Commandment,[5] I seize the occasion to impress their duty upon both children and parents, and I never fail to recommend the lesson to the children for further examination and thought.

---

[1] In the practice of Halle Pietism and the Francke Foundations, high wages and excessive claims for compensation were condemned as detracting from the good of the work of the Lord. To some extent, this drew from the medieval doctrine that it was a sign of greed and pride to earn more than Christian wages, namely enough to survive in one's own station.

[2] *Trägheit*, the sin of *accidia*, lack of fervor in prayer.

[3] Boltzius is again contrasting the law with grace.

[4] A book in the Apocrypha, not found in the King James version.

[5] Boltzius says 4th. See p. 10, n. 3.

A woman on the plantations moaned in her chamber and in solitude. I at first did not know the reason for this but shortly learned it. For she showed me verse 16 in the aforesaid 3rd chapter of Sirach: "Whoever forsakes his father is like a blasphemer, and whoever angers his mother is cursed by the Lord." These words had made her tremble in holy fear, for she had not acted toward her mother as befits a child. I told her that it was a major part of penance that the sinner should come to a recognition and strong feeling of his sin, but then not rest content but crawl to the feet, heart and wounds of Jesus, who has given Himself up for our sins. In connection with this verse in Sirach, I pointed her to St. Paul's epistle to the Galatians 3:13: "Christ hath redeemed us from the curse of the law."[1]

We considered the sad story of Adonijah from 1 Kings 2 as a mirror of our wicked and rotten hearts, where we indeed found ourselves confronted as a warning with lies, falseness, hypocrisy, much deceit and crooked paths, abuse of the friendliness of pious neighbors, rebellion and enmity against our masters, disobedience to parents, abuse of the name of the Lord, etc., and as well the threats and punishments which descended upon him in consequence. Here too, it is said that "Sin is a reproach to any people."[2] Since sins comes disguised in much deceit, we have been warned not to be deceived by sin, as was true for Adonijah, but harken to the voice of the Lord. And it is said for everyone among us, if he is true and honest, "there shall not one hair of his head fall to the ground,"[3] but if he shall be found to harbor evil, he will die. But who believes such warnings?

This morning, Brückner showed me a tiger skin of a light brown color, with a long tail and a few white spots around the neck.[4] The beast was heavy with two young and is larger than any dog at our place and taller than a wolf. It has sharp teeth, long feet, a long thin body and claws like a bear. The man had walked around a swampy area in the pine woods on his plantation, armed with an axe, and his dog had stirred up this tiger which ran like a cat up the next tree, which was not very high. He did not know what kind of animal he was confronting, and had called and whistled for someone to bring him a loaded rifle, and all the while the tiger had fixed him with his eyes, without moving a muscle.

---

[1] See p. 115, n. 3.

[2] Proverbs 14:34.

[3] 1 Samuel 45.

[4] This was a mountain lion (*felis concolor*), also called a puma or cougar. In Georgia it was called a "painter," from "panther."

Finally, he went home to fetch a rifle on his own, and when he came back, the beast was still hidden in the branches of the tree. He was lucky to hit it in the head, for else he might have run into serious harm. Had he known that it was a tiger, he would not have been quite so daring on his own and without help. These rapacious animals have caused much harm among chickens and pigs. This summer, four young colts were separated from their mothers in the meadows and we think they were eaten by these tigers.

Tuesday, the 14th of August. A man from the plantations complained with many tears that his wife did not fully obey him, which often caused him to fly into a rage and thus to commit a sin. He found many obstacles in his prayer and in his entire Christian faith. He would much like to be sure of his state of grace but could not make it, and thus he would not die in joy if that should soon be the Lord's will. As concerned his first complaint, I asked him for some details of his wife's behavior, and promised to come out shortly to speak to both of them. In the other matter, I examined him according to God's word as to whether he conformed to the Lord's order; and, since he bears the marks of a penitent soul hungry for grace, I instructed him from the gospel how he could take possession of the conciliation wrought by Christ and the mercy of the Lord that he has earned for us. I told him not to wait for some emotion or extraordinary sign. His faults and weaknesses of which he complained so much would not make him unable to receive grace, but chase him all the more deeply into Christ, the friend of poor sinners. He should fight against all doubt, fears, and suspicion of the Lord and gain from the gospels a full understanding of the unspeakably great kindness and helpfulness of the Lord Jesus. We prayed with each other and the man returned home full of new courage.

Because Kalcher and his wife have not been well for a number of days, I went to their house after this conversation to edify myself and them in prayer. Kalcher revealed to me his humbled heart and told me that his state corresponded to last night's lesson of the deposed Abiathar, 1 Kings 2:11.[1] For this man had grace before the Lord, as was attested to by Solomon, but he had come down in the world. This brought us to the aforesaid verse and the example of Demas.[2]

This our dear friend Kalcher previously carried a heavy burden in the orphanage with children and adults, which rested on his shoulders and left him little time for frequent prayer, silent examination of his soul,

---

[1] This is not 1 Kings 2:11. The story is told in 1 Kings 2:26-27.
[2] Demas, unidentified.

and meditation over the word of the Lord. It is true that he had little or no help in his management of the orphanage. Now the Lord has delivered him of this too heavy burden, and though his fever has set him apart from the people, and he now strengthens His work in him to my great joy and edification.

He also told me of another matter close to his heart, and here I repeated to him the last exordium as a good counsel of the Lord: "Commit thy way into the Lord"[1] (or push onto Him all that you encounter on your pilgrimage to the Holy Fatherland) and place your hope in Him for He will help you. That which we cannot throw onto the Lord (as it is said in another beautiful saying) we should roll and push onto Him as do our workers with their large logs. I knew and he knew with his wife that we had pushed much hardship and many trials away from us and onto the Lord. Thus he should do the same with his problems.

As we were talking, a girl was sent after me to call me home where I found a messenger from Savannah. Today this messenger brought me a letter from our good friend Mr. Habersham in Savannah, in which he wrote under today's date:

> The enclosed (it was a package of letters from Senior Urls-perger, Dr. [Gotthilf August] Francke, and Counsellor Wal-baum) was brought to me by our Capt. Grant of Charlestown, who had barely escaped capture by the enemy. He also brought two crates for you which, as you will probably find from your letters, were already dispatched from London in February. The ship was the only one among 15 to escape a heavy storm, but it was so badly damaged that it had to return to Dover for repairs. It is possible that saltwater has run into the boxes, and I suggest that you come down as soon as possible to see where things stand.

We have often recommended these crates to the Lord in our prayers and hope He will turn out things for the best, and this has confirmed us in our faith. He has planned everything well and set everything aright. Give our Lord the glory.[2] There is no letter this time from Court Chaplain Ziegenhagen, for he wrote separately when the crates were sent

---

[1] Psalms 37:5.

[2] *Er hat alles wohl bedacht und alles alles recht gemacht gebt unserem Gott die Ehre.* From the hymn *Er hat alles wohl bedacht* by Gustav von Mengden.

off, and Mr. Verelst had sent this letter separately with several enclosures to Col. Stephens. Today's letters were sent at the same time as the boxes.

There is also a package of letters for Pastor Driesler which I am dispatching as soon as possible. Prof. Francke's letter is dated from 15 November last, Counsellor Walbaum's letter, on 14 November, and Senior Ursperger's letter, 19 November of last year, to which is added the copy of a letter sent to him by Court Chamberlain von Reck.[1] We rejoice much at the letters, crates, and the edifying circumstances of their arrival here, and I hope that God may guide us in an enjoyable and blessed distribution of gifts.

Wednesday, August 15.   From Pastor Driesler I received a letter dated August 1, from which I gather that he is well. His granddaughter has some affliction of the throat, and he would like to send her here for a change of air if there is a safe means of travel. His news of the English preacher, Mr. Bosomworth, are troublesome. Since he has married Mrs. Musgrove, there is no end to his extravagances. He wants to travel with her to London and take along some Indians for display and to show his own importance; the commander at Frederica, Captain Horton, is doing his best to prevent this trip since it would mean considerable expense for the General [Oglethorpe], but the young man cannot be dissuaded. Mr. Driesler also reports that a party of Indians from the Nations has come down to Frederica. They report that the Indians who have until now been friendly to our side will go over to the French and become a danger to the English colonies unless a party were to travel to their people to confirm them in their loyalty to the English by means of promises and gifts. As in his previous letters, Pastor Driesler complains of the many irregularities in Frederica and he surely has some trouble with the members of his own congregation. When I wrote to him today before my own departure, I communicated several matters to him from the mail we have recently received and which may serve him as well as us.

Our worthy Senior Urlsperger writes the following to confirm our faith:

Recently, one of our German newspapers carried the news that Governor Oglethorpe had resigned his office. This caused some

---

[1] This could have been either Johann von Reck, representative of the Duke of Hanover and the King of England at the Imperial Diet, or his nephew, Philipp Georg Friedrich von Reck, who led the first and third Salzburger transports to Ebenezer.

fear in my heart, but I thought to myself, who knows the truth of this matter? And even if it should prove to be true, God Himself has not resigned His governance of Ebenezer. True, Oglethorpe was a good friend of Ebenezer, but who bestowed this gift on us? God. Can He not give us more or similar gifts? Yes. So now my soul, rest content. We all continue praying for you. The Lord will always prove Himself our Lord of old, and this is our trust. And may all people in Ebenezer say: Amen.

From Dr. Francke's dear letter, I let Mr. Driesler know the following passage, which was written for our necessary instruction and encouragement:

The miserable spiritual conditions at Purysburg and Savannah should cause little wonder since it is worse in many German places where there are superior institutions and more numerous occasions for the preaching of the word. Thus, you should not be discouraged from serving the people at the latter place with a word of admonition as often as your business takes you to Savannah. I gather from your diaries that they do indeed use the occasion to assemble at your services and sometimes are truly attentive. Now, as long as they are willing on their own to come and listen, you should not deprive them of your presence, for who knows if one or the other word shall not be blessed for the salvation of one or the other of these souls? I look forward to your news concerning the invitation to set up a school on the plantations in Savannah, and whether this proposal is taking shape. And if you should have rejected this proposal from a prejudice in your heart, you must nonetheless acquiesce in your blindness, for the Lord may yet open your eyes.

I do not doubt that Mr. Driesler will appreciate these words as well as others which I communicated to him from our letters, for he has inquired on several occasions whether we had not received news from our Fathers.

Friday, the 17th of August. Yesterday evening between 6 and 7 we departed joyously from Savannah in the name of the Lord, invoking the verse: "But it is good for me to draw near to God for I have put my trust in the Lord God."[1] This was very impressive for me in our present circumstances in which we have received our crates and letters. A man on the boat said that he was not in truth entitled to any of the gifts, for he had given up on the goods from Europe but now was torn between shame and joy at this wonderful benevolence of the Lord. Another person had told a pious sickly man that her mind had recalled these crates in her prayers, and she had implored the Lord to protect them on their journey here, and she had rarely doubted that one day they would indeed arrive.

The man in turn said that the grace of the Holy Spirit had until now confirmed this hope in his heart also. There is a good amount of linen and other useful things for the sickly Eichberger in these crates from Augsburg, which the wife of Senior Riesch has bought with half of the money that was still due to his wife from Salzburg.[2] He has had much misfortune this year with his cattle and his only horse, and since he needed another one for his fieldwork and for other business, he bought one from a pious Salzburger against part of the linen that he was expecting. If his package had been lost along with the rest of the crate, he would only have had to repay the seller at a lower cost. But how glad this man and his family will be, now that the Lord has heard his prayers and let everything arrive safely. He will join the others in praise of the great benevolence of the Lord. Let us say: "O give thanks unto the Lord; for he is good: for his mercy endureth for ever."[3]

Saturday, the 18th of August.   Yesterday evening several men gathered at my house on my request. They were to transport the two crates with gifts from Halle and Augsburg to our house. They did it with great joy and eagerness although they had a heavy load to carry uphill from the landing.[4] All rejoiced at seeing the crates; and, when we had them opened and unpacked, our joy and wonder at God's grace grew ever greater. For our friend in Savannah had gathered from the account of the Captain who had brought them to Charleston, at great peril and

---

[1] Psalms 73:28.

[2] Mrs. Riesch was the wife of Bonaventura Riesch, the senior of the Lutheran ministry at Lindau, where several Georgia Salzburgers had resided after the expulsion. Now, after ten years, we see one of the few cases of money being recovered from Salzburg. Because of questionable rates of exchange and of high prices in Georgia, money was usually transmitted in the form of manufactured goods that went through customs as charity.

[3] Psalms 106:1.

[4] The Red Bluff (Roter Berg) on which Ebenezer was situated was the highest in the area.

with many accidents on land and sea, that they might well have been contaminated by sea water, but we saw no damage to books, linen, medications, and sewn and ready-made goods.

However, there are a few things missing from the Augsburg consignment which are on the packing list from there. We assume that they were stolen in Deal by the mob who attacked the poor Captain and his cargo with force of arms, for it is clear that both boxes have been opened by force. The Captain himself said that they had been opened in Deal. We were busy until late at night sorting and inspecting the great blessing which the Lord has bestowed upon us, but had to leave the biggest part for this morning. We praised the Lord for everything and begged him for His blessing of our benefactors.

Last night, old Kieffer visited me and rejoiced that the Lord should have bestowed this wonderful Friday upon us. For just as our boat with its load of gifts docked at our landing, his son was bringing his father's and his own cattle (which is a fine large herd) overland from Purysburg to our neighborhood on the far side of the Savannah River. Thus, there was an occasion for those who had been called to carry the heavy crates to help Kieffer and his sons ford his cattle, while they in turn helped carry the crates and their content up the hill to our house. Both tasks went well. Young Theobald Kieffer told me that the Lord had maintained his cattle without loss throughout the cattle plague both here and in Purysburg, notwithstanding his own poor state of grace and merit, and had protected it on its way to our town.

In gratitude, he wished to give a cow to one of our poor and asked me to name a poor and pious person, for he would not like to make this choice himself. I suggested the late tailor Christ's widow who we hope will make good use of it. She has four untrained children and needs all the help she can get. Thus the Lord has indeed shown us His mercy in many ways these last few days. May He make us grateful and may everyone state in full truth : "But it is good for me to draw near to God: I have put my trust in the Lord, that I may declare all thy works."[1]

Tuesday, the 21st of August 1744 in Ebenezer.[2] After the sermon on Saturday, I showed my parishioners, who had gathered in large numbers, that today we were going to distribute the great blessing that had been collected for us in Germany with divine and gracious care and had been kept from great danger and had finally come to us here safely

---

[1] Psalms 73:28.

[2] The Halle copy at this point is headed "Extract from the Diary". See p. 37, n. 1.

and undamaged. I reminded them that on a Tuesday during this summer we had established and celebrated a day of repentance and prayer and had publicly implored the Highest that He graciously turn from us the threatened danger of a Spanish attack and grant us a period of grace to prepare ourselves communally for blessed eternity through the Christian use of the means of salvation.

Now, I said, our kind God has heard our poor sighs and prayer, and it is our duty to praise Him publicly for His undeserved protection and beneficent goodness. And, because He has just brought the two crates to us at this time through circuitous routes and danger and is thereby giving us a new sign of His fatherly grace and providence, we wish to make the day of distribution into a day of public praise of His name. In the morning, as is customary on Sundays and Holy Days, we will gather in the Jerusalem Church for prayer, reading, singing, and preaching of the divine word. This occurred today.

At a given sign everyone who was not sick at home gathered in the Jerusalem Church after eight o'clock dressed in clean white, and then the divine service began as is usual on Sundays, kneeling in prayer. We read in order Chapter 36 of Isaiah and we sang the first three verses of the hymn *O dass ich tausend Zungen hätte.* Before we had sung the song to its end, we read the very beautiful 145th Psalm instead of reading the epistle. The sermon was begun with a prayer, in which we praised our merciful God for not treating us according to our sins and for not punishing us according to our misdeeds, for then we would already be past our period of grace and in the depths of hell.

We would have deserved it if He had taken from us our religion, divine service, word, sacraments, our external peace, health, harvest, and mills, etc., but He does not treat us, etc.;[1] rather He shows us one kindness after the other, to which belong the wondrously preserved chests that have been brought to us. We praised Him in the name of Christ for His kindness and implored Him for grace to be applied according to His purpose; and we prayed for the dear instruments through whom He has shown us so much goodness. My text was Mark 7:37, "He hath done all things well."

I reminded the congregation that a week ago, namely the twelfth Sunday after Trinity, had learned from Mark 7 and from the words we contemplated in the exordium from Psalms 37:4-5 to know our Jesus, who had redeemed us dearly, as a Savior who made everything right.

---

[1] Allusion to Psalms 103:10, "He hath not dealt with us after our sins."

For from God's word and our own experience we could have said to His praise not only "He has made everything right" but also "He is making everything right" and "He will continue to make it right."

He showed Himself to be such a one already on Sunday and thenceforward in such souls among us who have given Him their souls, whom He has converted, justified, and sanctified. In them it can be said, to His praise and to the awakening of others, He has made everything right, He is still making it right (for His work never stands still). Even if they find much misery and many obstacles, there is still good counsel there. Commit thy way unto the Lord and trust in Him, He will make it right. But I also had to tell them that He had proved Himself in the Bible as a Jesus who makes everything right, as also in the case of our long-awaited chests with the gifts from various worthy benefactors.

The circumstances impressed me greatly and should rightly awaken or strengthen the faith in everyone through the word. I said that a week ago word had come from Savannah that our chests had been brought there safely from Charleston. At the same time I was advised in writing and orally that these chests had been in great danger of becoming lost but the Lord had so preserved them that not a single book or thread had been damaged in them. In this I reported several very edifying details known to me, some of which were reported above. We can now say, "He has made everything right." When they were packed and sent off, the minds of our benefactors would say with confidence: "He will make it right..." If anyone had said to the bystanders "Perhaps we are packing for the Spaniards, we are causing them a pleasure because the ship might be taken away," others would have said: "Behold the Lamb of God,"[1] "Here is Immanuel. Commit thy way unto the Lord."[2] We are putting the crates into the arms of Him who bears all things through His powerful words, He who is called and is an almighty Creator of heaven and earth. Perhaps (it was added) the Lamb of God printed on the caps that were sent here, which is a victorious Lamb and carries the banner as a sign of the continuing victory for our benefit. This gives us good cause for meditation and for trust in Jesus, who is Lamb and Lion so that they surely believed that He would deal with these crates on the perilous voyage so well that it will be said, "Well done."[3]

Just as those our worthy friends said in faith, "He will make it well," so we can now say to the praise of God to our and their joy, "He has

---

[1] John 1:29.

[2] Psalms 37:5.

[3] *Wohl gemacht*, allusion to the hymn mentioned on p. 118, n. 2.

done it well," even though we deserved, through our sloth, ingratitude, and other behavior, to be swallowed up or expelled by the Spaniards and to be robbed of these gifts. However, not only has our great Lord and Savior done well by us in this matter. Rather, since we traveled here from Europe, we have had innumerable other proofs, and through this account we led our parishioners back to their former years. As a clear example of this I cited what we heard in the prayer hour yesterday evening in the story of Abiathar (1 Kings 2:26), namely the man had deserved death, but he was exiled to his field and his estate and thus into solitude and was in this way torn by a high Hand out of the noise of Jerusalem and from evil companionship, in which he had been harmed and had caused harm. Here he had fewer obstacles yet enough opportunity to go into himself in his solitude and to prepare himself for blessed eternity. Thus, what other people thought was a misfortune was, through God's providence, a blessing.

In this way, I said,[1] the Lord has dealt with us sinners worthy of death. He has drawn us out of the noise and crass seduction of the world and brought us to our field and into solitude and held His hand over us so that in this time of war no one has been able to disturb us and we can use the means of salvation both privately and publicly for our salvation. For it is said, "He has done everything well." To be sure, He visits us in our solitude with many kinds of tribulation, many are physically sick, some have recovered from serious sicknesses, some are quite poor and are experiencing many other difficult circumstances, but here too can it be said: "He has done all well." For if things went according to the will of the flesh, in favor and health, etc., you would soon grow cool, etc. Abiathar was better off in bad than in good days. I know many in the congregation who sincerely praise God for their sicknesses, temptations, tribulations, etc., because they have had great spiritual profit from them. If we are too slothful to practice *anazopyreo*[2] then God comes with the bellows of external and internal tribulation and blows the ashes (which, although tender, are harmful) away from the glowing coals, otherwise they would well go out. Just as we can now say with certainty and joy "He has done all well," we can also say of the present: "He is doing everything well."

---

[1] The following passage is in the subjunctive, indicating that Boltzius is indirectly quoting his own sermon.

[2] To rekindle, light up again, show Christian enthusiasm. The word is written in Greek letters.

We are enjoying noble peace in time of war, the enemy's attack has been thwarted, we have health and strength, both adults and children, to appear in church in large numbers, we have had a harvest and the next is very near. The Lord cares for our mill and church by strengthening them, and for the latter a beautiful bell has been sent along with some money to paint the outer walls with oil paint. And who can relate all the blessing that God is granting us? Every moment there is a blessing through which we enjoy His favor. His blessings are so many that they have neither measure nor end.

Now, I continued, along with our present enjoyment of divine goodness there is no lack of all sorts of hardships and concerns through which heartfelt sorrow could arise, but Jesus has said, "Take therefore no thought for the morrow: for the morrow (and the goodness of the Lord that shall rise with it) shall take thought for the things of itself. Sufficient unto the day is the evil thereof"[1] (Jesus who knows what is best, says that). We should commit such ways unto Him and trust in Him. He will do it well.

I had my own concern, especially because of such listeners who, despite the rich use of the means of salvation, still remain without conversion and faith and consequently without grace or salvation. However, I do not lose courage with any of them but hope He will do it all well. Now if others in the congregation also have their concerns, especially some women (of which we now have several) who are approaching the time of childbirth, worry and care will not help, but rather the practice of the little verse: "Commit thy way unto the Lord." Likewise, "If it turns out that you remain true to Him, then He will deliver you, etc."[2] For the awakening and strengthening of their faith I could say that through some of the objects sent from our dear Saalfeld,[3] our heavenly Father had even provided for those who are still lying under their mothers' hearts, etc.

Finally, I read to the congregation something from the recently received little letter from Senior Urlsperger, from which we can learn how we should behave in a right childlike manner in all occurrences before our God and Savior, who makes everything right. The words read thus:

---

[1] Matthew 6:34.

[2] *Wirds aber sich befinden, dass du ihm treu verbleibst, so wird er dich entbinden.* From the hymn *Befiehl du deine Wege und was dein Herze kränkt*, by Paul Gerhard.

[3] See n. 2, p. 25.

Recently it was written in one of our German newspapers that Oglethorpe has resigned his office. This would have aroused great fear in me, only I thought: 'Who knows whether it is true? And, if it is, then God has not put aside His governance over Ebenezer. Oglethorpe was a good friend of Ebenezer. Who gave this gift? God. Then can He not give similar gifts? Yes. Therefore may my soul be put to rest.' Our prayers for you continue. The Lord will continue to show Himself as the old God. We should trust Jesus in this. And may all the people in Ebenezer say Amen.[1]

From this same little letter I also read the P. S. to them, in which stand some duties for our listeners which they need to have instilled in them so that they will not only know the will of our Jesus, who makes everything right, but also do it.

Tell my dear brothers of the entire congregation that I read the diaries with constant thanks, praise, request, and entreaty, according to how the circumstances are presented. Oh, if only it could be said of all who are still straying, 'Rejoice with me, for I have found my son that was lost.'[2] Children, be peaceful with one another, do not distress one another, fear God, honor and love your ministers, be content, do your duty, hear God's word gladly, diligently, and sincerely, do not scorn Holy Communion. Amen.

To this Amen we united our Amen and Hallelujah on our knees, prayed and praised the Lord with regard to this distribution and day of peace He had granted, and finally concluded with the hymn *Lobe den Herrn, den mächtigen König* and with the reading of the 37th Chapter of Isaiah. The distribution took place right after church in my chamber, but it would be too detailed and circumstantial for our friends for me to describe in detail the good order and great joy and refreshment that we observed.

I will report only this much, that 158 adults and 111 children from the most tender age up to the 15th year received a respectable part of these charitable gifts. Some received linen for shirts, some received

---

[1] Boltzius or his scribe seems to have forgotten that he had already quoted this letter on August 15.

[2] Apparently a combination of Luke 15:5 and 15:24.

green, brown, black, grey and other woolen cloth for clothing. Some received smocks, and also bonnets and caps, and some received yarn, buttons, light material for scarves or bonnets, ribbons, likewise printed linen and winter smocks. The bonnets for the women and children in the Augsburg and Halle chests were of such a great number that all of them could be supplied with them, and still enough remained over. The Lamb of God with the banner on the printed caps from Saalfeld gave me great joy in my dear Savior both in church and also in my chamber, when I spoke separately with the children before the distribution of their gifts; and I wish to remember this all the days of my life. I explained the picture to them from the Bible, and then we remembered humbly and gratefully the most important blessings of His redemption and reconciliation, which He achieved through His resurrection.

We held a conversation about the little verse "Behold the Lamb of God," also "You are virgins and follow the Lamb, you have His mind and it will happen to you as to Him, but oh bliss."[1] This was expounded partly through the last verse of the hymn *Auf, auf mein Hertz mit Freuden* and partly through Acts 6. Last of all, from the hymn that had been recommended to us, *Stilles Lamm und Friede Fürst*, we had the sixth verse: "If thou must stand on Zion, one will see me with thee, without pain, white and pure, there thou should'st be my Lamb, Light and Lamp."[2]

The children told me before the Lord with one voice that they wished never again to insult or dishonor the Lamb of God, which had redeemed them so dearly. We should say "Let no hour pass without praise and love."[3] Last of all we sang *Halleluja sey dir gesungen, O holder Hirt, O süsses Lamm*. Thereupon the children's linen, woolens, caps, etc., were distributed to them, who thanked us for them in a childlike way. I was, to be sure, tired, but much refreshed and strengthened in the little Lamb of God. Hallelujah.

Monday, the 27th of August. The schoolmaster Ortmann did not come to school today and, because I learned of it too late, most of the children had gone home. I visited him on his plantation toward evening and heard from him that he cannot walk because of some sores and swellings on his left foot, and therefore he will not be able to hold school for some days, in which he has so far been loyal and diligent in accord

---

[1] Allusion to Revelations 14:4-5.

[2] *Wenn du musst auf Zion stehen, müsse man mich um Dich sehn, ohne Pein, weiss und rein, da solst Du mein Lamm, Liecht ud Ampel seyn.*

[3] *Ohne Loben und Lieben vergeh keine Stunde.* Unidentified.

with his nature and weak forces. He has begun to dig a well, which is a very difficult task, and he may have contracted the harm to his foot from it.

One cannot get any working people even for money, and Ortmann does not have the means to hire anyone, for his salary is very skimpy, and he needs for his dire necessities whatever little else is given to him. He has written the exordium verses of this year in large Gothic letters on half-folios and quarto sheets and decorated the interior of his dwelling everywhere as if with wall paper, and I found this very pleasing. He was just finishing the task of writing more verses in this way and to paste them in his living room and bedchamber. He also spoke very edifyingly with me today about what our dear God had recently blessed in his heart. In his behavior toward his wife he is very weak. She is full of vices but can hoodwink him. If anyone is serious with her and works against her willfulness and evil nature, he takes her side blindly and becomes emotional right and left and loses the goodness he has achieved.

Tuesday, the 28th of August. Mrs. Helfenstein's oldest son came to our place at the end of last week to take up a plantation again. For, as he says, he and his family like Ebenezer better than anywhere else. I well remember the time that he and his family could find much fault with the orphanage and all of Ebenezer and said that our inhabitants were people with whom it was not good to live. Even though there is poverty, many difficulties, sickness, and other often severe hardships among us, they are not lacking in other places either.

In addition we here enjoy the advantage that we are in quiet and solitude, that we have God's word and his servants at hand and enjoy the sacraments both day and night. Also, in physical circumstances, be it poverty or sickness, we can find remedies and counsel at little or no cost. I consider it among the major physical blessings that we have two men skillful in medicine and surgery[1] with us. We receive so many splendid medicines from Halle that are given, willingly and without the least payment, at the prescription of Mr. Mayer to the poor who do not have the means to employ a doctor. He takes nothing for his efforts in prescribing our medications and adjusts himself according to the peoples' circumstances. Perhaps our dear God will one day put me in a position to give him some repayment. Now I am deeply involved because of the very important mill construction and have other things to pay for the

---

[1] Christian Ernst Thilo and Johann Ludwig Mayer. For Thilo, see p. 9, n. 1.

sake of the congregation. But God will surely help me soon so that we can say "He has done all well."

Some people along Ebenezer Creek have been supplied with very bad land, which, when it was surveyed for them, we thought much better than it turned out to be later on. I would like to help the good people who must find their sustenance from agriculture, if only there were some better land. The last time the surveyor was with us they received a few additional acres, yet they do not nearly have their fifty acres that every inhabitant receives from the Lord Trustees.

These people, who have settled here since the arrival of the fourth transport, still lack the means to acquire plows and oxen; also the stumps and roots are not yet rotten enough for a plow to be used profitably. Otherwise it would be possible, according to the suggestions of Jethro Tull, to turn the pine forest into useful fields in which they would gradually have advantages even over the so-called low land. We hear complaints everywhere that the bears, squirrels, raccoons, and other vermin are doing great damage to the corn,[1] and no shooting helps since much is spoiled at night.

In the pine woods only the deer damage the beans, whereas we would be entirely spared from these previously mentioned animals, for they keep themselves in thick forests where oaks, beeches, nut trees, etc. stand and the deer are also among them and devour the beans, leaves, and fruit, also sweet potatoes in quantities. It is as if they can smell men and gunpowder, for I have been told that, when people watch and lie in wait for them with a musket, they do not come for a few nights. However, when people sleep peacefully one night, they see the damage in the morning. The animals soon pay no attention to the scarecrows that we make with hanging clothes, caps, and straw men, nor are they very afraid of fires and dogs, even though some with good and large dogs (such as Kalcher has) save a lot of their crops. There are, however, not many of them in the community.

How gladly I would like to have a field near the city planted according to the new method, if only I could get the people. Already some weeks ago three men began to split two thousand rails for a fence, but they have been hindered often in this work by various happenings. These rails cost me £3 Sterling on the spot in addition to what it will cost to bring them here. To be sure, that is a lot of money, but they are earning it honestly. A lot of wood is still lying on the old land that is to

---

[1] By this time Boltzius usually uses the word *Korn* to mean Indian maize, as opposed to the so-called European crops, wheat, oats, barley, etc.

be plowed for me. So far, despite much effort, I have not been able to get any people to saw it into pieces and burn it. Everyone has a lot to do for himself, and I am happy that we have workers at the mill.

Friday, the 31st of August. Two brothers from Purysburg brought their ten year old sister to our school. They have more confidence in schoolmaster Kocher than in Ortmann, so they gave the little girl to the Salzburger Brückner, who, with his wife, will care for her with food and drink and receive a certain money each month in return. These brothers were formerly at our place for several weeks because of their work and received very much spiritual good, and therefore they have love for and trust in us, even though they are Reformed. They are entirely without good books, so they were pleased when I could give them an old Bible and a song and prayer book that someone had given me for a Halle hymnal. The hymnals that came to our hands through the care of our worthy Pastor Majer[1] have all been distributed and have caused great joy, for it is a great blessing for the congregation to sing the hymns from their own hymnals and also to have their devotions at home. Our young people are growing up and are also asking us for such dear hymnals, which I will not be able to supply until our dear God inclines the hearts of some benefactors to present our congregation with a new treasure of the extract of the two parts compiled by Pastor Freylinghausen.[2]

We also had great need of catechism books, and such a number of them have come along this time that we can make do for another year. Of the duodecimo Bibles that were sent us, there are still some left and I am pleased that I still have a small supply, for I sometimes hear of people in whom God's word finds a good place. The children have the promise that, if they love God's word and are obedient to it, I wish in due time to give them Bibles and hymnals and perhaps also *Treasure Chests*[3] (which are always demanded by the people who do not have them). The many little tracts and sermons that our worthy Prof. [Gotthilf August] Francke has enclosed in the chests are very dear to us and will be sowed under the governance of our divine Father as a good seed that will bear good fruit under His blessing and in His time.

---

[1] Pastor Johann August Majer, deacon of St. Ulrich's Church in Halle, benefactor of the Georgia Salzburgers.

[2] See p. 24, n. 1.

[3] See p. 24, n. 2.

Ebenezer, the 3rd of September 1744.[1]   Old Mrs. Rieser is preparing herself fully with hearty prayer and entreaty for her journey into her heavenly fatherland. She is now very frail, yet quite content with God's governance. She rejoices in her misery and thanks God for having granted her husband a great measure of patience, which he is showing to her even though her sickness has already lasted a long time. Formerly he became discontented quickly when she had the fever for a few days. Her sons, who sometimes caused her distress in healthy days, are tending her loyally and do not become tired or annoyed when doing all sorts of women's work because there is no woman in the family except for this sick mother.

I consider all these things a granting of her sighs and prayers, which she has performed loyally on her sickbed and elsewhere. The pains are not always equally severe, and God grants her intervals when she can pray and praise His name without hindrance. She considers it a blessing worthy of thanks that she can lie sick here in His will and among her own people. The oldest son has learned carpentry rather well from Kogler and is earning a good bit of money at the mill for himself and for his old parents. The two younger sons are working with their father on the plantation and hope to receive a good harvest.

It seems very strange to me that I am again without a colleague, since Mr. Gronau went to Savannah a week ago and from there on to the orphanage in search of sea air.[2] Since then I have received no news about how he is faring, but we think of him diligently before the Lord, who will surely send him back healthy to us to our joy. Since he cannot work with me on the adults and children of the congregation, he is praying all the more diligently, and from this I can clearly notice strength in my body and spirit.

Yesterday it rained heavily during the afternoon divine service and, since all the windows were open because of the hot weather, the noise of the downpour was rather loud and I found it quite difficult to speak in the heat so that, through fear of doing myself harm, I had to leave off before the hour was at its end. However, a few hours later, I again felt so much strength that I could hold the Sunday prayer meeting, at which we sang Allendorf's beautiful hymn *Halleluja, das Leben ist erschienen* very properly and without hesitation.

---

[1] The Halle copy at this point is headed "Extract from the Diary". See p. 37, n. 1.

[2] George Whitefield's orphanage, Bethesda, lay on the Jones Narrows, far from any fresh water.

Wednesday, the 5th of September. Yesterday evening the surveyor Capt. Avery came to the plantations via Abercorn. This morning before school I traveled out to him in order to see whether and how the important work at the mill will be begun. He had already assigned our workers their work and gave us hope that he would soon bring it to the point that the mill will operate even with this very low water, all of which seems almost impossible to me and others, for the water in our river has never been so low as long as our mill has been built. Therefore, if this man can make the mill grind with such low water, that would be something special.

Meanwhile I consider it the providence of the Lord that the water in the river is at its lowest during this now begun and very important construction. For now the master builder can see how far down the water drops and can do his best to put the mill in such a condition that we can have it run all the time. In addition, work is now much easier and cheaper than when the water is high. Also, it is the best time for our people to do this irregular work: in a couple of weeks the field peas will be ripe, which must be gathered without delay in dry weather. After that they begin to prepare the fields for European grains.[1]

Even though I now need every single shilling to pay the workers at the mill, I cannot fail to have other necessary work done because I have found people for it, who are very rare almost all year long. A thousand six-foot-long planks for a fence or enclosure around the Jerusalem and Zion Church have been finished. In place they cost £2 10 sh. Two thousand long rails, each twelve feet long, have been split for a large field in which new methods of agriculture are to be tried as a good model for the community and in which widows and other poor people will also have a few acres for wheat or barley. These cost £3 Sterling.[2]

Today I paid for eight hundred planks with which the physician's [Thilo's] dilapidated house lot is to be fenced. These cost 20 sh. Sterling. We are now also lacking the posts of pine wood for both the church square and for Mr. Thilo's fence; likewise, a kitchen must be built for him.[3] At present I am in great need of help from Europe, for such works must be paid for with cash money, which the poor people

---

[1] See p. 4, n. 3.

[2] Boltzius is contrasting the plank fence, which sometimes appears in early European sketches, with the split-rail fence, which appears to have been an American innovation.

[3] Because of danger of fire, the kitchens were usually built away from the house.

greatly need in their difficult housekeeping.[1] I am comforted by the
Lord Jesus' words: "Take no thought ... for our heavenly Father
knoweth what things ye have need of, before ye ask him."[2] At their
happy arrival the fourth transport brought us the beautiful little verse
from the house of our worthy Senior Urlsperger: "Be careful for nothing;
but in everything by prayer and supplication with thanksgiving let your
requests be made known unto God."[3] May God grant us grace to obey
this evangelical command and to believe in it, and then we shall see His
glory.

This morning I found Peter Reiter out of his bed and at a little work.
He told me, to the praise of God, that the Good Physician has not only
blessed the physical medicines on his miserable body but has also been
kind to his soul. He said he had felt quite well this week. Only his
sloth is causing him concern.[4] His wife also gave a good witness of
what is going on in her through the working of the Holy Spirit; and I
gave them both instructions from the word of God to penetrate ever
deeper into the heart of Jesus, which is both His will and our salvation.
We came across the beautiful 23rd Psalm and to the dear hymn based on
it, which we are now singing verse by verse in the evening prayer
meeting: *Der wahre Gott und Gottes Sohn...* .

Among other things I told them that it was, to be sure, a great
blessing of the Lord when we are made hungry and thirsty for Christ and
His mercy and thus have a spiritual appetite. This, however, is not the
first concern of Christianity, I said. Rather such a hungry soul must also
seat itself at the table of grace prepared by its Good Shepherd and let
itself be brought to the green pastures of His gospel. If it reads in the
Bible the dear gospel, which is pure milk and honey, it must not merely
gaze upon it, find pleasure in it, praise it, and rejoice in it, but rather eat
and drink it, i.e., simply and trustingly appropriate everything that is
proclaimed of Christ and His merited mercy. Then the poor grace-
hungry soul will become fatter than fatted calves. Nothing, I said, was
holding him back but his lack of faith, but, where there is recognition
and feeling of sin and hunger and thirst for grace, there is faith. Jesus
says: "Come; for all things are now ready."[5]

---

[1] *Haushaltung* denoted not just the maintenance of the house but also of the
whole farmstead or family economy.

[2] A composite of Matthew 6:8 and 6:25.

[3] Philippians 4:6.

[4] See p. 115, n. 2.

[5] Luke 14:17.

In the neighborhood I met a couple of pious women together who were performing a certain charitable deed, and I was able to hold a blessed conversation with them. One of them, namely Mrs. Bacher, who is used as midwife in the community, said that she had heard Mrs. Kalcher sing the hymn *Herr, so du wirst mit mir seyn...* She wished to learn the melody too, it well suits her as a midwife, for, if God goes in and out with her and gives His blessing to her task, then she need not be timid or daunted in any difficulty. I sang it with her and two others who were present, to my own edification. God also granted us much joy in our prayer so that we could entreat Him in the name of His Son for much goodness for us and for others and not doubt in the least that He has heard us.

Sunday, the 9th of September.   This has again been a beautiful, pleasant, and edifying Sunday for us on which, from the gospel Luke 7:11, etc, we got to know the Lord Jesus as our very best Friend in both life and death. At the afternoon repetition hour I acquainted my listeners with the exceptionally edifying hymn *Mein holder Freund ist mein*, and I closed with a couple of important points from the last words of the late Mr. Rieger, which have been very blessed for us and were appropriate to our today's material.

My dear colleague Mr. Gronau was absent from Ebenezer and from our meeting today as he was a week ago, for he has been sojourning at the orphanage at Savannah for the sake of his health. However, at the end of last week he sent me word that, if a boat came to Savannah tomorrow, he wished to come back with it. To please him a boat operated by just one man will be sent down early tomorrow morning, since he can easily come to Abercorn and ride from there to here. Therefore we hope to see him with us next Tuesday (God grant that he been strengthened in body and mind). We pray for him publicly and privately and always hope that our Great Physician will heal him and grant him to us for some time more.

A sickly person, who well knows the treasure of grace in our dear brother Gronau and wishes nothing more than his recovery, told me that she had heard a little boy in the neighborhood singing "There is no purpose in helping His hand, no matter how great the harm"[1] Since Gronau's sickness I have often thought of the words of today's epistle: "God is able to do abundantly above all that we ask or think."[2]

---

[1] *Seiner Hand zu helfen hat kein Ziel wie gross auch sey der Schaden.* From the hymn *Aus tiefer Not schrei ich zu dir*, by Martin Luther.

[2] Ephesians 3:20.

Today during the edifying story of Acts 9:32-35 I read the words *Omnipotenti medico nullus insanabilis occurit morbus.*[1]

Monday, the 10th of September.   We can see right clearly that old Mrs. Rieser is failing in her physical strength but is increasing in grace of God in Christ and that in all her suffering her heart is entirely comforted and that she is very well content with God's governance. She has given her heart to the Lord Jesus and is always concerned with Him, and therefore she lets herself be pleased with all His ways. She prays very diligently, and that is her best, indeed only, work, which will be a blessed seed toward eternity.   Along with her prayer her mind is diligently directed at God's word, she remembers the powerful verses of scripture and has some of them read to her by her family or cited from the sermons. She is a good preacher for the young people in the house with words and tears, and this, as she herself hopes, will do some good after her death.

She diligently instills into her children the advantages they have here over their miserable fatherland in Salzburg. They knew, saw, and heard nothing of the horrors that she had seen and in part experienced. They lived, she said, in solitude, are healthy, and are free and have the means of salvation abundantly. God's patience and forbearance with which He has followed her for so long lifted her very high today, and she lamented with tears that she had so often been untrue to God and His grace.

This week her husband is moving to his plantation not far from the town, therefore she asked me to give her Holy Communion before then. I told her that, with the planned move, she should remember with profit the little verse: "Here we have no continuing city, but we seek one to come."[2] I told her that it was no sign of wrath that she had to move from one place to another in her old and sick days. It was the same way with the patriarchs.   Her plan to take Holy Communion gave me an opportunity to tell her something about the beautiful words: "My dear Friend is mine, He remains devoted to me. For me the seal of His loyalty is His dear blood."[3]

Tuesday, the 11th of September.   At the previous distribution last winter we received a good number of the golden booklet *Short and*

---

[1] "For the omnipotent Physician no sickness is incurable."

[2] Hebrews 13:14.

[3] *Mein holder Freund ist mein, er bleibet mir ergeben. Das Siegel seiner Treu ist mir sein theures Bluth.* Hymn by Ulrich Bogislaus Bonin.

Simple Yet Thorough Thoughts on True Conversion, etc.[1] and a few more have been found in the last crate from Halle, and these we have been able to distribute to the members of the congregation. At the end there are some very beautiful new hymns, with which we made a beginning last night with the very edifying hymn *Hier kommt ein Schüler in die Schule*. To be sure, in town we do not have many copies of this excellent little treatise, but some of them will be borrowed from those which and are in the hands of the people on the plantations. May God also grant the same blessing on them that He himself has already laid, and will continue to lay, on the blessed *Edifying Thoughts on True Conversion*.[2]

May our gracious God replace in the bookstore of the orphanage at Halle all the blessed writings that have been sent to us so abundantly from time to time with thousandfold blessing. At our place we have very great advantages with regard to the Lord's wealth of goodness, but in the last prayer meeting we held we were loyally admonished to use them rightly, or else all the greater responsibility will follow.

We were reminded in the story in 1 Kings 2 that the people of David's and Solomon's time on whom there was such a great wrath, as we have seen in the case Adonijah, Joab, Abijah, Shimei, and formerly in Abner, Amaha, Absolom, Ahithophel, and Ammon, lived either in or near Jerusalem, where God had His fire and hearth, and at a very blessed time. However, because they remained unrepentant in spite of all that, they departed more and more wickedly from God's judgments in their contrary manner fell into physical and eternal misfortune. A persistently unrepentant man rejects the grace of God and God himself, who offers Himself as the greatest Good through His word, and this is a terrible sin.

My dear colleague came right after twelve o'clock via Abercorn to our plantations, where I had the pleasure of seeing him again and welcoming him. He was stronger in body and spirit than when he went away and, because the sea air was so good for him, he is planning to go from the Savannah orphanage [Bethesda] at the end of this week to Carolina with a pious captain and to visit some of the plantations situated on the sea, perhaps even to Charleston and Frederica. The people in the Savannah orphanage show him very much kindness and give him all possible support on both water and land for his recovery. I gladly let him travel because that seems to be the best means for him

---

[1] *Kurtze und einfältige Gedancken von der Bekehrung. Author and date unknown.*

[2] *Erbauliche Gedanken von der wahren Bekehrung.* Probably the same as above.

to recover and because the Lord has so strengthened me that I can
perform my duties without interruption. Mr. [Ludwig] Mayer is doing
me a very great favor by copying the diary and making the extract for
Prof. [G. A.] Francke.[1] May our dear God repay him for this in his
body and soul.

Wednesday, the 12th of September. The authorities have paid more
attention to my last letter than in previous times. They have sent our
constable Bichler a written plenipotentiary power or warrant to arrest the
wicked servants in Old Ebenezer and to bring them down to Savannah,
where they will be dealt with according to the law. One of them has
already run away and has ridden to Carolina, but the other, also a Swiss,
is still in Old Ebenezer and will be fetched today by Bichler and his
people.[2] I wrote a few lines to Col. Stephens in which I reported two
more coarse things this person had done secretly at our place and which
he will not be able to deny.[3] Both youths have been so wicked that we
cannot marvel enough at the divine forbearance which He is showing
these wicked ruffians. They consider all their tricks and wickedness as
nothing before the Lord. And thus it goes with many Germans in this
country. They spend their time idling about, which is an opportunity for
much evil. In the local fortresses and in the service of the Trustees in
Old Ebenezer they get their sustenance and thirty shillings per month
with idling, and there is no blessing in such unrighteous money. They
spend it for clothes and sin, and therefore one might say, "Easy come,
easy go."

Thursday, the 13th of September. Today old Mrs. Rieser received
private communion. Yesterday morning I visited her to speak to her
from God's word for her preparation. I found her somewhat strengthened in body and spiritually content on her bed, on which she had done
some light work. During the conversation I noticed that she uses
everything that she sees and hears for the praise of God, for prayer, and
for intercession. She had heard that Peter Reiter has such a sickness that

---

[1] These extracts were forwarded to the Fathers in London, Halle and Augsburg.
See Introduction, p. viii.

[2] Martin Dasher and Heinrich Meyer had disturbed the peace by parodying the
Salzburgers' hymns during divine service and cursing and defying the pastor. Meyer
escaped and fled up the Savannah River, where he killed an Indian in a drunken brawl.
Dasher was taken to Savannah at great expense but merely put on probation and told not
to annoy Boltzius any more.

[3] He had debauched a Swiss girl named Magdalena Meyer under her mother's
roof while everyone else was at church.

he often has a wet bed as if from dropsy. She thanks God that her sickness is not accompanied by such inconvenience.

Because there is no woman in her house and she must be tended by her sons, such a sickness would be much more difficult for her than the one she now has, and therefore she thanks God for her own cross, which suits best on her own shoulders. I said that, because she let the ways of the Lord please her eyes, this was a sign that she has given her heart to the Lord and that she should continue doing it through His grace, for she would not regret it. It is written, "My son, give me thine heart, and let thine eyes, etc."[1] The deeper the heart penetrates in God, the more content one is with God's ways.

She said further that, when she is lying on her bed and contemplating, it seems to her as if all corners, nooks, and crannies in her dwelling are full of her sins, yet she remembers the lovely hymn *Wenn dein hertzliebster Sohn, O Gott, nicht wär auf Erde kommen*, etc., especially the words "In His wounds I refresh myself and come to Thee in joy." I told her that, whenever she remembers her sins and they cause her worry and disquiet, she has all the more calling to come to Christ, the Friend and Physician of sinners, and to crawl down deep into His wounds; for He himself says, "Come unto me, all ye that labor and are heavy laden, and I will give you rest."[2] His blood, I said, speaks better than Abel's,[3] namely, it cries for conciliation and forgiveness.

Last week she heard the miserable person from Old Ebenezer screaming and jumping about near her hut like a drunken Indian, and this sinful behavior moved her to tears, sighs, and prayers. On that occasion she told her children they should ask God to preserve them from such company and to keep them at our place. And thus she spends her time constantly in God-pleasing works. At the Holy Communion service today I told her and her family something for their edification about the lovely words of our Lord Jesus: "Do this in remembrance of me,"[4] or, as St. Paul explains it, "For, as often as ye eat of this bread, and drink this cup, ye do show the Lord's death till he come."[5] For her edification I left with her the beautiful Communion hymn *O Jesu unsre Wonne*, etc., which her family was to sing to her or read aloud, since she cannot do it herself.

---

[1] Proverbs 23:26.
[2] Matthew 11:28.
[3] See Matthew 23:35.
[4] Luke 22:19.
[5] 1 Corinthians 11:26.

Sunday, the 16th of September.   On this 17th Sunday after Trinity it has been just three years since we consecrated our Jerusalem Church, and we have used it up to now in great physical peace and for the great edification of our souls.   Especially on this day each year we rightfully remember this great blessing of the Lord and praise Him for it publicly, as we did three times today.   In doing so, I reminded them what seemed remarkable in comparing 1 Kings 2 with the present circumstances of this time.   To wit, in last evening's prayer meeting we heard that, at the order of the wise Solomon, Shimei had dwelled for three years in Jerusalem (which the Holy Ghost calls a long time).

There he was near the divine service and had opportunity and means enough for his conversion, but the unhappy outcome teaches how poorly he spent this time: he remained a worldly minded unconverted man, who loved his servants more than the oath of God and the command of his king, and this cost him his life.

Now we have, as it were, lived for three full years in Jerusalem and have had enough opportunity and means in this Jerusalem Church to win our salvation with fear and trembling.   However, many have let themselves fail in this and are still standing in their carnal and worldly dispositions.   Such people should hasten and save their souls, because it could soon be said of them "Behold, these three years I come seeking fruit on this fig tree, and find none.   Cut it down; why cumbereth it the ground?"[1]

At the same time I gave our listeners new instructions as to how they could become good people in this good time granted by the Lord. Because examples make a good impression, I read them one in the afternoon catechization lesson from a written sermon by Prof. Dr. [A. H.?] Francke concerning the 4th commandment.[2]   This had come to our hands in the last crate along with other edifying reports.   It was very edifying, and from it they could learn how they could spend their time in church right blessedly.

Monday, the 17th of September.   In the night between Saturday and Sunday Bichler and his people returned home from Savannah, but he told

---

[1] Luke 13:7.

[2] Following Lutheran (and Roman Catholic) usage, Boltzius numbers this as the third commandment.   Honoring one's father and mother includes the clergy, and therefore church attendance.   This was probably August Hermann Francke (d. 1727), whose publications were far more numerous than those of his son, Gotthilf August, the director of the Orphanage during Boltzius' tenure in Ebenezer.

me only this morning how things went before the authorities since he did not wish to trouble me with it yesterday. He himself had to stand guard over the rascal whom he had to take down at the order of the authorities until it was convenient for the gentlemen to hear him. He did not deny his wicked deeds, yet they absolved him and sent him back to Old Ebenezer on our boat, where he continued his evil deeds in the company of a young girl he had seduced from us.[1]

Such un-Christian behavior of the authorities, which makes nothing of coarse vices and disorder, moved me to write the following letter to Col. Stephens under today's date. "Honored Sir, etc., Necessity and the obvious disfavor of the Savannah authorities toward me and my congregation recently forced me to report the following to the Lord Trustees before the conclusion of my letter of 3 August of this year: My Conscience, etc. This evening I set on paper various particulars of the behavior of the authorities toward me and my congregation, which I shall soon send to the Lord Trustees in the form of a letter. I would gladly bear it if it concerned only me and my family, but, since it concerns my office and congregation, I cannot remain quiet, for I cannot be responsible for the actions of the local authorities before God or before the Lord Trustees and our other patrons.

"These examples of their behavior toward us that I have written down make it very clear that they would rather destroy and overthrow my congregation than to support it according to the purpose of the Lord Trustees. I shall forward a copy to Court Chaplain Ziegenhagen so that he will know everything word for word what has been written to the Lord Trustees, for it would be too extensive to insert it here, and to translate the passage into German would cost me too much of my strength and time, which I must conserve in every way in the absence of my dear colleague. Since yesterday I have borne in mind the lovely words: "Take counsel together ... for God is with us."[2]

Wednesday, the 19th of September. For some time God has been visiting Rottenberger's wife and children with all kinds of sickness, and her husband has had a certain very dangerous accident. From it Mr. [Ludwig] Mayer has judged that a divine goodness has been shown, otherwise he would have lost his life, for she narrated the circumstances as being very dangerous and frightening. I told her that the people of Savannah[3] in Acts IX had let the marvelous goodness of God that He had

---

[1] Magdalena Meyer. See p. 138, n. 3.

[2] Isaiah 8:10.

[3] The name Savannah must have been a scribal error for Lydda. See Acts 9:32.

shown to the sick Eneas serve to convert them to the Lord and that that was just what He was expecting of her and her husband.

I reminded them of what I had recently read of her and her husband in the 9th Continuation of the Ebenezer Reports,[1] namely that our dear God had used the edifying example of her late kinsman, Madreiter, to show their souls much good. What blessed people they would be if they had dealt loyally with this grace! I recited for her several times the little verse "Because thou art lukewarm, and neither cold nor hot, I will spew thee out of my mouth."[2]

In our evening prayer meeting we now have a sorry example of Shimei, who did not convert to God but only from his obvious wickedness through hypocrisy and for the sake of social respectability and even used the means of salvation publicly in order to please King Solomon. He himself had to admit that he had heard a good opinion, i.e., that Solomon and God meant well with him and his soul. However, he spoiled things with God and Solomon and himself, and this is the nature of all unconverted people.

Even though he knew that death would inevitably follow transgression of the king's command, he still risked it and put his life and everything in jeopardy just to regain his servants.[3] Of him one might say, "If the farthing is my gain, let the hundredweight go."[4] In this he is followed by all those who sin against their conscience for the sake of their bellies and earthly things and lose their souls and salvation because of it. Oh, what a dangerous thing is an earthly and carnal mind! Just as the wise Solomon and his governance proved to be not only a Solomon[5] and King of Peace but also a King of Justice, so too our Lord Christ, who had already been prefigured by Solomon and Melchizedek.[6] He is a King in Salem and a Melchizedek, i.e., a King of Peace and righteousness.[7] Thus he shows himself now, and thus He will show Himself when He comes to judge the quick and the dead (Jeremiah 9:24).[8]

Kornberger announced that his wife bore twins this morning, a little son and a little daughter, whom he wished to have baptized in Zion

---

[1] *Detailed Reports* 8:287.

[2] Revelations 3:16.

[3] This story is told in 1 Kings 2:36-46.

[4] *Ist der Heller mein Gewinn, fahre der Centner immer hin.*   A proverb.

[5] A play on the name Solomon, which means "peaceful."

[6] In the patristic tradition, clerics of the early modern period saw all characters of the Old Testament as prefigurations of those of the New.

[7] Melchizedek means "righteousness."

[8] This is not Jeremiah 9:24. It is 2 Timothy 4:1.

Church this afternoon. The baptism took place. He wished to name the little boy Johann Friedrich and the little girl Hanna Friderica in commemoration of the grace and goodness of the Lord that He has shown in maintaining peace so far, and I and others found this edifying. It cannot but please me when, in such important matters as the naming of children in baptism, our congregation does not act through habit and without consideration but with caution and Christian reflection. Other children are also pleased when they hear that the children who are brought to baptism receive a lovely name. They always ask about it and rejoice in it.

Two little boys were taken along to prayer in Kornberger's dwelling, and one of them told me that a woman had prayed "Lord Jesus I belong to thee" and also the two verses "God so loved the world, etc."[1] and "And Moses lifted up the serpent in the wilderness."[2] I was pleased that the visit to Mrs. Kornberger was made with prayer and that these two children had taken notice of it.

Thursday, the 20th of September.   After school this afternoon I visited Metzger's family, which is rather numerous. I examined the son and his young wife from the catechism so that both she and the others might recognize how much they need instruction from the catechism. There are still other people along Ebenezer Creek who lack recognition in Christian dogma and cannot come to the evening prayer meeting all week because of conflicts. As long as my dear colleague has been sick and has had a weak voice, the edification hour has been discontinued on this side of the plantations. However, today I have resolved in the name of the Lord to apply a couple of hours at noon every week to repeat the Sunday sermon with question and answer for one hour with old and young on the plantations along Ebenezer Creek and in the second hour to teach them briefly the basic truths of Christian dogma or to continue to build on the foundation I have laid. May the Lord grant His blessing on it and grant me strength of body and mind.

With the children in school I now have the *Golden A.B.C. Booklet*[3] printed in the back of the *Order of Salvation* that the late and dear Pastor Freylinghausen published.[4]   Every point there is annotated and has

---

[1] John 3:16.

[2] John 3:14.

[3] *Güldenes A.B.C. Büchlein*, children's catechistic primer by Pastor Sommer of Schortewitz.

[4]   Johann Anastasias Freylinghausen, *Ordnung des Heyls, Nebst einem Verzeichnis der wichtigsten Kern-Sprüche*. Halle, 1724.

provided me with beautiful material to teach the children *Doctrinalia &
Moralia Theologica*[1] and doctrine effectively. Therefore I have almost
resolved to go through it briefly with said people. Because I shall have
still more work in this way, I shall, to be sure, have less time to visit the
people in their homes. However, if the Lord strengthens me, it will not
be left undone. I must watch out for my health.

Friday, the 21st of September. A married Christian couple asked
me to visit them this week because they intend to go to Holy
Communion. I found the wife alone in the house, but the man had
already arranged to be called from the field when I arrived. They had
prayed a short time before and read a piece of the lovely little tract
Edifying Thoughts on True Conversion.[2] She told me that she was
worried that she had not, as it says in the said booklet, converted any
further than to Moses. In hearing the last stories treated in the prayer
meetings, when old sins were brought to mind and disposed of, she
remembered her former coarse sins, and she feared that they were not
disposed of in God's judgments.[3] It is so difficult, she said, to take
comfort in the belief in Christ and His full repayment.[4]

I recited for her a couple of verses in which it stands that in the
divine order even the greatest sinners are received, for through Christ a
general pardon has been merited. The gospel, the "joyful message of the
merits of the Lord Jesus" are the means through which faith is effected
and strengthened. These joyful tidings, which are proclaimed in Bible
verses and evangelical songs, also apply to her, I said, and she must
cling to them against all feelings. It is said, "Sin is recognized through
the law and strikes down the conscience; the gospel comes to hand and
strengthens the sinner again. It just says, 'Crawl to the Cross,' etc."[5]

I told her it pleases our dear God and must be useful for her that she
is being led in the dark. The joy and feeling of grace will soon come,

---

[1] Basis of the faith and a good life.

[2] In carefully listing the applications of the tracts and books received from
Halle, Boltzius renders account of the good use to which the donations on behalf of
Ebenezer were put. Many of these were channeled through the book store of the Halle
Orphanage to supply the American and East Indian missions with edifying literature.

[3] Boltzius is saying that she is still "legalistic," or fears the law of the Old
Testament more than she trusts the grace of the new.

[4] I.e., the atonement of our sins through His death.

[5] *Es wird die Sünd durchs Gesetz erkandt, und schlägt das Gewissen nieder,
Das Evangelium kommt zur Hand und stärckt den Sünder wieder; es spricht nur kriech
zum Kreutz.* From the hymn *Es ist das Heil uns kommen her* by Paul Speratus. Another
contrast of the law versus grace.

if not sooner, then on her deathbed and with the greatest certainty in blessed eternity. Now, I said, we must say "Without feeling I shall trust, until the time comes to see Him,"[1] likewise, "If I see no comfort, I shall refresh myself in belonging to my Jesus."[2] She belongs to Him, I said, in many ways as stands in the lovely hymn *Mein Gott du weisst am allerbesten...* She is, I said, in divine order for she recognizes, laments, regrets, and bewails her sins, is ashamed of them, and has a sincere desire for Christ and His grace, which grace she must not throw away through the feeling of her many weaknesses, that are taking her courage away. She has much physical suffering and tribulation, which she thinks she has merited through her sins, yet she considers them very minor in comparison to her spiritual suffering, and she would gladly bear it all if only she could be assured of the merciful forgiveness of sins.

From time to time she tastes the peace of God and is very well, but then she comes again into darkness. Among her real sufferings she counts the fact that her sick suckling child hinders her from performing her prayers properly on her knees. When she finds some time for that late in the evening, sleep overcomes her, and this causes her new worry. I instructed her in this from God's word, as her husband had already done. She showed me in her *Treasure Chest*[3] a verse that had come to her hands several times in succession: "Take heed of your spirit."[4] I told her that our spirit is a false spirit, so she must not believe it, whether it speak from the law or the gospel, rather the unerring word of God must be her teacher.

I was unable to tell her what she wished to know about the seven horrors that are lodged in the heart according to Bunyan's life[5] (It stands on the same page of the T.C.) because I have not read this work completely. I am planning, however, to read it in the English edition. I told the two married people what a great sinner this Bunyan had been, about whom people could talk far and wide because of it, yet God's

---

[1] *Ohne Fühlen will ich trauen, biss die Zeit kommt ihn zu schauen.* First verse of the last strophe of the hymn *Es ist ein Heil uns kommen her*, by Christian Friedrich Richter.

[2] *Solt ich k. Trost erblicken, will ich mich damit erquicken, dass ich meines Jesu sey.* From the hymn *O wie selig sind die Seelen, die mit Jesu sich vermählen*, by Christian Friedrich Richter.

[3] See p. 24, n. 2.

[4] Malachi 2:15.

[5] The reference is to an extract from John Bunyan's life (*The Pilgrim's Progress*, 1678 and many editions) published in the *Schatz-Kästlein*. See p. 24., n. 2.

grace manifested itself in him such that he became a blessed tool for the saving of many souls.

Monday, the 24th of September.   This morning I held the edification hour for the first time at Ebenezer Creek, and in it I both showed what I would lay as a basis and what teaching method I would choose; and I also gave instructions how they should make use of this good opportunity.   At the beginning of each hour I repeat half of a major point, thus in each week an entire point; and I can finish repeating the catechism in six weeks.   In the Monday hour I will repeat through question and answer the sermon given on the previous day, but on Thursday I will lay the *Golden A.B.C. Book*[1] as a basis of the edification and also proceed with it in a catechistic method, and in this even the adults would not be embarrassed.

In this first hour I laid as the basis of edification the first words of yesterday's Sunday reading, 1 Corinthians 1:4.   "I thank my God always on your behalf for the grace, etc., that in everything ye are enriched in him, in all utterance, and in all knowledge, even as the testimony of Christ was confirmed in you."   May our dear Lord strengthen for us here a right edifying beginning; and I trust in Christ that He will mercifully bless the end.   I let first the men, then the women, then the children answer.

Tuesday, the 25th of September.   The sick old Mrs. Bacher informed me last Friday through her daughter of the state of her soul. She was fighting hard in her conscience because of her former wicked and hypocritical life.   Her heart had been as hard as steel, she said, and no gospel verse would help.   Finally the Lord had mercy upon her and granted her the forgiveness of her sins in the blood of the Lamb.

When I visited her [Mrs. Bacher] yesterday evening on her plantation, I found her sitting on her bed, and then she told me in detail how she had remembered the sins of her childhood, youth, and later life and especially that she had so often misused Holy Communion hypocritically and in her mouth-Christianity and gravely sinned.   Now, she said, perhaps God no longer considers her worthy of hearing His word publicly and enjoying Holy Communion, for which she so greatly yearns.   Her daughter and son-in-law, Theobald Kieffer, had done her very good service through their encouragement from God's word.   In her are found all signs of repentance and faith, and therefore the gospel

---

[1] See p. 143, n. 3.

applies to her: "Daughter, be of good comfort, thy sins are forgiven."[1] For Jesus preaches penitence and forgiveness of sins.

I edified myself with her from the dear words that I had read a short time before, Isaiah 45:22 ff. "Look unto me, and be ye saved, all the ends of the earth, ... In the Lord have I righteousness and strength." These should be appropriated by those whom the Lord has been able to bring to repentance on bended knees and humiliation. I also told her that, if she again got into difficulty because of her sins, she should investigate whether she is standing in divine order, then she could make her own all evangelical promises even if she did not at once feel any joy. "The sacrifices of God are a broken spirit, a broken and contrite heart,"[2] which was clarified for her in the example of the great sinner in Luke 7.

Wednesday, the 26th of September.   I have known since last week that Mrs. Rheinländer's children and those of old Mr. Kieffer and also Zettler's serving girl have lived in disunity and unfriendliness toward each other. This has caused the parents unrest, even though they themselves may be partially to blame for it. Therefore the two older girls could not go to Holy Communion last Sunday; and today I had them all at my place, presented to them their un-Christian nature and instilled into them the verses "Blessed are the peacemakers,etc."[3] and "Follow peace with all men, and the holiness without which no man will see the Lord, etc."[4] Likewise, what we had in school today. A male or female disciple of the Lord endeavors to be pure in his love for God and his neighbor.

They promised to regret their offenses against each other, to forgive everything, and to improve themselves so that I would not be saddened again. In good hope of their improvement I gave them some little books. I gave the girls the late Professor [A. H.] Francke's funeral sermon song on the words "The maid is not dead, etc."[5] in which the very edifying life of the late Miss Wiegeleben is found. I gave the two boys another lovely little book and promised them to take note of their good as well as of their bad behavior, of which they would enjoy the fruits. May God let this my simple effort as well as these edifying little tracts be blessed in the souls of these children!

---

[1] Boltzius seems to be translating Matthew 9:22 freely.

[2] Psalms 51:17.

[3] Matthew 5:9.

[4] Hebrews 12:14.

[5] Matthew 9:24.

OCTOBER 1744

Tuesday, the 2nd of October. Already some weeks ago Scheffler let himself be recruited as a soldier for six months at a fort or small fortification between Savannah and Frederica.[1] Now he has returned to fetch his wife and two small children. He is a very miserable[2] man who has only made debts and now cannot repay them. He obligated himself to me to satisfy all his creditors between now and Christmas, and we are letting him go under this condition. If he does not become orderly, he will not be able to get along here or anywhere else. He is taking no blessing from Ebenezer, just as he has brought none here.

The word of the apostle in Romans 2:5 apply to him and to his wife, too: "But, after thy hardness and impenitent heart, thou treasurest up unto thyself wrath against the day of wrath etc." May God have mercy on these sinful people. It appears that Ruprecht Zittrauer will keep him company, even though he is still keeping it secret. He does not wish to work either, and therefore the idle solder's life suits him better than the work in Ebenezer, where only those who work get to eat. I remember that the grace of God had pulled quite mightily on these two men, who are coarse old sinners, in their sickness and had brought them to a recognition and feeling of their misdeeds. However, afterwards one could say of them "When the sick man recovered, he became all the meaner."[3] Physical and spiritual judgments are accustomed to follow upon this.

Before coming here with the second transport, Ruprecht Zittrauer had been in Prussia, but he did not wish to do any good there either.[4] He himself said that he had run into Polish territory and that on his way back to Germany he had acted mute, dumb, and stupid and had received beggar's bread and was never stopped. He is otherwise very ignorant and yet tricky, mendacious, and devoted to drink, with which he would have committed excesses if only he had the means and had not been restrained by necessary supervision and discipline. His wife is no better; and thus one blind person is leading the other, and finally they shall both

---

[1] Probably at Ft. Argyle on the Ogeechee River, now located on Ft. Stewart.

[2] For Pietists and Lutherans in general, the word *elend* usually meant "sinful and unconverted."

[3] *Wenn der Kranke genass, je ärger er was.* A proverb.

[4] The majority of the Salzburger exiles had gone to East Prussia. Escaping was dangerous, for the King of Prussia, Frederick William I, had paid for their journey and settlement and considered desertion tantamount to treason.

fall in the ditch.[1] I am sorry for the two small children and for other honest people in the community.

Saturday, the 6th of October.   Yesterday after the prayer meeting that my dear colleague Mr. Boltzius held in his present weakness, our God and Father, who has been reconciled through Christ, brought me back to Ebenezer rather lively and strengthened.[2] To be sure, He has until now done great things for my soul and body. Oh, how often He has refreshed me in my pilgrimage and especially in the orphanage at Savannah, which is called Bethesda. There He let me see and hear and even experience much good, and this house has been for me a special house of mercy for my soul and body. He has also strengthened me right noticeably in body so that I could observe it clearly toward the end.

A few weeks ago after my last sickness I traveled from home very weak, but I have returned again much strengthened. Only my spiritual powers are still weak, also speaking is difficult for me and there are some other things wrong. But perhaps the Lord will bless what I still have to take for it at home. After all, He has given me the one, and He will also give the other in due time. In me He has also shown that, as the Son of Man, He has the power on earth to forgive sins. May He not let me forget what He has done so far for me, poor man, in body and soul. May He also richly reward His children for the good they have done me, and especially bless the Orphanage, our dear Bethesda, and let it remain for many a house of mercy for soul and body.[3]

May he bless the supervisors there, also Mr. Whitefield, and grant him much for maintaining it. May he also bless my worthy colleague and repay him for all his love for me, miserable man, and strengthen him again abundantly and preserve him to the great blessing of us in Ebenezer. May He also reward all our dear listeners who have remembered me diligently before the Lord and may He bless all our dear Fathers and friends in England and Germany. I thought that, when I came home, I wished to take some medicine and refrain from official duties until my health were more constant so that I would not become weaker right away and, as it were, have to begin all over again and leave Ebenezer once more, as has already occurred.

However, because it has pleased the Lord to let my dear colleague fall sick this week, He will grant as much strength as will be necessary.

---

[1] Allusion to Matthew 15:14.

[2] Note that Gronau is writing this entry.

[3] The name Bethesda meant "house of mercy." Gronau had recovered temporarily while there as the guest of George Whitefield's oeconomus, James Habersham.

It must go not according to human, but to God's counsel, for He conducts everything gloriously, He has not yet overlooked anything in His governance. Last night my dear colleague had severe pains in his lower body, and today he is so weak that he must lie in bed almost all the time. Our Father does not treat us according to our sins but according to His grace and mercy. May He accept him and us and let us be and work together for some time more so that we and our parishioners can be better prepared for Holy Communion, the wedding of the Lamb.

Thursday, the 11th of October.   Yesterday evening our boat returned home from Savannah, and it delivered my letters to the friends to whom they were addressed. The engineer, Capt. Avery, is very sick, and therefore he cannot come up here, as much as he would like to. However, he sent orders as to what should be built so that the work can proceed with the good weather and while we have low water. Our friend, Mr. Habersham, who is in serious domestic circumstances, has again lent me some money to pay the construction workers; and I consider this an especially great benefaction at this time. May God repay him for this.

He recently wrote me, and I was told by in detail by Mr. Gronau and others, that a large ship full of German people had come from Rotterdam to the vicinity of Charleston and had been captured there by a Spanish corsair and taken to a Spanish port. They had previously fallen into the hands of the French, who had merely plundered them and let them go again so that the poor people are doubly miserable. It is said that the government of Carolina will ransom these unfortunate Germans, who wished to settle in Carolina.[1] We hear nothing but sad reports from sea and land, even though nothing has come from Europe for a long time.

This morning I received a long letter from our dear and worthy Pastor Driesler from Frederica, who is yearning for news from Europe. He is very frail physically so that he can barely preach only on Sundays. His wife and granddaughter are also weak, so he is requesting some medicines from Mr. [Ludwig] Mayer and from us, which will be sent him at the first opportunity. I have always feared that he is working too hard and has too little rest and physical care, which would have been

---

[1] This appears to be a garbled version of the capture of the *Two Sisters*, Capt. Steadman, off the coast of England, which was taken to Bilbao. Some of the ransomed passengers, including the future governor of Georgia, Johann Adam Treutlen, reached Georgia in 1746.

necessary for him in his approaching old age after so many hardships in this hot country. Little can be had there even for money, seldom any fresh meat and other things. His house stands next to the dwelling of Mrs. Musgrove, now the wife of the Anglican minister,[1] where a great swarm of drunken Indians lie day and night and cause much trouble. It is all very miserable. Still, people of all stations have a high regard for this servant of God, and the commanding officer [Horton] recently said to someone that the English and Germans had love for and fear of Mr. Driesler, whereas he would have to be satisfied with fear, if he could achieve even that. He cited some lovely details from which we can see that he has not conducted his office in vain so far. His weakness goes much to the heart of adults and children. They weep about it, lament their disloyalty, and promise much good; and they pray to God for his recovery. Even Englishmen have walked the good ways to true conversion, and Mr. Driesler wishes them loyalty and constancy.

I have sent him excerpts from letters from Germany, such as those of our worthy Senior Urlsperger, Prof. [G. A.] Francke, and Counsellor Walbaum for his edification and information, also in the new continuation of our printed diaries and mission reports,[2] and this has so pleased him that he can hardly express himself about them. The commanding officer [Horton] continues showing him much kindness as best he can, only the good man is deeply involved with the undisciplined soldiers and does not know what to do.[3] Just as Mr. Driesler was closing his letter, a sloop arrived with foodstuffs from New York, which was very welcome.

Thursday, the 18th of October. This morning, after completing some other business in Savannah, I visited Col. Stephens and found him more friendly than I have seen him recently. He allowed me the things that belong to the decayed sawmill in Old Ebenezer, and I consider this a great benefaction, for there are still a lot of useful things there that we will be able to use in all sorts of ways and which would otherwise spoil in a short time. As soon as possible I will ride there with the carpenter Kogler and remove to a dry and safe place everything that can be fetched at high water with a large boat.

---

[1] Mrs. Musgrove had married John Musgrove and later Jacob Matthews, before marrying the Anglican minister Thomas Bosomworth.

[2] The *Ausführliche Nachrichten* and the *Der Königlichen Dänischen Missionarien aus Ost-Indien eingesandte Ausführliche Berichte.*

[3] When English officers raped some German girls, the recorder, John Terry (Jean Thierry) said that Driesler had caused a woman to accuse him of rape.

In the morning of the day after tomorrow he will send a packet of letters via Charleston to the Lord Trustees, and he offered to enclose mine. However, I plan to write only at the end of this or the beginning of next week; perhaps we will meanwhile have the pleasure of receiving some news from Europe, for which we have been waiting with yearning. On account of the mill construction I had to get money with a bill of exchange, concerning which I have given Court Chaplain Ziegenhagen word in a little letter. I did this in the good hope that our dear Lord has granted something to him, Senior Urlsperger, and to Prof. [G. A.] Francke for our necessity and that the bill will be paid without delay.

Money is very scarce in the colony, yet there is a friend in Savannah who advances us cash money, without which nothing could be constructed at the mill, for our workmen are poor and need the money they earn, and thus the mill is a special benefaction for them. It is a very noticeable providence of God that Capt. Avery performed the last work of his life at our mill, which work is so well arranged that the skillful carpenter Kogler will gradually be able to carry out all subsequent construction very easily, to the great advantage of our entire community and other people in the land.[1]

This morning, when I visited the widow, Mrs. Avery, she told me and another friend how much her husband had loved our people and how much pleasure he got looking forward to serving us further until the entire mill construction was completed. But it had pleased the Lord of life and death otherwise. He had prepared himself right well for his transition from life to eternity, since he had noticed a good time in advance that he was not going to recover from this sickness.

Friday, the 19th of October. After my work I visited a woman who was just reading her *Treasure Chest*,[2] from which our dear God was granting her many treasures of edification. She hungers and thirsts mightily for grace and makes the unexpected death of Capt. Avery very useful for her preparation. Recently she had a right sensitive assurance of the grace of God and granted a little drop of her life to sweet eternity, and in this condition she wished to depart from here. However, she gradually lost this sweet sensation, and this caused her unrest.

I directed her to divine promises that apply to her in God's plans and which should be more certain for her than all the joy and moral assurance of God's mercy she has felt. Her past and present sins cause her much worry, struggle, and disquiet. However, since everything has

---

[1] Avery had died suddenly in October.
[2] See p. 24, n. 2.

been atoned, paid, and merited by Christ, and we are fully reconciled with God, she should just believe and make comforting use of the merits and mercy, which, however, do not come easily to a bowed and contrite soul.

Wednesday, the 24th of October.   Kogler has moved from the orphanage out to his plantation with his family, namely with his wife and two children,[1] and is establishing his own household there. I have hoped to receive letters from Europe from which to receive some instructions or at least suggestions as to what I should do for Kogler. For he has often been mentioned in my letters, and he had moved into the orphanage so that he might have all the more time to serve the community in all necessary construction with his skill; for, if he were to devote himself to cultivating his field and raising cattle, he would be all the less able to pursue his profession.   However, since it is neither necessary nor possible to continue the orphanage in its previous circumstances and because I have received no answer or instructions from Germany concerning the Koglers, I have had to let him begin his former farming again.

To be sure, I already see and feel the harm in discontinuing or sloppy tending of the mill construction, but I can do nothing to help. For I can go no further than I have the means for it. The members of the community cannot contribute anything to the many expenses that are required for the cultivation and development of our plantation city.

Because nothing has flowed from Europe for a long time and we have no help at all from the authorities in Savannah or from anybody else, I am often in great tribulations and do not know where I should get this or that. Mr. Thilo has long been requesting a kitchen, which has now been built and has cost much money, but it is indeed well and durably built. Now he wishes to have his house lot protected by a good fence, for which I have already bought long planks for 20 sh. Sterling and have had posts and poles prepared. Much other aid has been given him in the hope that he will leave off his selfishness and become all the more useful to the community. This has quickly run into big money. I still have to hope for the good effect of all that has been spent on him.

This morning I wished to visit Kogler and his family but did not find him at home. Meanwhile I spoke with her[2] and her honest neighbor, Mrs. Kornberger, some edifying words about the little verse "We have

---

[1] Barbara, née Rossbacher; Georg and Maria.

[2] It was common usage to say "I called on Schmidt and told her," meaning Mrs. Schmidt, even though she has not been mentioned.

here no continuing city, but we seek one to come."[1] So far she has had divine services and good opportunities very near, and our dear God has wrought much good in her, which she should apply to denying herself and the world and to directing her entire heart and spirit to the search for and contemplation of the New Jerusalem, as all the faithful here have done so from the beginning.

Mrs. Kornberger is very much concerned with her salvation, she knows that she formerly deceived herself with a false faith, and therefore she now fears self-deception as much as the devil himself. When she heard the verse "Delight thyself also in the Lord; and he shall give thee the desires of thine heart,"[2] she wished for and requested one thing, namely, that she might become one heart and one soul with her husband and have only one mind that is aimed only at what is necessary. Then her husband would have patience with her weaknesses and they would be able to accommodate themselves to their domestic cross. God granted us all much grace for joint prayer and for His praise.

When I was finished there, I went to young Lackner to consecrate his new dwelling with the word of God and prayer. We sang *Danckt dem Herrn ihr Gottes Knechte,* etc., contemplated Hebrews 13, and felt abundantly the blessing and assistance of the Lord while singing, praying, and contemplating the divine word. In this beautiful chapter there are lovely verses that very well suit the circumstances of the consecration of this new dwelling and of the two married people. Their friends who were invited from the neighborhood received much good to take home with them, especially the last words: "Grace be to you all."[3]

Saturday, the 25th of October. This morning those young parishioners who live in town or on the near plantations gathered in Jerusalem Church to attend the harvest and thanksgiving sermon, which was based on Hebrews 13:15-16, "By Him therefore let us offer the sacrifice of praise in God continually." The divine service was begun and ended with humble prayer, and in the sermon we were reminded of both our spiritual and physical blessings and of our duty, which consists of hearty spoken and practical thanks to God and of not forgetting the need of one's neighbor, for with such sacrifices God is well pleased.

By the last words of the text "forget not to do good and to communicate: for with such sacrifices God is well pleased," we were reminded that these words were not written to rich people but to the materially

---

[1] Hebrews 13:14.
[2] Psalms 37:4.
[3] Perhaps shortened from Romans 1:7.

poor Hebrews who had been chased from their houses and farms and deprived of all their possessions because of the wickedness of their Jewish kinsmen, just as collections were made in Jerusalem among the Christians from the heathens for the poor saints, in the same spirit: "Forget not to do good and to communicate" and a similar admonition stands in Ephesians 4:[28], "Let him who stole, etc. ... rather let him labor, that he may have to give to him that needeth."

At this point we looked up verses from Leviticus 19:9, 23:14,22, Deuteronomy 24:19, in which the Lord God commands all Israelites who receive a harvest to remember the poor. And thus our people were also admonished to come to the help of those who are still poorer than they are with the blessings they have received from the Lord. If it is done with obedient, willing, and joyful heart, then such sacrifices of Christ well please the Lord and He loves such givers. In conclusion I asked the congregation to contribute something of their means for the better maintenance of the two schoolmasters, Ortmann and Kocher, which should consist of each householder's donating annually a bushel of corn (weighing approximately 50 pounds), even if he is not sending any child to school, because every Christian and friend of God must rightfully contribute something for the maintenance of the churches and schools.

Since this is a small thing but the total would be a great help for the schoolmasters, I hope that no one will refuse this. The parents who have children and send them to school will add another bushel for all their children and thus pay two bushels yearly. For the support of the ministers in the church they do not, as they knew, have to pay anything at all because God has inclined the hearts of the worthy members of the most praiseworthy Society[1] in England to provide for our stipend. For that the congregation should thank the Lord all the more and beg Him to reward them.

After church three men, who are still weak beginners, called on me and announced that they wished to pay their share with work or with money because they could not spare any of their crop. Along Ebenezer Creek there is mostly sandy soil, and the rain was lacking there longer than on the other plantations. Therefore some of them harvested very little.

In today's sermon they were directed away from the *causis secundis* and to the hand of the Lord, who has always known how to maintain the poor among us. He will also do it from this harvest to the next in such

---

[1] The Society for Promoting Christian Knowledge.

a way that, when they look back, they will have to marvel at His wonderful providence. He gives it to His friends in their sleep, and He has said, "I will never leave thee, nor forsake thee." Therefore, be satisfied with what is there. I promised publicly to pay for those who, because of poverty, cannot give anything to the schoolmaster as much as God gives me the means. I wished to spare them from this demand, if need did not drive me to it. May God test their faith, love, and obedience by this; And He can replace it thousandfold.

I had hardly come home from the church when an Englishman brought me a letter from a captain of a corps of Rangers who wishes to found a new city on the Ogeechee River named Williamsburg after himself.[1] He described for me the lack of foodstuffs in Frederica, from where he and his people were to be provisioned. Therefore he asked our people to let him have 200 or at least 50 bushels of corn, which he would have his people fetch as soon as possible. He wished to have a part of it ground if our mill was operating. He will be given some 50 bushels.

Our people could very easily sell their Indian and European crops because very few crops are grown elsewhere in this country, if only they would learn the way to cultivate and raise a lot of crops. This can not take place until they apply themselves seriously to plowing. Some have already prepared the woodwork for plowing and are just waiting anxiously for their plowshares. They can accomplish very little with the hoe, especially in the hottest summer time, when the Indian corn and the beans must be cultivated. They may well get sick because of the widespread and deeply rooted crab grass. For that reason many in the community are very poor. If I could not let them earn something for daily labor, they would have to seek work in some other place.

The pay that is given them can therefore be seen as an alms, yet very many necessary and useful things can be accomplished in Ebenezer, such as the present mill construction. May God continue to awaken benefactors in Europe who will practice with regard to our inhabitants: "Forget not to do good and to communicate, for such sacrifices please God." In this lasting time of war, when merchandise and other goods are exceedingly expensive, it is very difficult for our dear people to gain strength and reach a point of not desiring any more help. Therefore I surely hope that they will finally not only reach that point but also reach such a position under divine blessing as to demonstrate to others who

---

[1] Nothing came of this scheme.

may wish to come here to take their retreat in this quietude the context of our today's sermon. God in heaven will recompense our worthy benefactors in Europe for what they have done so far in Ebenezer. The glory of God demands that they not abandon us now but give further assistance.

Saturday, the 27th of October. Toward evening yesterday I again visited Johann Schmidt's fatally ill wife and found her very weak and miserable. She no longer talks, but she understands everything that is called out to her. He testified that she was entirely calm and patient during her greatest pain. Already several weeks before her sickness she had become quiet and aimed her mind toward death and eternity, as if she had already noticed in advance that she would close her life in this pregnancy. Now there is surely no more hope of her recovery, and her husband is showing great resignation and is bearing his cross with right great patience.

God has shown very great mercy to this woman. She came to us with the third transport very ignorant[1] and had no desire for God's word. Because of the sad conditions then in Ebenezer everything was distressful for her, and therefore she made life bitter for her husband in many ways. However, our dear God so blessed the truths of the catechism in certain lessons that she came to a recognition of her blindness and wickedness. In this God used her husband and other Christian people as tools to lead her ever further and to Christ.

She often marveled at her great blindness, obstinacy, and sinful paths and nature, and at the same time at God's forbearance and patience toward her. She lamented the corruption of her heart and hungered inwardly for Christ, who also stilled her hunger and fed and refreshed her with the crumbs of His grace. As distressful as Ebenezer was for her at first, just as pleasing it became for her later, after she had found her spiritual birthplace. Because she had grown up in coarse ignorance and much disorder and even entered marriage in a disorderly way in Austria,[2] she had many very evil habits, errors, and frailties. Therefore only some among us recognized the grace that the Lord had placed in her. These were people who had frequent occasion to speak to her and engage her in a spiritual conversation.

Sunday, the 28th of October. Mrs. Schweighoffer has been dragging herself around for a long time with an evil condition and, because she has let up on the use of the means of salvation, the ailment

---

[1] *Unwissend*, unconverted and ill-trained in the way to repentance.

[2] The third transport consisted mostly of Upper Austrians and Carinthians.

has increased and has now been joined by a violent fever, by which she has been greatly debilitated. Since she abandoned the first love and strength of Christianity through a lack of watching and prayer but later turned herself righteously to the Lord, she cannot achieve a proper certainty of her state of grace and joy in faith. She must struggle with all sorts of anxiety, fear, and doubt. Nevertheless, our dear God does not leave her without a glimmer of grace.

When I visited her, she right heartily regretted her disobedience to her ministers and the evil example she had given others through her obstinate behavior and she sighed for grace. I told her various things from the gospel about Christ's reconciliation, which applies to her; and, from the example of the woman with the issue,[1] I told her of the kind of faith that so appropriates Christ as if He had died and fulfilled everything for such a person alone.

Jesus humbles her outwardly and inwardly under His cross and wishes to draw her to Himself entirely through these tribulations so that it can finally be said "The marriage of the Lamb is come, and his wife hath made herself ready."[2] Since she thought that she had insulted and distressed us ministers and other believers, I told her that we and they had long since forgiven and forgotten everything and that we did not like for her to think of it again or to worry herself about it. Rather she could much better look to our heavenly Father in Christ, who grants such love from His abundance into the hearts of His people and she herself surely used it with all her strength.

She knows, I said, how great her mother-love is for her children and that she would gladly carry them to heaven in her arms. What will her heavenly Father and Savior not wish to do for her, or what has He not already done, for He is like both mother and father. It is written: "He that formed the eye, shall he not see?"[3] Also, "He who put love into the heart of father and mother, should he not love?"[4] Numerous verses and examples attest to that.

Monday, the 29th of October.   Today I received via Ebenezer a letter from Mr. Broughton, the present secretary of the praiseworthy Society, which was dated March 24 of this year and was therefore seven months en route. This worthy successor of the late Henry Newman

---

[1] Mark 5:25.

[2] Revelations 19:7.

[3] Psalms 94:9.

[4] *Der Vater und Mutter die Liebe ans Hertz gegeben, solte der nicht lieben?* Unidentified.

wrote to us in a very friendly way and reports that our letters of last year please the Society and that they heartily rejoice at all the good that God is showing us in the land of our pilgrimage. He also writes that it the express desire of the Society for us to send in a journal from time to time from which they can see the condition and state of our community.

He finally reports that the Society has dismissed the schoolmaster Ortmann from his service and that his salary was to end on the first of May 1744. Full power will be sent to us to choose a person as schoolmaster who can instruct the children in both German and English, if such a person can be found. Ortmann himself is to blame for this dismissal, not only because he got into a lot of disorder, especially with Thomas Stephens,[1] and lied to and calumniated our community and could not be persuaded by me or others to recognize and apologize for his offense in a letter to the Lord Trustees or to the Society. His wife is to blame for his misfortune. The measure of her sins will soon be full, for in the years when Ortmann was schoolmaster she caused much annoyance and distress, and the whole story of her life stands in the words: "Because they have no changes, therefore they fear not God."[2]

May our dear Lord now show us a man who can take over the work with the children in the school. My and my dear colleague's minds are set on our dear Mr. [Ludwig] Mayer, if our heavenly Father will incline his heart to take upon himself this sour and difficult, yet blessed and God-pleasing work. All the members of the community would rejoice at this choice, since they have true confidence in him. This would also be a means for him to support himself all the sooner. Since Mr. Thilo must also be taken care of and the congregation is still small and stands in a difficult beginning and many tribulations, the contributions for his support, to be sure, are not the way one would want them. With the first of November our and the schoolmaster's salary begins, so the new schoolmaster can take up his work at once.

Now that God has strengthened my dear brother-in-law and co-sponsor[3] Mr. Gronau again, I have already discussed with him last week a new arrangement in the school for the good of both the large and small children, for which of course Ortmann could not offer us a hand. He

---

[1] Ortmann and two others had signed a pro-slavery petition brought to Ebenezer by Thomas Stephens, the undutiful son of the Trustees' secretary in Georgia. See Trevor R. Reese, *The Clamorous Malcontents*. Savannah, Ga., 1973.

[2] Psalms 55:19.

[3] *Gevatter*. Each was godfather of the other's children. Boltzius and Gronau had married the sisters Gertraut and Catharina Kröhr.

wishes to, but cannot do what suits a competent schoolmaster. The point about sending in an English diary to the Society strikes me as rather difficult, since I would have to neglect other necessary work in order to write such a diary or else tax my strength too much. Still, I have a desire to obey this hint and calling. Perhaps it will redound to the glory of God and the edification of my neighbor. The worthy members of the Society have been the great and dear benefactors of the Salzburgers from the beginning of the emigration, and they have shown themselves as great and dear benefactors to us ministers and our congregation throughout these eleven years. Therefore it should be a joy for me and my dear colleague to live to please them in everything if the Lord grants us time, strength, and means to do so.

Wednesday, the 31st of October.   Schoolmaster Ortmann did not come to school today to teach the children, nor did he tell me that he would be absent so I might act accordingly. When he was speaking with me yesterday about his dismissal, of which Mr. Broughton had written him in a personal letter, he recited the services he thought he had rendered the school. He paid little attention to what I said. In the above-mentioned printed tract of Thomas Stephens he attested with his signature that he knew of no example of anyone who could support himself in Ebenezer by the work of his hands. It is surely a judgment on him and his naughty wife that he will not enjoy any of the corn and beans that our inhabitants contribute to the support of the schoolmaster after the sermon of harvest and thanksgiving. He is to be pitied, for his wife is bringing him into poverty and all sorts of need even though one can get along well with him. However he did not teach school very well. This we have always regretted. His English is quite useless, but he does not like to hear this.[1]

A Christian woman who had visited Hans Schmidt's wife before her present and very great weakness told me that she had talked a lot about her sins and the deep perdition of her heart and had bewailed and lamented them. Catharina Holtz, who had been in her service for some time, walked into the hut at just that time and Mrs. Schmidt spoke these words to her movingly: "Do not postpone your repentance until you get sick, etc."[2] Thereupon she became quiet and gradually very weak, yet her eyes were always aimed at heaven, and she pointed to her breast with her hand. Through her husband she told me that she was sorry that she had insulted a certain person concerning a sponsorship and wished to

---

[1] He had learned his English as a marine aboard ship.

[2] Paraphrase of Sirach 18:22.

forgive her. I have not had time today or yesterday to come to her, but I hear that physically she is faring very badly and miserably.

NOVEMBER 1744[1]

Thursday, the 1st of November.   Yesterday evening my dear colleague came safe and sound from Savannah and brought me a friendly letter from Mr. Habersham in which he sends us a greeting from our dear friend Mr. [Thomas] Jones saying that he is sending us, through Mr. Whitefield who has now gone to New England, Mr. Henry's exegesis of the entire Holy Scripture in five folio volumes.[2]   He is always sickly, whereas he was always healthy here.   Mr. Whitefield is now expected shortly in Savannah, and this is causing great joy among his friends.   Also, money has come to Savannah from the Lord Trustees from which a part of our debts can be paid.   Col. Stephens will also send us the money for the orphanage's silk, and this will be a great help with the mill.

From two Christian friends we have received a fine gift of clothes for our wives.   We have heard good news of General Oglethorpe and his health and many other good reports.   Thus the end of last month and the beginning of this month have been blessed for us in many ways.   Things may be very bad with the war in Germany,[3] but we can learn nothing certain about this.   I rightly consider that one of the great blessings that our dear God has shown us at this time is that He has inclined Mr. [Ludwig] Mayer's heart to accept the work in the school in God's name, and this has caused joy among children and parents.

I have now answered secretary Broughton's letter and announced that we have employed Mr. Mayer in place of Ortmann and reported some things about his good character to report to the Society.[4]   His work will consist of relieving my dear colleague, who holds the catechism hour from eight to nine, of beginning the school with prayer (from nine to ten), repetition of the catechism of the already learned verses,

---

[1] The extant manuscript for November 1744 contains only this entry for November 1.

[2] Matthew Henry, *An Exposition of all the Books of the Old and New Testaments*, printed for J. Clark and R. Hett, 1725.

[3] The Second Silesian War, 1744-1746.

[4] The Society for Promoting Christian Knowledge also paid the salary for one schoolmaster.

and application of the first hour from nine to ten to the advancement of the larger children in reading. He will also let the little children recite once, which in the future will be done between ten and eleven. In the meanwhile the larger children are to write.

If Mr. [Ludwig] Mayer could also hold a little school hour in the afternoon, it would be spent with reading, with practice in English, and in other useful ways, as seemed to suit the children's circumstances. He has a desire to learn the English language, and in this we will give him as much help as possible.

JANUARY 1745[1]

Ebenezer, 1 January 1745. In yesterday's evening prayer meeting we used the two verses from 2 Peter 15-18 to conclude the old year, "The long-suffering of our Lord is salvation ... But grow in grace, and in the knowledge of our Lord and Savior, Jesus Christ." May He remind us of these words throughout the year and strengthen us in His mercy and recognition, so that we may stand firm and victorious in all trials and temptations which we will yet face in the short portion of our lives that is still ahead of us. We shall need much of this on our deathbed. Now that he is fastened to his bed and his cross during his long sickness, how my dear colleague [Gronau] profits from the treasure of grace and blessed recognition of Christ which he has collected over these many years. May He continue to bless his beautiful example in me as well.

Old Mrs. Rieser, who has now been miserably sick and tied to her bed for many months, also admires with many tears the wealth of God's grace and patience; and she praises the Lord for the rich blessing He has shown her during her life and her illness. Of her, too, we shall say after her departure and dissolution, which she impatiently desires, "Her pain, grief and misery are coming to a blessed end. She has carried the yoke of the Lord, has died and yet lives."[2] For the New Year's text today in the morning and the afternoon we used as a point of departure the verse from John XII, "I am come a light in the world..." He not only came into this vale of tears, but into a poor and humble station at his birth and circumcision, and from this floweth an immense comfort for us poor and

---

[1] The Halle original says "Continuation of the Diary" following this date.

[2] *Ihr Jammer, Trübsal und Elend ist kommen zu einem seeligen End. Sie hat getragen Christi Joch, ist gestorben und lebet doch.* From the hymn *Nun lasset uns den Leib begraben* by Michael Weisse, from an old Moravian hymn.

miserable sinners who have run into such terrible grief because of our sins. This comfort lies in the name of the dear Lord Jesus, which bears with it life and full contentment.

In the past year, our congregation saw 29 children born, 8 persons died, that is one man, 3 women and 4 children; and 3 couples were married. Our congregation at Ebenezer now consists of 270 souls, among them 117 small and large children. From 1734 to this day, 128 children have been born into our congregation and baptized,[1] 131 persons have died and 56 couples have been married.

Wednesday, the 2nd of January. A pious Salzburger who kept watch at Mr. Gronau's bed last night told me with much joy that our merciful Lord had given him a generous present for the new year from the sermon we preached. We had a most edifying conversation. He has resolved to learn the core verses with his family during the course of the coming year, and he will let nothing interfere with this if God gives him grace and perseverance.

I received an English letter from Abercorn which was written on behalf of a German man called Johann Martin Lohmann. He writes that on Christmas Day his hut and all its content were consumed by fire. He requests some help to get back on his feet. He lives below Savannah on an island called Skidaway. I presume he is the smith who sought and received our help while he was still in Purysburg. At the time, he pretended that, while it had rained on the fields of others, his field had remained dry and thus he had lost all money. He is a wicked man who has caused great mischief. At last, when he became too well known as a cattle thief in Carolina, he moved to this colony.

We have written several letters to our friends and Fathers in Europe at the end of the year, which were sent this morning to our friend Mr. Habersham in Savannah, together with the German and English diaries.[2] He will take care to expedite this packet from Charleston to London. The letters were addressed to the secretary of the Society, Mr. Broughton, to Court Chaplain Ziegenhagen, Senior Urlsperger, and Professor [G. A.] Francke. May God protect it all!

Thursday, the 3rd of January. When I went to the plantation yesterday afternoon, Gschwandl told me that four Indians had frightened

---

[1] The German phrase *als Glieder unsrer Gemeinde geboren* probably refers to children baptized and may exclude those who died before receiving the sacrament.

[2] During this period the Trustees had required an English version of the diaries as well, putting considerable hardship on Boltzius and his assistants. These diaries are not known to have survived.

his girl coming back from church service and afterwards shot one of his best cows for the sake of its bell, which they stole. A few days ago Mrs. Ortmann told me that the Indians who come from Old Ebenezer had shot a large pregnant sow belonging to the Ortmanns. This is the pitiful situation in which we live, and nobody can help us unless it be the Lord Himself. Mrs. Ortmann traveled on New Year's day to join her husband in Savannah by way of Abercorn. Thus, she shunned the blessing that the Lord has offered on this first day of the year through the preaching of His gospels, and this will not work to her good.

Mrs. Grimmiger, who was so severely ill, has recovered again and can take care of some housework. She claims that she has recognized with much gratitude that the Lord has not yet called her to eternity. She has made many good resolutions, showed us something from Arndt's *Christianity*,[1] where she had read of the repentant conversion to the Lord, and cried bitterly because she had for so long been unable to come to church. I admonished her in those things necessary for her salvation and warned her of such matters as she and her husband had previously been involved in.

Friday, the 4th of January.   Last night, Mrs. Riedelsberger was delivered of a daughter who was baptized in the Jerusalem Church this afternoon. Her husband had been sent to Savannah with our letters on Wednesday, and he will return to an unexpected joy at his home. Mr. [Ludwig] Mayer has resumed copying the lost diary.[2] This will cause him much trouble because he has much work and is daily engaged in copying and continuing the English and German journals. But he does it gladly and I am much relieved by his help. May God strengthen him in his manifold work and truly reward him for the trouble he has taken with us and our congregation and friends.

As a matter of conscience, I may not omit any part of my daily journal, for in my original instructions I was expressly enjoined to maintain a detailed diary.[3] More than that, experience has taught us that our marvelous and great God has used the printed diaries as a means

---

[1] Johann Arndt, *Vier Bücher vom Wahren Christenthum*... Reprinted many times throughout the 17th and 18th century.

[2] The reference is to one unspecified part of the 1744 diaries, which are reprinted in this volume for the period from Feb. 24 to Nov. 1.

[3] These lengthy and detailed instructions on travel, comportment, relationships to colleagues and flock, and the maintenance of a diary were given to every missionary sent from Halle as part of his call. The one for Boltzius and Gronau is in the Missions-Archiv, Franckesche Stiftungen, series 5A.

through which our congregation has received many a gift from generous hearts. May He continue to show us His mercy also in material things; for we need much for the mill construction, and our people here are too weak to contribute more than is necessary for the miller's livelihood. Since we have had no news from Europe for a long time and money is scarce in this country, I intend to interrupt the construction of the lower run for the rice mill so as not go too deeply into debt.

Praise be to God, who has protected us so well that our grist mill is in good condition and of great service both to our congregation and to the others who make use of it. It is my sincere wish that all among us will use this and other benefactions of the Lord to recognize His kindness and providence and shy away from ingratitude towards Him and man, for this has caused us unspeakable damage, as I have learned in the case of the orphanage and elsewhere. Today at the end of the edification hour at the Zion Church I mentioned several points concerning this matter for the improvement of everyone, if the Lord so wishes.

Saturday, the 5th of January. Pastor Driesler wrote me today and his letter was forwarded from Savannah by messenger. He writes that the dear Lord is blessing his office but is also bestowing upon him much suffering, but that this does him no harm. I too am the object of much criticism by some who judge me quite harshly, but Mr. Driesler knows well how to bear this burden. He remembers a great sinner who, much to the surprise of others, has turned to the Lord. I replied to him yesterday and am waiting for an opportunity to send my letter.

In this new year we have had several warm days as if it were spring. The nights are pleasant, neither cold nor warm. It is now time to plant mulberry trees, and I have planted a good number and have had the older ones fertilized and pruned. But few among us are inclined and skilled for this type of planting, which I much regret, for this shows wilful disobedience of the wishes of the Trustees, who urge silk culture for this colony. The people also lose much of the advantage which the mature trees will yield in the future.

Sunday, the 6th of January.   Today we celebrated the Feast of the Epiphany, in grateful memory of the great and invaluable gift that the Lord our God showed our forbears by delivering them from the wilderness and other[1] darkness and bringing us into the light of the gospels and also maintaining us and our children in this heathen country. From this we came to understand, both through the preaching of the

---

[1] The word "Popish" has been deleted here, presumably by Urlsperger.

gospel and a demonstration of our duties, the blessing that we have received in Christ's becoming flesh. In this context we studied the last part of the 14th Chapter of Zacharias, v. 16 *et seq.* that all heathens who have been brought into the congregation of the Christian Church should come out every year to pray to the Lord Zebaoth and to celebrate the Feast of the Tabernacle of the New Testament or a feast of thanks and joy, as we are celebrating today. Whatever creatures on earth do not come out to praise the King, Lord Zebaoth (as did the firstborn among the heathen, the three Wise Men), it will not rain on them, and they will deprive themselves of the edification that is in justice and of all the means of salvation, which are richly provided by the preaching of the gospel.

Last night we considered in the story examined so far the apparition with which King Solomon was blessed by the Lord and in particular the Messiah at Gibeon,[1] for which he with his servants and subjects showed himself fully grateful in Jerusalem before the house and ark of the covenant, likewise verses 18 and 19, a fact which the gross disdainers and also the separatist spirits[2] would do well to remember, for they rob themselves of a great blessing by missing public services, a fate of which people were warned.

A woman has suffered much in her spirit, particularly regarding a certain gross vice. While she begged the Lord's pardon again humbly and in tears, invoking the name of Christ, she also prayed Him to instruct her ministers in His mind and His tongue how to speak to her about this. When I visited her unexpectedly yesterday so that she could reveal her desires to me, she was all the more impressed by my instruction from the gospels, because she saw in this that her prayers had been heard. She prays that the Lord will keep her in His mercy and assist her with His grace in her hour of death, whether it comes sooner or later.

Today we based our morning and evening sermon for this day of celebration on the dear verse: "Look unto me and be saved, all the ends of the earth; for I am God, and there is none else."[3] We showed that

---

[1] 1 Kings 3:5.

[2] The reference to separatists is deleted in the text in accordance with long-standing practice at Halle and out of consideration for English readers. Pietism, although often accused of separatist tendencies, in fact avoided schism and stayed within the Lutheran confession. There were no separatists, i.e., sectarians such as Baptists or Mennonites, at Ebenezer.

[3] Isaiah 45:22.

Jesus wishes dearly for all men to obtain the state of grace, but that most remain in a state of sin through their own fault and may even be wholly lost to perdition.

Monday, the 7th of January. My dear colleague Gronau has grown weaker and weaker for the last few days, causing us to throng all the more closely to the fatherly heart of the Lord with our poor prayers of support. The Lord Jesus looks upon his soul with great kindness, which causes him to shed tears of joy. He regrets that he cannot pray much because of his great weakness, but the Holy Ghost in his heart and his Immanuel to the right of the Father are praying all the more fervently for him. As a true member of the invisible Christian Church, he benefits from the prayer of all believers and from his own frequent and urgent prayers on his sickbed, for the merciful salvation goes on at all times.

A pious woman who owes much to his intercession, word, and example used the expression that he had filled much oil into the lamp and the vessel during the days of his health, from which he can now benefit; this served me as a salutary reminder. Every night a Christian man watches at his bed and is of service; and several men, both in the town and on the plantations, have offered to spell each other in this task. I do truly feel as if this time he will pass into the silence and the joy of the Lord.

May our dear Savior take pity on me at this time. From a simple and deeply pious Salzburger woman who had visited another sick woman to pray with her, I heard the beautiful and well founded judgment that one could clearly feel that she was growing in her strength and increasing in it, and that this was a blessing one could earn if only one could cross over to Him one day. If only we could feel this in all our listeners, who have been given such rich pasture from the grace of the Lord.

Last Friday, we learned that a mare was lying on the road from Old Ebenezer to Abercorn. It is said to belong to a poor man on our plantations, and it may well be that this evil deed was perpetrated at the same time as the shooting of the cow. Our rangers went out on Saturday and found the dead horse in the area of our old cowpen. They searched for thirteen hours, and it seems that the Indians could not catch the horse right off, since they shot it three times. These are the sorrows which the Lord places on us as a trial, and they have without doubt a salutary cause which He has intended for everyone to see.

Yesterday we read Isaiah 45.   "I had the evil and therefore it is
better to humble oneself under God than to lose courage."[1] ...   "The
right hand of the Lord can change all things."[2]

Tuesday, the 8th of January.   Dear old Mrs. Rieser much likes me
to visit her, and we see in her too the good that we observed yesterday
in the woman we have mentioned; for she too grows and increases on
her heavy sickbed in the grace and the recognition of Christ.   She is
weak in her body and longs for and looks forward to her dissolution,
because she is sure of her salvation in Christ.   Every verse that is given
her from God's word is dear and sweet to her and presses itself deeply
into her heart.   Among other matters, she asked me, if I were to write
to Augsburg, to thank the people there on her behalf for the many
spiritual and material benefits that she, her husband, and her children
received in the Evangelical poorhouse there.[3]   In the material world, it
meant much to her that the poor had a good bed and a well set table, and
she regretted her own ingratitude and that of others.

On her sickbed, she wishes to ask the Lord for a blessing on her
benefactors in the poorhouse.   She recommended her children to me and
asked me to punish them if they were bad, but I hope that they will let
themselves be punished, convinced, and chastised by the word of the
Holy Spirit.   She passes on to her old husband and to her children and
others here the impressive lesson of her youth, that is, to use their
strength and their bodies better than she did.   I instructed her oldest son,
whom I found at her bedside crying into the book, to read to his mother
slowly and clearly the words for her funeral sermon: "Rejoice greatly,
oh my soul,"[4] for this hymn would follow her to the churchyard if she
were the first to leave us.

Today we have finished with 1 Kings, both in the Zion and the
Jerusalem Church.   The Lord has offered us much edification from this
text.   May He be praised.   I presented the last part, dealing with the
most prudent judgment of Solomon in the matter of the two harlots[5] as
follows: This much blessed King on this high holy day of the Epiphany
may well have held an open table with his retinue and servants, or so one

---

[1] *Ich hatte das Übel ud also ists besser unter Gts Hand zu demüthigen als sich
den Muth nehmen zu lassen.*   Not found in Isaiah 45. Cf. "Humble yourselves therefore
under the mighty hand of God, that he may exalt you in due time." 1 Peter 5:6.

[2] Psalms 77:11. The King James version is worded differently.

[3] See p. 58, n. 1.

[4] *Freu Dich sehr, O meine Seele.* Hymn by Christian Weise.

[5] 1 Kings 3:16-28.

may assume. Since the poor people had profited for a long time because of the many buildings undertaken by their king and had brought forward their petitions, these two women were encouraged to bring their dispute before the king, presumably at the end of this feast.

This wise lord will have noticed from both words and expressions who was the mother of the child, but he thought of a scheme to draw out the real mother's stronger love and affection into the light of day and thus convince all those present. He demanded a sword, without saying how he would use it; and this may have acted like a whipping on these two sinners, who in their bad conscience and great fear may have thought that judgment was to come over them and their lives because of the sin of whoredom, which is so clearly forbidden under Deuteronomy 23:2,17. We may compare this to the wise Joseph, who let his brothers feel the whip.

The lessons which we learned from this story were, among others, these three:

1. Just as under the wise government of Solomon, with both divine service and policy in good order,[1] there were nonetheless some sinful and offensive persons, whose sin was therefore all the more offensive and irresponsible. This should not be placed as a burden on the whole congregation, nor should the good that exists be denied, as often happens, so that dutiful and honest authority is twice offended. But such offensive women then held on to the fruit of their wombs, although St.Paul says of the last and horrible times of 2 Timothy 3:3 there would be .... [2] who in a manner of speaking divest themselves of the vestments of their natural love and treat the fruit of their wombs both before and after birth like barbarians and worse than animals. The Lord Himself speaks of this in Isaiah 49:15, in a manner hardly credible for us: "Can a woman forget her suckling child?"

2. The patience and charity of the Lord regarding the birth of children out of wedlock is all the more amazing in that such bad mothers not only give birth as easily as those born of married parents, but they are born whole and sound and with all their limbs. We recalled at this time the special providence of the Lord for little children; for, if that was not all encompassing, few would keep their sound limbs and escape

---

[1] Boltzius uses the word *Polizey* in its Early Modern German meaning of arrangements for public order and civil welfare, not as a body of policemen or constables. The word "police" often used in English translations for this period limits its scope unduly.

[2] Illegible.

being smothered (as in this story) or otherwise hurt from lack of care. This should encourage all parents and children amongst us who are sound of limb and body.

3. There still are many involved disputes where even the guilty party wishes to be in the right, and therefore judgment may have to be postponed until the right Solomon arrives. I closed with 2 Corinthians 10.[1]

Wednesday, the 9th of January.   My dear and very ill colleague received Holy Communion this morning, having revealed unto me himself and through others his earnest desire for this sacrament.   He harbored a small scruple, which he discussed with me and then was content.   Early on His heart had turned towards the beautiful words: "For I determined not to know any thing among you, save Jesus Christ, and him crucified."[2] I reminded him that a good while ago in his severe illness Jesus Christ was his crucified relief and element, which he had subsequently confirmed in an evangelical and impressive manner for our edification in the catechisation for the passion story.   We then remembered the words: "But of him are ye in Christ Jesus, who of God is made unto us wisdom, and righteousness, and sanctification, and redemption."[3] All this is closely intertwined and interdependent and therefore we may not sorrow if a believer feels that sanctification and renewal are coming at a slow pace; for we have all in Christ.

The Father Himself has created Him thus for us, and thus He is all ours.   When with the last word, "redemption," I returned to his main verse: "And the ransomed of the Lord shall return ... they shall obtain joy and gladness, and sorrow and sighing shall flee away,"[4] he cried from the bottom of his heart and was most quiet.   While in close communion with this my sick brother and colleague, the image of the blessed Dr. Anton[5] in his last days has again grown vivid for me, for they resemble each other in many ways; and indeed God has given him much grace from the writings of this dear theologian, in particular from his *Evangelical House Talk*.[6] Several days ago he told me that he felt

---

[1] Verse number not legible.

[2] 1 Corinthians 2:2.

[3] 1 Corinthians 1:30.

[4] Isaiah 35:10.

[5] Dr. Paul Anton (1661-1730), born in Upper Lusatia and a follower of Jacob Spener. In 1686, together with A. H. Francke, he founded a *collegium philobiblicum* for theological students at the University of Leipzig. Since 1695, Professor of Theology at the newly founded Friedrich University at Halle.

[6] Paul Anton, *Evangelisches Haus-Gespräch von der Erlösung*. Halle, 1730.

like Lazarus: "He already stinketh." His tears prevented him from speaking. I thought he was referring to the poor Lazarus in front of the rich man's house, and I offered something to my colleague from this story for his instruction and comfort, and he became quiet.

Last night he repeated our words from the day before and said that, because of his bothersome flatulence, he had felt like the Lazarus who had been in his grave for four days and of whom his blessed sister had said to the Lord Jesus, "By this time he stinketh."[1] But he had realized that this was one of the reasons why the Lord Jesus had been dissatisfied with him and had corrected him. In this connection, I used for his and my own benefit the words: "Said I not unto thee, that, if thou wouldest believe, thou shouldest see the glory of God?"[2] He has often proved His glory in this my poor brother and He can well do it again and return him to us once more, although he is so close to death. We must believe and hope where there is no hope, as did Abraham with his dear Isaac, whom he knew in his heart to be dead. Last night, he also said, "I would like to die, this is always in my mind. I would like to depart and return to Christ; but, since my dear friends desire to have me around longer, I would be content to become well again and would much like to bring more souls to Christ."

Thursday, the 10th of January. This fall and winter we have plowed much land in our area and planted European grains. If the Lord is with us and gives us a blessed harvest and if the German grains such as wheat and barley can be sold here, this will encourage our people to pursue their farming more industriously. For they will then have a better living as if they only planted the native crops here, such as corn, beans, and rice. Recently we heard from the story of 1 Kings 3:14 that, if we walk in God's ways and obey all His statutes and commandments and walk in the steps of the faithful, we will not only be on the road to spiritual and eternal but also temporal happiness, for godliness will help in many ways and promises both this and our future life. It is in this order that our gracious Lord promised Solomon a long life, to which belong health and sustenance, even if *cum exceptione crucis*.[3] He can easily prevent the Indians from hurting us further.

He may even direct the hearts of the Lord Trustees to take matters more seriously if there should one day be peace with Spain and France. For, if their cows and horses were shot and carried off, they would incur

---

[1] John 11:39.
[2] John 11:40.
[3] "Even if with the exception of suffering."

great obstacles in farming, since they have borrowed horses for this purpose. Several horses are missing and it is believed that they were caught by the Indians. We hear few cowbells in the woods; for, since the Indians chase the cattle for these bells, the people ought to let their cattle run without them, but then they are all the more difficult to find. We are waiting eagerly for plowshares. Today I let two men have the orphanage's plow[1] for 30 shillings, although it had cost us 50 shillings to have them made by our smith, who knows little about this type of work and thus had to spend much time on it. He has two plowshares.

Friday, the 11th of January. A young woman wished to speak to me before the service in the Zion Church. She had something on her mind concerning Holy Communion, and she desired instruction with a humble and eager heart. For a long time she had let herself be kept away by the words: "He that eateth bread with me hath lifted up his heel against me,"[2] for in her honest mind she finds herself full of faults and defects, distracted by her household duties and much else. Then, when her mind is jolted out of the edifying mood into which the sermon of the Lord's word has put it, she applies this verse to herself. I therefore corrected her from the Lord's word and referred her from Moses to Christ, who does not despise His feeble children for their faults and much less does He cast them away.[3]

After the service, a man waited for me so as to speak to me by himself. His concern was the following: I had been on his plantation a little while ago and, among other matters, had asked whether he and his wife eagerly repeated Luther's small catechism for themselves and put it to good use, and he had answered with a "Yes." But this had not been the truth, and this lie had become an infernal fire in his conscience, He had remembered several stories, among them that of Ananias and Sapphira,[4] also verses like "Thou destroyeth the liars."[5] ... "All liars shall have their part in the lake which burneth with fire and brimstone."[6] Now he suffered greater fear than ever before in his life, even worse than when I had first awakened his conscience during his first act of repentance, and he was urged to confess. His fear and great disquiet had

---

[1] The word, almost illegible, may be *Dreg-Pflug*.

[2] John 13:18.

[3] Another contrast of the law and grace. See p. 144, n. 3.

[4] Acts 5:1-5.

[5] Psalms 5:6. The King James Bible says, "Thou shalt destroy them that speak leasing."

[6] Revelations 21:8.

also stirred his wife's conscience about something that appeared trivial but nonetheless offended against the 6th Commandment.[1]

I told him briefly that he should take comfort from my demeanor. Since he was full of remorse and quite dejected, I would not treat him roughly but take to my heart the pain in his conscience which he had brought upon himself. I would gladly forgive his trespass, but he should rest assured that the most gracious and tender man and Friend of sinners, Jesus Christ, would gladly offer him greater welcome than the most friendly mortal man. He and his wife should continue in their prayer so that they might grow strong in grace.

Saturday, the 12th of January. Last night after the prayer hour I was informed that my dear colleague, Mr. Gronau, was becoming weaker. I immediately went to see him and, with other pious people there, prayed for and with him. The heat in his body had abated somewhat so that he could hear and understand everything and join our prayer. Then he said full of joy: "Now I am forgiven all sins." He praised his Savior, gently bid goodbye to his dear wife and other friends, continued in prayer and the praise of the Lord and died in Him with raised folded hands after ten o'clock in the evening.

My friends will easily understand how much I am bowed by this separation, yet I must nonetheless praise the Lord for His grace, which has supported me in my loss. Last night in the sick room I asked and obtained this blessed brother's forgiveness for my many sins which I have committed since we were called to this congregation by allowing disorderly and violent emotions to occupy my heart and by omitting many a good deed. When I prayed this morning with the three men who watched last evening and through the night over the departure of my dear brother, we shed many tears and here, too, our heavenly Father strengthened and filled my heart.

May He now awaken us all to the good which we have seen and heard of this our brother, for his word and example has been much blessed and thus is not only irreproachable but most edifying. May He fulfill in the poor deserted widow and her two children what we know from Proverbs 3:33 and at the end of the ten commandments: "He blesseth the habitation of the just ... and showing mercy unto thousands of them that love me, and keep my commandments."

---

[1] See p. 10, n. 3.

From Mr. Thilo I heard that he had shown some Letechia,[1] and I only wished that he had treated this dear and compliant patient in the manner which the blessed Dr. Richter has directed for such sicknesses. But Mr. Thilo does not like the *essentia dulcis* and the *pulvis vitalis* [2] and he told me expressly that he could not follow the instructions of other, even the most experienced, authors but must follow his own counsel, for else he would not be a good *medicus*.

We must be patient, therefore, and silent. He [Gronau] was a bright and burning light in his life, as all honest and even the unconverted souls among us agree. All his speech was most edifying, and his patience in his long illness was extraordinary. Even in his feverish fantasies he never said an uncouth word, much less committed absurd things. He accepted all instructions and was easily dissuaded from delusions caused by his fever. In his good periods, which were frequent, he begged the Lord Jesus from his heart to deliver him from delusions and strange schemes, and the Lord granted this prayer. His only raving speech, which sounded hard but which he made in a friendly manner, was directed toward Mr. Thilo: "You could well help relieve my suffering if you only would. For even if you use a thousand beautiful and fine words that you mean me well, I cannot believe it." Mr. Thilo said to me: "He can't get bleeding off his mind,"[3] and indeed he wished for it fervently and seemed convinced that it would improve his health. For he had not been bled for three months. The last words which I called out to him after pronouncing the blessing was: "If everything joins together against me, Thou art my salvation, who will damn? Love will take care of me, let it take care of me."[4]

Sunday, the 13th of January. By the Lord's mercy, this has been a sad but blessed Sunday. We have accompanied to his chamber of rest a true Israelite, Israel Christian Gronau, my dear colleague, brother-in-

---

[1] Unidentified. Possibly it is a corruption of *laetitia*, happiness (in the Lord).

[2] Two of the most famous of the so-called Halle Orphanage medications. Boltzius refers here to the course of treatment advocated by Christian Friedrich Richter, who had first manufactured these medications and propagated their use in a self-help text highly popular among Pietists and sold throughout Europe in translation. See Wilson and Poeckern, as cited in n. 1, p. xi.

[3] The physician Thilo did not approve of the indiscriminate practice of bleeding or of over using the Halle Orphanage medications. Instead he relied on his own medical judgment. This was a source of considerable friction with Boltzius.

[4] *Tritt alles wider mich zusammen, Du bist mein Heil, wer will verdammen ... Die Liebe nimmt sich meiner an. Sie nehme sich auch meiner an.* From a hymn.

law,[1] co-sponsor, and dearest friend of my heart. He surely is among those of whom it is said: "They who walk in righteousness will come in their souls to peace, and their bodies will rest in their chambers."[2] His body joins two dear little children, Katharina and Israel Christian, who both died at a tender age, in our churchyard, but his dear soul is now with them in the paradise of joy.

After the bell had tolled this morning, his body was carried out in a coffin accompanied by many men and women and set down in the shade near the Jerusalem Church. We gathered in the church and commenced our service, as is usual on all Sundays and Holy Days, with a prayer for our children. When the first hymn, *Alle Menschen müssen sterben*, had been sung in a most moving manner, Mr. [Ludwig] Mayer read the 9th chapter of John verses 1-45, whereupon we sang: *Der Bräutigam wird bald rufen*, which edifying hymn the blessed man had made the school children learn by heart shortly before his last sickness, for he much valued such evangelical hymns. Instead of an exordium, I briefly informed my dearly beloved and deeply grieving audience (whose tears resumed when I began speaking) that I would now start upon a labor such as I had not yet undertaken in this my office. That is, I would offer the funeral and memorial sermon for their dear teacher who had been called home, who was also my dearly beloved colleague and my brother-in-law and co-sponsor.

Grief filled my heart to bursting and my tears choked off my voice, but it was nonetheless necessary to praise the work of the Lord that He had done in him and in us; and, while I had begged the Lord for mercy, strength, and help, they should now join me in prayer so that I would be strengthened in this important labor at his grave. We rose together, praised the Lord for the grace He had shown the blessed deceased in days of sickness and health, and begged for ourselves and our listeners that which we would need in our present circumstances. And I must count it as praise for the Lord Who heard my prayer that He has, despite my yesterday's weakness, given me humble but real strength and much comfort and edification. My text was Hebrews 13:7, "Remember them which have the rule over you, who have spoken unto you the word of God," for which reason the dear apostle impresses on our minds and that of the Hebrews both the great gift lying in His word and the important duty to use it well. The great gift lies in the fact that He gave

---

[1] They had married two sisters, Gertraut and Katharina Kröhr, who came with the Salzburger transports.

[2] Isaiah 57:2. The King James version differs greatly.

him and us teachers or (according to the Greek) such who would lead them and who prove themselves as *Brautwerber* and *Brautführer*[1] as sub-shepherds[2] and as spiritual fathers and mothers by word and example and revealed to him the word of the Lord and the counsel of salvation clearly, thoughtfully, and with the Lord's blessing.

This great gift our congregation has now enjoyed for a total of eleven years, which made it easy to convince them (for everyone among us is fully convinced) that our blessed teacher has in fact proven himself in his whole thinking as a *Brautwerber-* and *führer* and a faithful sub-shepherd with young and old, in private and in public, and has shown them all the most tender fatherly and motherly love. He fully understood from the Holy Scriptures and his own living experience the counsel of the Lord as to man's salvation, and this enabled him to teach clearly and thoroughly repentance before the Lord and faith in Jesus Christ. He also was a shining light for everyone one in his irreproachable and edifying life.

Here we had to ask whether all among us had indeed used this great gift of the triune Lord, that is, of the Father, who sent out and uses His servants as a spiritual testimony for the children and educator and spiritual father; of the Son, who uses them as His sub-shepherds, and of the Holy Ghost, who makes them right good *Brautwerber* and *Brautführer*. We also asked whether the office of this dear tool of the Lord has in fact been blessed in all of them. Since He gave them this great gift for so long, they could well recognize that He loved them all and would gladly accept them in His grace if they would only bring in through His grace that which they have neglected, and here their own conscience would be their best counsel.

Here I cited to them my own guiding verse, which our gracious Lord again blessed in me yesterday: "Where is such a God, as thou art, who forgives sins and excuses the misdeed of the others of his heritage."[3] And He has indeed forgiven their trespasses to many other repentant and faithful sinners who are His bountiful inheritance according to Psalm 16[:5] and who, like our dear brother, have already returned to their rest in the heavens. And He will also do just that for the others among His inheritance who are still part of the Church Militant. We may hope for

---

[1] Groom's advocate and groomsman. See p. 159, n. 3.

[2] Since Christ is our shepherd, his ministers are His sub-shepherds.

[3] *Wo ist solch ein Gott, wie du bist, der die Sünde vergiebt und erlässt die Missethat den übrigen s Erbtheils pp.* Micha 7:18. This is not found in the King James version.

all good things from Him in the future, for He is merciful and will take pity on us again.

The second point, the great duty toward the deceased teachers and therefore also our dear Mr. Gronau, I had to postpone until the afternoon. It consisted of three parts. 1. Think of them, with respect, love, and gratitude to the Lord. 2. Contemplate their end and their prior life as Christians and ministers. 3. Follow them in their faith. At the end, I told them a few special stories of the merciful guidance of the Lord in his material and spiritual life which he had slowly and carefully confided in me; such that our faithful Lord had wonderfully sustained him in his material poverty, both at school in Halberstadt and later at the University in Halle, and that he had taught him the meaning of the famous verse: "Do not be afraid, my son, because we have become poor. You have great wealth if you fear God, etc."[1]

He had mercifully protected him from pressed recruitment into the army although he had been in danger on several occasions. He counted it as a great gift that his dear father, parson in Croppenstedt, had instructed him in the ways of the Lord but that the blessed Israel Clauder had sponsored his baptism and had given him the gift of his intercession, admonishment, example, and a hymn he had written, *Mein Gott, du weisst am allerbesten*, etc., from all of which he had received much blessing and edification.

When he arrived in Halle, he was pious but uninstructed, and he still regretted how often he had offended the Lord when He attempted to shake his own false justification and bring him to true humility. The conversations with the blessed Inspector Kraneke and with other honest students of theology gave him a good hand for his true conversion. The music hours at the orphanage penetrated his heart, for there he often heard and was made truly aware of the beautiful words from Psalms 69:7, which gave him a full experience of the heart of his Savior and made him taste the forgiveness of his sins. From this time on he opened himself to the Lord with life and soul and soon moved into the orphanage as a tutor and inspector. Finally he was assigned as a traveling preacher to the Salzburger emigrants who were traveling to Prussia through Halle and Berlin. At this time he learned to understand the spiritual treasure of these dear people and, when he came back to Halle, it seemed as if he would receive a call to be their teacher in Lithuania. But he returned and at the same time received the vocation as an adjunct

---

[1] Tobit 4:21.

and catechist for Ebenezer.   Thus, he was indeed destined for the
Salzburgers, not there but here.

It is clear as daylight, moreover, how he excelled among us in a
simple and pure faith, honest love to God and man, zeal in prayer,
faithfulness in office, patience and forbearance against everyone
(following the example that the Lord had set towards him), heartfelt
humility, contentedness and resignation in the Lord's will, extraordinary
patience in his suffering, particularly in his last and protracted illness,
collegial and warm friendship, and a most exemplary life. And therefore
it is said justly and well: "Think of our teacher who taught you the word
of the Lord, contemplate his end and follow him in his faith, for which
all of us have received and been offered sufficient grace."

We concluded this morning's church service by singing, in two
choirs, *Denn seelig seyd ihr doch ihr Frommen*, and afterwards both old
and young formed a procession and followed the body, which was
carried to the graveyard in order and silence by six pious Salzburgers.
The body was then entrusted to the earth to the sound of the hymn: *Nun
lasset uns den Leib begraben, der Erde, die unser aller Mutter ist*. We
prayed again at the end and concluded with: "The sighing and groaning
and the thousand tears that have flowed, they should finally accompany
me to thy bosom and hands and to eternal rest. Thou, the light of mine
eyes."[1] In the afternoon service, we sang: *Er mag das Hauss, das aus
der Erde*, etc., then we read the 84th Psalm. Next we sang again: *Wie
wohl ist mir O Freund der Seele*, and again after the sermon, *So bin ich
nun nicht mehr ein fremder Gast*. In the evening prayer hour, we sang
his wedding song: *Herr Gott Zebaoth tröste uns, lass leuchten dein
Antlitz über uns, so genesen wir, Amen*.

Monday, January 14.   Last night the old Rieser woman was
liberated from her long and arduous but nonetheless blessed sickbed, and
her soul has been brought to its eternal rest. Her emaciated body, which
had been ravaged by her grave illness, was interred this afternoon in the
churchyard in town; and God used this occasion to give us a new
treasure of edification.   May our merciful Lord also grant a large
blessing to her old husband and her sons from her prayer, beautiful
example, and strong admonition. The song, *Freue Dich sehr O meine
Seele*, which was partly sung, partly contemplated, during her funeral
service, is really most suited to her, for it expresses not only her love

---

[1] *Dein Seuffzen und dein Stöhnen, und die viel tausend Thränen, die da
geflossen sind, die sollen mich am Ende in deinen Schooss und Hände begleiten zu der
ewigen Ruh. Du meiner Augen Licht.*

but also her Christian soul most impressively. She rejoiced that she would die with Mr. Gronau, her highly regarded teacher, and she is buried next to him. To her other side is the body of the blessed Mrs. Schmid and her little child, which died soon after baptism. During classes today, I repeated with the children the main points of yesterday's funeral sermon and tried to impress on them further the example of their blessed teacher. May the Lord bless all this in them and me.

Tuesday, the 15th of January. Before the edification hour, five men joined me before Leineberger's house and offered their services for the supervision of the mill. They assured me that they would manage it as if it were their own. They live not far off and they are good and Christian men. Like others in the community, they much desire a millrace which will operate even during low water; but I cannot take up a loan for this. However, I offered them a couple of horses belonging to the orphanage if they should manage to sell these profitably.

A woman sent word through her honest husband that she owed to the blessed Mr. Gronau as the tool of the Lord that she is now in Ebenezer. In the first sermon on the plantations which she heard after her arrival from Carolina, God had touched and pulled on her heart, so that she never wished to move away again, although she had at first not liked our solitary way of living.

Köcher gave me a written piece in which he renders a most beautiful testimony of the blessing which the Lord bestowed on him from the prayer and edifying life of his blessed teacher. We shall enclose it in our next letters to Europe. Also, a woman had a letter written to a minister in Augsburg in which, as she told me, she gave similar testimony.

Wednesday, the 16th of January. We have written several reports to our Fathers and friends in England and Germany in which I recounted the death of my dear and esteemed colleague. In particular, I have petitioned the Lord Trustees and the Honorable Society to continue in their love for and generosity to his esteemed widow, my-sister-in law and co-sponsor, and her two little children. To my great surprise, Mr. [Ludwig] Mayer has already copied the lost diaries from February 24 to April 18.[1] My heart praises the Lord for this, for He has clearly strengthened him in this and his other work. We shall dispatch our present reports, the old diary and the present continuation, written in both English and German. May our merciful Lord grant us our heartfelt wishes. We cannot bear the loss of another packet. Sending off mail is

---

[1] The reference is to the diaries for 1744, in this volume.

hard work in view of our many tasks, while with the help of the Lord it is an easy matter and a pleasant occupation to enter into our diary each day that which the Lord bestows on us and among our congregation. These words should always ring true in this place: "Bless the Lord all His works in all places of His dominion bless the Lord, O my soul."[1]

Thursday, the 17th of January.   I encountered some men who had undertaken a useful task out of love for Mr. [Ludwig] Mayer, and I asked them what had occupied their minds over the course of the day's work.   Did they know of a good Bible verse?   One of them confessed to his shame that he had not been eager and faithful in this regard.   I reminded both of what we had heard on Tuesday in Zion Church, when we again heard the verse: "I am come that they may have life, and that they may have it more abundantly."[2]   He came to us and for love to us left the heavens and their glory, and we shall now come to Him and abandon the world and its sins.   He calls, "Come unto me, all ye that labor and are heavy laden ..."[3]   For in His house there is plenty.

In the important lessons from Solomon which we are treating now, it is always said from the mouth of the Christ the Lord: "Behold, a greater than Solomon is here."[4]   Our great King with His Kingdom and its riches, as also the story of the blessedness of His servants and subjects, are made clear to us from this typical Bible story.   And this is the means the Holy Ghost uses to enlighten us in Christ.   No King is Thy equal, Thy all-powerful Kingdom is up there and never down here.

My dear blessed colleague had the beautiful habit of lovingly talking to those he encountered on his errands and of using this opportunity to implant in their hearts a heavenly blessing.   This has often left a deep impression, as I had learned even during his lifetime.   His heart was always full of Christ, and his mouth spilled over.   He also had a simple heart so that the simple among us loved to talk to him and deal with him. Among some of us it is as with the seed in the field, where some grains appear to be lost but open later and flourish.

The late Mr. Gronau was in charge of the bills for the construction of the church and the money for the orphans, and I went over these yesterday with Mr. [Ludwig] Mayer. We rejoiced in the accuracy which was revealed in these documents.   In all external matters and in those pertaining to his office, as in his entire Christian life, Mr. Gronau was

---

[1] Psalms 103:22.
[2] John 10:10.
[3] Matthew 11:28.
[4] Matthew 12:42.

clearly and constantly revealed as a Christian, and in this he sets a beautiful example for me and others. He was equipped by nature and God's mercy with beautiful gifts which were exactly suitable for our Ebenezer congregation and for me, his colleague.

Friday, the 18th of January.   Colonel Stephens and another good friend sent their condolences in letters that expressed their sadness at the great loss which we must suffer because of the departure of our dear colleague. Both advised me that there is not currently any opportunity for [sending mail to] Charleston, but they suggest I send a packet with letters and they will take care of it. The Colonel also writes that he had better news for me now than previously, for the packet of diaries from February to April does not seem to have been lost but arrived in due course. This is good news indeed but I would have liked to have it earlier and before dear Mr. [Ludwig] Mayer had to go to the trouble of copying the diary in sixteen days. I shall use this as a caution not to recopy anything until we have news from Europe. Until now, this took so long that we never knew if and what has arrived or been lost. But I shall send the old copied diary along anyway.

I also received a letter from Mr. Driesler in which he expressed his wish to hear from me. I am surprised that my letters of the 17th and the 20th October and the 4th of this month have not yet arrived.[1] He movingly pictures the miserable and sinful conditions there and also his own need, and his words moved me to warm pity. May God help him! He has a good heart, and I think he trusts people too quickly and considers them honest, but when the opposite turns out to be true later on, he is aggrieved and dejected. He is in straightened material circumstances as well because everything is quite dear and he has not taken in a penny since his arrival. He complains that he has no way of sending letters to Europe. For they fear that he would report to Europe the incredible misdeeds and horrors that take place there.[2]

I have previously offered to enclose his letters with mine if he can send them here, although I too am not as secure as I would wish. The English preacher [Bosomworth], who is still in Frederica, causes great offence; and we can only wonder that such things are permitted to

---

[1] These letters were from from 1744, and the January one had been written nearly a year earlier.

[2] Transcriptions of three of these letters are in the Driesler file of the Georgia Historical Society in Savannah.

someone who wishes to be called a minister. Things may get better once
the General arrives, a hope also cherished by Mr. Driesler.[1]

MARCH 1745
Immanuel[2]

Ebenezer, March 2, 1745. Yesterday evening and today I had the
pleasant opportunity to write a few letters to our friends and Fathers and
therein, in part, answer their own blessed letters and, in part, report our
circumstances.   I wrote to Court Chaplain Ziegenhagen, Secretary
Broughton, Mr. Albinus, Senior Urlsperger, and Professor [G. A.]
Francke.   On Monday I intend to send these to Colonel Stephens for
dispatch together with the German and English diaries, of which Mr.
[Ludwig] Mayer has again made a clean copy. Our benevolent Lord,
who is a Lord of all things, gave us a sure opportunity to dispatch our
packet to Charleston and from thence to Europe.

In the afternoon I travelled to the mill for exercise and in order to
join our workers at the end of their labor with prayer and for the praise
of the Lord. I came too late, however, for they had finished early to
attend to their own tasks. The wooden structure for the large new mill
house, which is to house not just a gristmill but also a barley and rice
stamp, has been fully prepared and the parts will be put in place shortly.
The pieces which will be replaced will be used for the low-water run, for
which they are well suited.   Apart from the large shed where the
woodwork and iron parts for the sawmill are being kept yet another solid
building has been finished this weekend where strangers can find lodging
and store their grain and flour. We praise the Lord for His assistance so
far rendered. I encouraged the miller and his wife to praise the Lord for
His great works which are always before their eyes. The water in the
river is now quite high, but this no longer effects any change in the mill,
whether it run high or low. The workers now have returned to their own
fieldwork, and must yet help those for a few days who must build a
threshing floor. Therefore they will not be able to return to the mills for

---

[1] The reference is to James Edward Oglethorpe, who did not return to Georgia.

[2] "Immanuel" is followed by the notation "Continuation of the Diary". The
pages for the second half of January and for February could not be found. But the
March diary was clearly read with a view to publication. It contains several editorial
changes and many place and proper names were crossed out to avoid embarrassment to
European sponsors.

another fortnight. Perhaps we shall receive some new support in the meantime so that we may continue at an even brisker pace.

Sunday, the 3rd of March. We have again announced to everyone that next Saturday will be given over to celebrating our annual memorial and thanksgiving ceremony, and we encouraged our listeners to prepare well for this day. In the last quarter of an hour of the afternoon sermon I told them that our glorious Lord in His merciful providence had begun to prepare us for our celebration and given us a token of His love for our heart and mouth. For He had put into our hands three letters from Europe, that is, from Professor [G. A.] Francke, Mr. Albinus in the name and according to the intent of Court Chaplain Ziegenhagen, and from the Honorable Society, which contain much proof of His providence for Ebenezer during this miserable and dangerous time of war.

Also, we learn that our spiritual Fathers and friends live and continue in their constant and warm affection to us. Thus, our munificent Lord has 1. showered onto Halle a large blessing in books, tools, linen and other things which have been dispatched in a large crate; 2. The Court Chaplain has taken care of plowshares, harness for the draft horses, and scythes, which he will forward together with the crate and which will greatly improve our agriculture. 3. Mr. Mayer concludes from certain expressions used in his letters from Memmingen that our good friends in Augsburg have also prepared quite a joy and a shipment for us. But we know nothing for certain yet, since last summer's letters are still outstanding.

A letter of Dr. [G. A.] Francke from June of last year to which he refers in his most recent letter has not arrived. From this I gather that other letters, too, are still on their way. 4. The secretary of the Society [Broughton] informs us that a certain esteemed benefactor in V.[1] has transmitted to the Society the considerable gift of £15 sterling which I have permission to draw on my name. I mentioned in this connection that our workers at the mill have for some time now worked in hope of payment; but, although I had asked the Council in Savannah for help on the Trustees' account, nothing had been received because of the great dearth of money here in this country. Now the Lord had made up for this dearth by this great gift and from afar, for nothing could be found here.

---

[1] The name of the city of Venice was suppressed. It was the home of a number of German mercantile houses which made donations to Ebenezer and the clergy of the Pennsylvania settlements.

The man who conveyed to me the refusal of our request to Savannah also brought me the letter from the Society, from which I well recognized the providence of the Lord just mentioned. They well knew the great gift which the Lord has so far given us in regard to the mill, and this should encourage both old and young to praise the Lord. For those among us who remain ungrateful, gifts shall be followed by punishment. Josuah 24:20. There are a number of important points in the two beautiful letters by Mr. Albinus, and we shall make these known shortly for the praise of the Lord and the edification of the congregation. They should now consider whether there were many congregations in Christendom to whom the Lord shows His miraculous bounty from near and afar as spectacularly as He does for us.

In the evening prayer meeting, which we now conduct daily between 5 and 6 o'clock, I read to my brothers in prayer the strong and instructive song which the esteemed Court Chaplain had sent me as a proof of his fatherly love and which is well worth being made known to others who read our diaries. For this reason I take the liberty of entering it here, although I do not have his permission.[1] After I have finished the *Golden ABC Book* in school, we will use it for the benefit of the children as an excellent compendium, to teach them in an easy and understandable manner the articles of faith and the treasures of Christian doctrine with the entire order of salvation. They will learn this golden song as in play just like the *Golden ABC Book*, so that we can sing it to a known melody.

Monday, March 4. This morning I was busy both before and after school to pack our letters and diaries and send them off to Col. Stephens for dispatch. I sent Mr. Driesler's packet to Savannah by a friend, with the request to forward it to the commander in Frederica as soon as it is safe. I wrote both to him and to Mr. Driesler this morning. The man who is taking the packages to Savannah left this morning after 11 o' clock and will deliver them to the Colonel, if not today then quite early tomorrow morning.

Mr. Thilo had a catalogue of medications to be sent to London, but he came too late, when all had been sealed and wrapped. It was not possible to break open the package to the Society and the enclosed one to the Court Chaplain, although he urged me to do so, for the Salzburger messenger waited for them with impatience and I was in a great hurry to

---

[1] See Appendix II.

return for the edification hour on Ebenezer Creek at 11 o'clock.[1] He was requesting medications in the amount of £5 Sterling which the Society had granted him for this purpose some time ago.[2]

This morning I visited the sick Austrian Pletter and found him a little more alert than during recent days, but his illness is still in a dangerous stage. As I entered their house, his wife was just repeating to him the beautiful words of the Lord Jesus: "This sickness is not unto death, but for glory of God,"[3] which she had remembered well from her own illness. The patient much liked my visit and our joint prayer, and I reminded him of the dear cooing voice of the Lord which we heard on the day of Epiphany in these words: "Look unto me, and be ye saved."[4] He could repeat the whole verse by heart and promised me to deal in his spirit as the old Israelites had dealt with the brazen serpent.[5] He drinks much cold water, which may well not be good for him, but he is surfeited with thin broth; he has a craving for tea, however, for which I gave him a few shillings as a gift because he is quite poor.

Riding home, I encountered an unmarried woman with a bundle of wood which she was carrying home with great difficulty. Yesterday she listened to the beautiful verse in our exordium, "Thou hast wearied me with thine iniquities,"[6] and therefore I reminded her to apply to herself in her burdensome work the labor and trouble to which the Lord Jesus had gone in his internal and external sufferings and to be like the servant who devoutly remembered the wood of the cross that Christ bore for her whenever she carried wood home from the forest. Yesterday, we treated the gospel for Invocavit Sunday regarding the great labor, trouble, and burden borne by the Lord Jesus once he assumed his teaching office.[7]

Tuesday, the 5th of March. A woman eager for edification told me that she had waited impatiently on Sunday to hear whether I would include among the benefactions the Lord has shown our community the fact that the Lord had heard our prayers and given three assistants to

---

[1] The Salzburgers' settlement along Ebenezer Creek being remote from Ebenezer, religious services were often conducted for them there.

[2] We have no documentation of the medicines Thilo ordered from London, since such imports would have displeased the Fathers in Halle, who ran their own pharmacy.

[3] John 11:4.

[4] Isaiah 45:22.

[5] See Numbers 21:8, 2 Kings 18:4, John 3:14.

[6] Isaiah 43:24.

[7] The "he" here surely refers to Gronau. However, because of the stress on the similarities in the lives of Jesus and Gronau, it is not always possible to determine the referent of a pronoun.

dear Pastor Mühlenberg.[1]   For she believed our congregation would
rejoice as much at this news as if they themselves had received a great
gift.   We shall not forget to praise the Lord for this as well.   I had
written Driesler about the good news, so that he also might rejoice and
praise the Lord.   May God give them true unity of the spirit through the
ties of truth, and they will effect much good through the mercy of their
Savior and their sufferings and trials will be less heavy!

Old widow Schweighofer has recovered sufficiently from her last
dangerous illness to get up and about.   I told her something from our last
sermon and today's edification hour concerning the passion story, so as
to awaken her to a childlike trust in her dear Savior.   For He has
suffered and labored greatly not only for the offenses that constitute
original sin but for daily transgressions as well; on His cross, He had,
in a manner of speaking, cared first for His most bitter enemies when He
called: "Father, forgive them."[2] And by this He proved a faithful
physician who directs his heart and mercy to the most endangered among
his patients.   Her daughter is much chastened by her sins and longs for
Holy Communion, but she did not have the heart to register publicly in
church with the others.

Wednesday, March 6.   On Monday, the son-in-law of old Mr.
Kieffer [Valentin Depp] moved into our town for good with his wife and
children. He will live in the house of Schrempf, his brother-in-law, until
he can build his own dwelling.   I visited him and made sure that our first
act was to pray together in his dwelling with all who were present at the
time. The locksmith Schrempf has put up his shop on land designated
for his house and will build there by and by.   Until now, he has lived on
the property of Lochner,[3] his stepfather, in a hut which he had bought
from him.   Lochner in turn moved to his plantation and is devoting
himself to tilling his fields. Lochner [4] is not a good man and will not be
brought to repentance whether by the word of the Lord or physical
chastisement, although he is not short of good feelings, resolutions, and
promises.

Those among us who convert to the Lord and are efficient in their
profession are slowly getting enough for their nourishment and live
contentedly with the Lord's blessing.   Those who against their own

---

[1] Peter Brunnholtz, Johann Nicholas Kurtz, and Johann Helfrich Schaum, who
were sent to Pennsylvania with the support of G.A. Francke and Court Chaplain
Ziegenhagen.

[2] Luke 23:34.

[3] See p. 11, n. 3.

[4] The name was deleted in the manuscript.

interest despise the Lord's counsel do not do well, however, and then blame *causas secundas*. Yesterday, the old Swiss carpenter sent me a letter and told me about his discord with his neighbor, Engel.[1] Both want to take Holy Communion next Sunday, so that I found it necessary to ride out the long way to their lodgings at the farthest end of the plantations, from where I returned so late that I had to miss the prayer meeting. This I regret most seriously since we now find our edification in contemplating the dear and most important story of the suffering and death of our beloved Savior. May God bless my labor, so that these souls shall be reconciled. May He grant that both parties place their affairs on a sound basis and keep the peace. The old man is now of a somewhat improved disposition; and, if he walks in accordance with his talk and the forgiveness which he proclaimed, it will be easy to deal with him and he will not find so much fault in my judgment of their discord.

Thursday, the 7th of March. From Savannah I received on our boat several pleasing letters from dear Pastor Driesler and several of our Savannah friends. The first writes most edifyingly and is much pleased by my poor letters. He has held a memorial sermon for my dear deceased colleague and the Lord has blessed his listeners in this. He offers us heartfelt comfort in our loss and in eager and urgent prayers begs the Lord with his family to strengthen my poor soul and body and to send me another Gronau for a colleague. He himself is well but has several problems.

Although General Oglethorpe wrote to the commander there, nothing has been done for Mr. Driesler's financial support. He says that most of his letters to Europe are being kept back because it is feared that he is reporting too much detail of the excessive offenses committed by both high and low. If our wise and merciful Lord were to direct his labors to another place, he would be most grateful for His merciful guidance, but if this should be His wish, he would gladly continue to work and suffer where he is.[2]

Since now is the time to collect and bring home run-away cattle, four honest men from the community have resolved jointly to assume this task for the love of the congregation. They will ask a reasonable wage. If God blesses their endeavors, this will be to the great profit of the congregation, for several among us lost one or the other head of cattle several years ago. If these could be found and returned here, it would

---

[1] Hans Jacob Engli.

[2] This following paragraph was deleted from the manuscript.

greatly benefit the poor people, for they have lost much of their domestic cattle through the cattle plague.[1]

A young man complained in bitter pain that he was in doubt as to his Christianity and the seriousness of his repentance. Since God had forgotten him and let him feel his sins, for which he had gained forgiveness from the gospels,[2] he had remembered much more. He also felt his inability to believe in Christ, and now he had to set his wife a good example, but how could he do this if he himself were in such poor shape? I said, among other things, that he will have prayed to the Lord on many occasions that He should reveal to him his wicked heart and his entire powerlessness to do good. Now that He has granted his prayers, I continued, he had a new call to flee to Christ as his only Helper. Faith was the work of the Lord, I said, and therefore he would have to continue praying. The words of the song gave him much grief, he said: "Leave all and turn to Christ." I explained these to him and gave him the beautiful preparation of the late Professor [A.H.] Francke on the dear words in Revelations 22:17, which were spoken directly to his heart.

Friday, the 8th of March.[3] There have been many and well-founded complaints concerning our miller; and, since he does not improve but increases in his faithlessness and injustice, which causes much calumny in other places, we have again talked to him about this state of affairs. He defended himself and gave up his job. We accepted this gladly and easily found another quite honest and converted man who has the trust of everyone in the congregation. He will have no trouble learning a miller's trade, and thus we have more reason to welcome rather than to regret this change.

The children in school have quickly and gladly learned the instructive and edifying song which we mentioned under date of March 3. They will recite it in public tomorrow afternoon, that is, on our day of memory and thanksgiving, instead of one of the psalms which we usually choose for such occasions. They sing it quite well and we receive a good and edifying lesson from it. Schoolmaster Kocher has copied it so that he may teach it to his children as well. Several people intend to copy it for themselves, so that the text will be quite familiar among us, which pleases me much. I hope that I will be able to please dear Pastor Driesler with it, who likes to share in our edifications. Mrs. [Elisabetha]

---

[1] Known as "blackwater."

[2] The original passage read: "and had tasted forgiveness."

[3] The following paragraph was deleted in the manuscript, probably because the dishonesty of a Salzburger miller would have caused raised eyebrows in Europe.

Mayer has hoped from one week to the next to join the congregation in public in Holy Communion; and, since she had anticipated that her physical condition would improve soon, she deferred private communion for several weeks. Today, however, she received the Lord's supper in her house because her physical weakness persists. She is not always bedridden but has relief during several hours and can just find time to take care of her household tasks. However, illness and pain often attack her quite suddenly, just as had happened back in Germany. She bears her lengthy cross in patience, and I am much edified by her words. In turn, the Lord blesses my words to her, as she has told me herself. He much and generously blessed in me, to a greater recognition of the love of our Lord Jesus, the hour which I spent today with her and her dear husband for the purpose of her communion. There was occasion for prayer, song, and a short sermon.

Saturday, the 9th of March. It is now eight[1] years since the dear Lord brought us to this country and showed us in both Old and New Ebenezer countless material and spiritual blessings. These we recognized today in our annual commemoration and thanksgiving service. Before dawn, He blessed us with a warm and fruitful rain which lasted until eight o'clock in the morning. But this great blessing, which was eagerly awaited for the growing corn, did not deter our listeners from enjoying the even greater blessing of public worship. Their consciences would not have suffered an absence, although the way from the plantations to Jerusalem Church was somewhat more burdensome than during dry weather. After prayer and the reading of a chapter from the New Testament, we sang: *Jesus Christus Gottes Lamm* etc., read the 121st Psalm instead of the reading from the gospel; and then we sang: *Sollt ich meinem Gott nicht singen*, etc. The morning text was from Titus 2:14[2] from which we learned about the great love of Christ and its salutary object. In the afternoon, we spoke about the important text in 2 Corinthians 1:14-15, in particular the great power and love of Christ for us poor miserable sinners. Here the Lover, the beloved, the act of His love, and its final purpose were considered as well.

Between the first and second hymn, *Nun bitten wir den Heiligen Geist* and *Lasset uns den Herrn preisen und vermehren*, Court Chaplain Ziegenhagen's lovely hymn was recited twice by the children. After the sermon we sang *Hallelujah, Lob, Preis, und Ehre*. May the material we

---

[1] The reference is not to the the Salzburgers' arrival in 1734 but to their move to New Ebenezer.

[2] Acts 2:14.

contemplated on this our feast of Commemoration and Thanksgiving be appropriate not only for the present time. We were also led to the true main benefaction which the Lord God has let us pray until now, namely, to become grateful for it with heart, mouth, and entire way of living. If we believe in this faithfully, then all the other benefactions will come to our aid. How could the Father not grant us everything along with His Son our Savior?

In the last quarter of an hour I imparted to the congregation some things from the lovely letter of our dear Mr. Albinus, from which we could see how much good we have received from the hand of the Lord in these dangerous times of war and how much we are still to receive. Likewise, that the Lord had sent righteous men to our dear Pastor Mühlenberg as a help in church and schools.

Before and after the prayer in the evening prayer hour we sang the excellent hymn *Lobe, lobe, meine Seele, den der heisst Herr Zebaoth*, we thanked Him on our knees for His spiritual and physical blessings, prayed for our worthy benefactors both near and far, implored Him to bless the words we had heard, and begged Him for everything that we shall need in this pilgrimage.

Before the prayer hour an old man came and revealed to me that, while he was listening to the dear gospel, our merciful God had granted him repentance and tears for his sins and that, God willing, he planned to go to communion tomorrow, whereas he had previously wished to postpone it one more time. He made bitter complaints about his wife, who justified herself and neither recognized her sins nor wished to give them up. I instructed him how he was to conduct himself toward her with words and conduct. It was a very important and comforting verse that we sang in the prayer hour from the previously mentioned hymn: "When the enemies assail us so that there is struggle from without and we are distressed by fear, they must withdraw (that means the stone of pious Ebenezer); Hitherto hath the Lord helped us, thus far we have come. I am much too small for Thy gracious light to be illuminated with such gracious splendor."[1] Hallelujah!

---

[1] Boltzius is quoting from the previously mentioned hymn *Lobe, lobe, meine Seele*: *Wenn die Feinde uns anfallen, dass von aussen Streit es gibt, und von einer Furcht betrübt, müssen sie zurücke prallen das heist denn der Stein der frommen EbenEtzer, bishieher, bishieher hilfft uns der Herr, bis hierher sind wir nur kommen. Viel zu, viel zu klein bin ich, dass mit so grossem Glantz mir leuchten soll dein Gnaden Schein. Halleluja!* This refers to 1 Samuel 7:12, "Then Samuel took a stone, and set it between Mizpeh and Shen, and called the name of it Ebenezer, saying, Hitherto hath the Lord

Sunday, the 10th of March. Yesterday before evening a very strong west wind arose that became most violent during the night and brought us a very unpleasant chill that we had not expected at this time. There was ice, and it presumably harmed the tender mulberry leaves and surely harmed the grape vines and their tender seeds[1] and leaves; and it appears that the cold will last several days. Yesterday it was so warm in the church that we could open all windows and doors. However, today we could again learn what a blessing it is to have such a well protected church as ours is. The Zion Church is not yet provided with glass windows and sills, it also lacks regular pews and a balcony, which items are to be supplied when our good Lord grants the means for them.

Today Holy Communion was celebrated with fifty-six persons, and the Lord made this Sunday into a blessed and joyful day of grace for us. Because we celebrated our Commemoration and Thanksgiving Day yesterday, we treated today's Reminiscere gospel, Matthew 15:21, in accord with the circumstances of the time in which we are living. From it we reminded the congregation, which had assembled in large number, of some especial blessings that the Lord God had shown us so far and through which we should be encouraged to praise Him. These were: that He has saved us from heathen and popish blindness and has brought us to the light of the gospel and to complete freedom of conscience, that He has burdened us, for our own good, with all sorts of suffering and tribulations, that He has not let us be mired in them but rather has always graciously kept us and heard our prayers, and that He has given us friends in many places in Christendom, who, as true disciples of Jesus, seek our good through their intercession.

In the introit[2] we called to one another from Sirach 50: "Now bless the God of all, who in every way doth great things." That He does great things for us not only here but also at a distance has been made known to us to our joy and praise through His especial providence over us and in the pleasant letters from Europe, also from the last one. In the afternoon I had a brief quarter of an hour left over that I applied in announcing to my dear listeners from the letter of instruction from our dear Dr. [G. A.] Francke and the enclosed specifications of the charitable gifts which are to be found in the dispatched chest. How

---

helped us." The words EbenEzer means "stone of help."

[1] *Saamen*. Boltzius apparently means the young buds or still undeveloped grape clusters.

[2] By *Eingang* Boltzius can mean either the introit or the introductory part of his sermon.

much good and how many manifold blessings our good and pious God has prepared for us in Halle through the service of this His loyal servant, who was sick but has become well again.

We were edified by this fatherly providence and we rejoiced in the Lord because of the specified gifts; we also wish to pray now and afterwards, when the chest arrives, and to accept them; and then our joy will be ever more perfect. He gladly gives us the physical, but far more gladly the spiritual, His Son, and with Him everything that is a true blessing, which the believing Israelites (Sirach 50:23) accepted with right eager hearts and encouraged one another to the praise of our merciful God.

I believe that for many salvation-hungry parishioners among us it was true today that "now that the church service is over and blessing has been imparted to us, we will go home with right and walk God's ways freely."[1]   Thus this day has been for us a true Reminiscere and Commemoration-Sunday, for not only has our dear God reminded us most emphatically of His gifts and blessings of the past and present time, but we can also apply to ourselves the words "The Lord hath been mindful of us: he will bless us."[2] May He, according to the wealth of His mercy, think of our dearest benefactors in all places of His kingdom, and may He bless them with thousandfold spiritual and physical blessings for the love and affection they have borne for us.

Monday, the 11th of March.   This morning a sister of Paul Klocker's little boy told me she had visited this her little brother and found him in bed very weak. He is brooding over the little verse: "I come quickly."[3] His foster father, the righteous Glaner, expressed his sorrow to me that this promising child has become so dangerously sick. He would (as he expressed it) gladly give his cow if only he could be cured. He told me the following about his love for God's word. Whenever he (Glaner) went to church, this little Paul would ask in a childlike way, "Father, where are you going?" "I'm going to church. Mr. Boltzius will say a lovely verse for you." When he returned, the child would ask, "Father, what sort of a verse has Mr. Boltzius sent me?" Mrs. Glaner, who can read, had to recite it for him until he could memorize it. Then he would run to Glaner and say, "I already know my little verse" and recite it to him several times. In this way he as well as

---

[1] *Nun der Kirchendienst ist aus, und uns mitgeteilt der Seegen, so gehen wir mit Grund nach Hauss, wandeln frei auf Gottes Wegen.* From a hymn.

[2] Psalms 115:12.

[3] Revelations 22:20.

his wife have learned many beautiful Bible verses. The child likes to pray and can handle the verses he has learned although he is scarcely four years old.

Yesterday I heard a very different story from another child. When it was asked whether it loved its stepfather, it said, "My father is in heaven, but my stepfather is not good, he strikes my mother. Question: "Where is your little sister?" The child: "Also in heaven." Question: "Do you want to go there, too?" "Yes, if my mother goes. She must go, too." I hope to learn from the neighbors whether it is true that the husband, who has otherwise walked good paths, has degenerated so far as to live with his wife in such disorder to the scandal of this five-year-old child; and I plan to talk with him further about it. The people think much too seldom of the verse "Be sober, be watchful ... your adversary walketh about."[1] I now have several of our congregation in mind who have made a serious beginning in their Christianity. They have, unfortunately, fallen asleep again and are degenerating into disorder and hypocrisy.

Tuesday, the 12th of March. I was told that recently a young man had sinned through frivolous speech while working at the mill. Today, when he came to me, I reminded him from God's word that it was a sin. At first he considered it a trivial matter, thereby revealing his ignorance and the poor nature of his heart and putting material in my mind and mouth to make him recognize his danger. He finally accepted my counsel and went from me with a good resolution. When people work together and do not guard themselves, they easily become useless and involve themselves rather deeply. If space is left for one sin, then many of them will be there, as we have learned from the lamentable story of Juda in several prayer hours.[2] The people generally shy from His name, but not from His spirit. Unconverted people, or those who have received the grace of God in vain, resemble this unfortunate man as one egg resembles another. This we have shown in detail to further a true repentance. Pletter is still lying very miserable on his sickbed. He can hardly hear anything, and speaking is very difficult for him. He seems to be very calm in his heart like one who has found peace. His wife had the good thought that it was very dangerous to postpone his repentance until his sickbed. The time for planting is near, and she does not yet

---

[1] 1 Peter 5:8.

[2] Not identified.

know how her field will be planted. I referred her to the verse "Call upon me in the day of trouble," etc.[1] and promised her a little help.

Wednesday, the 13th of March.   Court Chaplain Ziegenhagen has sent a gift of money to the schoolmaster Kocher, who wrote him a letter last year and admonished him sincerely to execute his office faithfully and honestly. Mr. Albinus sent him the words 1 Timothy 4:6: "But godliness with contentment is great gain," which I read to him twice. Mr. Albinus' letter concluded as follows: "We should faithfully work in the service of the Lord and for the salvation of the children, and our reward shall be great in heaven. As often as I touch upon this matter of the instruction of our children my heart revives, because it revives in me the blessing which I had for my own soul in instructing the children at the Orphanage and the Paedagogium at Halle. And that is why I often request this favor of the Lord, that He might make of me a schoolmaster (If this be His will.)" I then wrote to Pastor Driesler and forwarded to him the beautiful letter of our dear Mr. Albinus, for I know that he hungers for edification. I will do the same with the beautiful hymn of Court Chaplain Ziegenhagen. A young woman hungry for the faith is copying it.

This afternoon I visited the sick child Paul Klocker. I found him lying on his bed near the cradle of little Benjamin, Glaner's little son, whom he loves greatly and likes to rock. The motherly inclined Mrs. Glaner praises God for all the good that has been done for the little boy in healthy days and sick days. He is very patient and quite satisfied, gladly takes the medicines prescribed, and prays and sings with much pleasure the verses he has learned. He recited for me the verses: "I cried unto thee, and thou hast healed me."[2] Several days ago he said, "Pray diligently for our dear God to make me well again." Glaner was not at home. Yesterday and today he has been looking for two cows that ran away because they are now chasing after young grass, who knows how far, and the people have no cowherds in this region. He has got lost several times in the forest and, because he has been away for a long time, she has prayed and wept in the meanwhile. Soon afterwards her prayer was heard, for her husband returned home again.

Thursday, the 14th of March.   Yesterday God granted us a much desired rain with light thunder, for which we rightfully praised Him in our evening prayer hour. Afterwards it rained almost throughout the

---

[1] Psalms 50:15.
[2] Psalms 30:2.

entire night. The newly sprouted grain[1] stands very beautiful in the fields and glorifies the wisdom, goodness, and omnipotence of the Lord in a lovely way. Because on well cultivated land a large bush, almost as big as a hat, grows from each and every little grain of wheat, rye, and barley. Afterwards the ears sprout from them and the sprouting grain seems to be standing too thick everywhere. To avoid this while sowing, Jethro Tull's [2] machine would be very useful because it can distribute the seeds everywhere in the right order, close or far apart, very quickly. However, we can not make one because none of us has ever seen one. He calls it a drill, a wheat or turnip drill. With three such machines, everyone in the congregation could be served all year long because, according to his description, one can sow many acres in one day. It makes a shallow furrow, lets the seeds fall in at the desired intervals, and fills up the furrow again, and all this at one time. One can sow deep or shallow, it all depends on how the instrument is set.

The last freeze[3] damaged the leaves on the young mulberry trees somewhat as if they were burned, but on the strong trees of this kind we see no damage. It will gradually be seen how it stands with the buds, which usually come out before the leaves. As for the seeds on the grape vines, we are uncertain as to whether they were ruined by the hard frost. I lack a man expert in wine culture, and as a result my vineyard has made no real progress. Because I have to use all sorts of people in it who do not share the same knowledge, they are of more harm than use.

Friday, the 15 of March. Old Mrs. Bacher can not yet go out because of her physical weakness, and it is a great sorrow for her that she cannot come to church as previously. Therefore she wishes she could live in the town and she hopes meanwhile to be able to attend the prayer hour and divine service. She has a great swelling in her breast and in her legs. Her son-in-law Theobald Kieffer, is planning to build a house in town, and therefore it will probably gradually become possible for this old widow to come into town and be near the church. She was just reading in Martin Möller's *Contemplation of the Passion*[4] as I came

---

[1] By 1744, most of Salzburgers had converted to winter wheat and rye sown in the fall. See the entry for March 15.

[2] See p. 82, n. 2 and 3.

[3] The German word *Frost* means either a freeze or else hoar frost. Here it means the former.

[4] The Latin version is entitled *Soliloquia de Passione Jesu Christi*.

to her. She is diligent in reading and praying and is very content with
the chastisements God has laid upon her so far.

Along with the warm penetrating rain we are again having cold
winds and freezing at night, yet as far as we can see the young grapes
have not been greatly harmed. Some leaves low on the vine look as
though they have been boiled. Today the wind came from the east and
was very cold. In the evening the sky was covered over, and this lets us
hope that there will be no freeze. Today, to my amazement, I already
see blossoming the barley that the Salzburgers sowed seven weeks before
Christmas along with the wheat. The cold may be harmful for the tender
blossoms, but everything is in God's hand.

General Oglethorpe strongly advised our people to plant their wheat
before Michaelmas in early September. As Columella[1] wrote, it had to
have *duos soles*, or two summers. This is practicable in Italy but not
here in this country, as we have learned from experience. If freezing
weather were to come at the end of March, then the blossoming wheat
would be in danger. Experience is a good teacher. Our people sow
wheat and rye in October and November, but they sow their barley
shortly before Christmas and their oats somewhat later. Today, when I
saw the barley in ears and some of it in blossom, I remembered from
Leviticus 13:10 that, at God's command, at their Easter Feast in the
promised land the Jews had to cut already ripe barley and bring it as a
sacrifice to the Lord. That can very well have been possible, since
Palestine lies in the same climate as our land does.[2]

Saturday, the 16th of March. Today it rained all day long gently
and penetratingly, and this has been very good for our fields. There is
a promise of a good and fruitful year, for which we should rightly praise
the Giver for His blessing. In the planting of the corn, which is now
being sowed, we are hindered by the fact that the plowshares have not
yet arrived, for which I have long since written. Those that the worthy
Court Chaplain Ziegenhagen procured for us are presumably on their
way. I have, however, written to Pennsylvania several times and have,
to be sure, received answers and promises, but no plowshares.

A merchant in Savannah promised me already six or seven months
ago to help me get some plowshares in New York. For lack of these
most of the people will have to get along with hoes in planting corn, in
which the work is great but the profit little. The desire of all the

---

[1] Junius Moderatus Columella, a Roman agricultural writer active in the first
century AD, whose advice was recommended to Boltzius by James Oglethorpe.

[2] Jean Pury and other promoters had stressed the fact that Georgia was on the
same latitude as the Holy Land.

Salzburgers to plow their fields is very great now that they have seen the value of it daily in the fields. That which is cultivated with the hoe is not nearly as much as when the plow is used. Even the land that they have scorned and considered not worth cultivating (when nothing could be accomplished on it with the hoe) is now bearing, to everyone's amazement, such abundant wheat that it is standing much too thick and has already had to be mowed five times, and this does not please the farmer. He did not put any manure on the field but rather did it three times in the previous year and plowed it under.[1]

All knowledgeable people now consider the pine land[2] valuable and promise themselves, with God's blessing, to cultivate the most beautiful wheat fields in it. If the Trustees ever send working people to this colony (for others are not worth much in this land) and enable them to use the plow soon, they will not only remain strong and healthy but also be able soon to support themselves well. And in this way no Negroes will be needed in this country. As long as the people have to plant the corn with the hoe and do not apply themselves to European grains, they will remain weak beginners who will scarcely be able to earn as much in a year as they need for themselves and their families.

When we came into this country the low land covered by oaks and nut trees[3] was always praised and the pine woods were always scorned, and this caused our inhabitants great harm to their health and sustenance. They could not use a plow on the so-called good land and they worked so hard in many ways until they lost their strength.[4] Also, they lacked the means to get plows.

Sunday, the 17th of March. Last night Zimmerebner's wife bore a young well-formed daughter who was publicly baptized this morning before the congregation. I was told that during the birth the woman had been in difficult circumstances and had thought she would die. She was afraid of death; and her husband said that the late Gronau and I had sincerely warned her and showed her the way to her salvation but that she had not wished to obey but rather remained of a worldly disposition

---

[1] The last two sentences are barely legible and are rendered as closely as possible.

[2] *Förlwald*. Called in the local dialect piny land or pine barrens. Boltzius was wrong in championing the piny lands, since they played out after a few seasons when the humus was blown away.

[3] The Salzburgers removed from Old Ebenezer to New Ebenezer partly because the oak trees there indicated better soil.

[4] Boltzius means that, because of the dense roots, it was not possible to plow the land where oak trees had stood, whereas it was easier to do so in the former piny woods, where the roots rotted more quickly.

and would now fare badly. These distressing circumstances had driven
this righteous and heart-converted man to prayer (for he always prays
diligently) and God had heard his prayer for help in freeing his wife. I
hope she will let this fear of death and legalistic terror [1] serve for her
true conversion.

It can, however, not be denied that grace has already accomplished
much in this woman, who had come here in great blindness and had
formerly walked in the dreadful snares of Satan, as is known by those
who knew her previously. She respects the righteous nature of her
husband and joins him diligently in prayer and in the word of God.
Through her baptismal sponsor I sent her the verse from today's introit,
Hebrews 2:14-15: "Since then the children are sharers in flesh and
blood, he also himself in like manner partook of the same; that through
death he might bring to nought him that had the power of death, that is,
the devil; and might deliver all of them who through fear of death were
all their lifetime subject to bondage."

Already for some time now the daughter of the late Mrs. Kieffer of
our place has had a cancerous growth on her nose and is otherwise
greatly afflicted. In such a state she is in very miserable circumstances,
yet she can go around with a bandaged face and diligently seeks good
opportunities for edification. Last year she took treatment in Savannah
from Dr. [Patrick] Hunter but noticed very little improvement. She lives
in the house of the widow Christ, to whom I pay ten shillings annually
for her; and other good people[2] contribute all sorts of foodstuffs for her
sustenance so that she cannot suffer any want. She also occasionally
receives some money. I am much concerned with her hardship and will
also contribute everything possible and will see to it that something is
attempted for her cure. She is a young person of eighteen years and was
so badly harmed through an inappropriate salivation[3] by a surgeon in
South Carolina.[4]

Monday, the 18th of March. I visited the sick [Johann] Pletter and,
to my great joy, I found him in a better condition than when I saw him

---

[1] *Gesetzliche Furcht* is the fear of "legalistic people" (those who fear the law
of the Old Testament more than they trust the grace of the New Testament).

[2] Boltzius means "other people, who are good." He is not including himself.

[3] A treatment to cause the flow of saliva by irritating local masticatories or by
means of a mercury preparation such as calumel.

[4] A surgeon used occasionally by the Salzburgers was Jean Baptiste Bourquin
of Purysburg, a Swiss who had served for nine years in the Duke of Wellington's army.
He tended to perform quite drastic operations.

last week. First of all he recited for me the verse that has been fulfilled in him: "Jehovah hath chastened me sore; but he has not given me over to death."[1] He went on to say that he had lain for the entire time in great fever and without the use of his sound understanding and had therefore not known how he was faring and what was happening to him. Thus he stood before the gate of eternity: in his whole life he had never felt the way he did this time. Nevertheless, God assured him of His mercy; he often remembered the verse: "Behold, the Lamb of God, that taketh away the sin of the world!"[2] and therefore his sin. Whenever he looked upon his sins he remembered these dear words: "Behold, I have graven thee upon the palms of my hands."[3] He clung firmly to such promises and surely believes that they must also be fulfilled in him.

He said he had already died to the world and that he saw himself as one who no longer belonged to this world. Therefore he suffered no inner worry or disquiet because of his children, wife, or anything else. He would like to have died, but now he sees that God wished to make him whole again for this life, which life is connected with much sorrow, disquiet, and danger. Shortly before my words of encouragement, God granted him the beautiful words in the *Treasure Chest*:[4] "In the Lord I have righteousness and strength."[5] He believes that he has been saved because God has heard the prayers of others for him. "For," he said, "the prayer of the righteous availeth much if it is serious."[6] He thanks most heartily for the good he has received; and this moved me to have a gift of money and of white bread flour given him.

Tuesday, the 19th of March.[7] Yesterday I received the sad news in a letter that the Prussians had suffered a great defeat and that even the King of Prussia had been dangerously wounded.[8] This news came to Charleston from Jamaica and New York. Even if things may look bad in our dear Fatherland, may the Lord hold His hand over Prussia and other lands in which we have so many intercessors and patrons, and may He lets His church suffer no harm even in the noise of battle but emerge from it cleansed and purified.

---

[1] Psalms 118:18.

[2] John 1:29.

[3] Isaiah 49:16.

[4] See p. 24, n. 2.

[5] Isaiah 45:24. The wording differs in the King James version.

[6] James 5:16. The King James version differs greatly.

[7] The following paragraph was stricken from the manuscript.

[8] This refers to one of the battles in the Second Silesian War.

How much we would rejoice and praise our Lord in a special thanksgiving feast if we should hear of a general peace treaty among the powers by land and sea. We have especial cause for a thanksgiving ceremony because in this dangerous time of war we are so marvelously enjoying the noble jewel of peace in this corner of the earth. If only it would continue for us! Then the congregation would have peace, and would dwell in the fear of the Lord, and would be filled with the comfort of the Holy Ghost.

The English schoolmaster in Savannah[1] sent me the petition of the German people around Savannah to the Trustees, in which they are requesting the young Reformed preacher [2] and in which the first name is Ortmann, who first composed the petition and collected the names of the people.[3]

A few years ago they sent General Oglethorpe a letter requesting a very miserable person; but, because I could not possibly approve of the testimonial I had received from the Purysburg minister, nothing came of it.[4] They wish a minister to their liking. May God grant them as He wishes!

Wednesday, the 20th of March. Col. Stephens has sent me a very friendly letter and assured me in it that he is seeking the best for our congregation. He requests that this spring two more young women be sent to the Italian woman [Camuso] in Savannah to learn the reeling of silk, which, if possible, should be done tomorrow. Then we will see whether this year they will be instructed better than last year.[5] Col. Stephens, like us and many more, believes that she wishes to keep her art to herself and not teach anyone even though the Trustees have assured her they would so compensate her that she would be taken care of in her

---

[1] John Dobell, a friend of Boltzius, who supported him in his opposition to slavery.

[2] This was Johann Joachim Zubly of St. Gall, who later became the leader of the Dissidents in Georgia. The name was suppressed in the manuscript, along with that of Ortmann.

[3] This petition was brought by the people of Vernonburg and Acton to Col. William Stephens on 26 Feb. 1745. Stephens approved the request and forwarded it to the Trustees, but they had already appointed Bartholmäus Zouberbuhler to the position.

[4] On 3 December 1739 Zouberbuhler had come to Ebenezer to ask for a recommendation to preach to the Reformed around Savannah, but Boltzius had refused because of the company Zouberbuhler was keeping. The phrase referring to the recommendation from Purysburg is also deleted in the manuscript.

[5] Mary Camuse (Maria Camuso) was the tyrant of the filature in Savannah. Boltzius claimed that she used the Ebenezer girls for other chores and would not let them learn her secrets.

old age. Col. Stephens has no advice concerning our wild cattle and cannot help us obtain persons knowledgeable about the forest, yet the cattle manager in Old Ebenezer has a command from the Council to bring our people their cattle when they find them in the forest. According to that, our people will have to do whatever they can, which is a rather dangerous business. May God avert all injury! They are trying diligently to keep any more cattle from going wild. It is better to have few cattle, but tame ones, than to abandon them to other people.

A pious woman called on Mr. [Ludwig] Mayer concerning her physical condition and later called on me to reveal her present condition to me. She knows all sorts of verses and tries with them to cling steadfastly with a firm faith to Christ, "the Lamb of God, who taketh away the sin of the world."[1] The spirit of God is very busy in her soul, and my conversation with her was not without worry. She has her cross with her husband, who sometimes turns his mind to the world; and she must treat him with prayer, good conduct, and quiet rather than offer words, otherwise she just makes evil worse. The soft and quiet spirit in Christian women is also the adornment that is delectable before God.

Thursday, the 21st of March. The widow from Piedmont [Barriky] who is residing in Purysburg with her children,[2] has sent me a letter in which she is offering her services in reeling silk. But she is the same one who called on me last winter and wished, indeed, to work with silk here but demanded excessively great pay for it. However, she will not promise to teach our young women honestly the art of reeling silk. I wrote back to her that she had announced herself too late because two skillful, knowledgeable, and industrious girls were sent in a boat to Savannah this morning in order to learn silk reeling from the Italian woman there if she will teach them loyally. At least she[3] cannot pretend to the Lord Trustees that she wished to teach her art to others if anyone wished to learn. She does not spare untruth, as I have seen from Col. Stephens' letter, in which she claimed before the Council that it was not her fault but that of the girls that they had not learned anything, for it is apparent that she employed them only in outside tasks and became angry whenever, during the reeling, they watched her fingers and wished to imitate her.

It would be of great value at our place: 1) if one of our people understood the art of reeling, and 2) if the Lord Trustees, for the next

---

[1] John 1:29.

[2] This was Mrs. Barraquier, generally known as Mrs. Barriky.

[3] Mrs. Camuso.

couple of years as in the beginning, would give the bounty, namely four shillings for a pound of raw silk, so that the people would be in a position to prepare more pieces of land for mulberry trees and to provide them with good fences. They would also be able to build special chambers in which to raise the silk worms, which must be kept not only clean but also warm in winter and airy in summer, and do whatever else is necessary.

Without such aid as the Lord Trustees gave in former times, the silk reeling will get off to a slow start. I note with pleasure that several people in the community are now convinced of the value of this work and regret that they did not plant such trees sooner, which would now be large and able to bring much benefit. They are now earnestly applying themselves to European crops like wheat, barley, oats, and peas. Because such fields are already cultivated in the fall and winter, they have time in the spring to care for the silk worms and also to plant Indian corn if they do it with plows, as has already been done by several of them and will be done by all if God grants them plows.

This is a very blessed land in which people can easily support themselves if they take up their work wisely and in the fear of God. For they can cultivate the land profitably almost all the year. For example, in fall and winter they plant their European grains, which are harvested in May. From the time of planting up to the harvest they have not the least trouble because the growing grain does not let any weeds grow. In the spring the women and children can occupy themselves usefully with silk worms. Because the worms require very little work in the first three or four weeks, they can help the men and boys with cultivating their fields with local crops with the plow. For this they have already had to prepare the land in winter, clear it of trees and bushes, and fence it in.

After the great wheat harvest they begin making hay, which grows abundantly and as one would wish. The peaches also ripen now, of which we have an almost unbelievable quantity every year. From it the people would distill brandy for their own use and for sale.

At the end of August and in September comes the harvest of our local crops of corn, beans, gourds, rice, and sweet potatoes. Also the turnips, which are planted at the end of June and in August, are large and thick so that men and cattle have their pleasure in them. I say nothing of the garden vegetables, which grow very abundantly if just a little industry is applied to them. Without horse and plows the people cannot get half as much use out of the good land, and they also contract much harm and deterioration of their health through getting overheated and chilled. Therefore I wish innumerable times that God would put me in a position to give some assistance to the industrious workers to help them get plows and horses and other things for their farming. For some of them are very poor and physically weak. By working with the hoe they have lost much strength and accomplished little good. *Dominus providebit.*[1]

Friday, the 22nd of March.	Yesterday shortly before the prayer hour, when I was coming home from the plantations, I heard that a sick woman had sent for me. I went to her immediately and heard what I had already feared, namely that she had not been sincere in her previous confession of her sins, to which her conscience had driven her, but rather had concealed some matters. I never insist upon such confession; but, if the people are driven from within, I warn them against falsity and trickery, which are evidence of impurity in the confession and do not allow the heart to come to any lasting, well-grounded comfort.

This is what she did here. This time she assured me she was no longer holding in her conscience any of the sins that formerly oppressed her and that she did not wish to take them into eternity with her. Therefore she spoke freely with many tears and sighs as well as with much trembling. With great emotion she desired the announcement of merciful absolution in the name of Lord, which I announced to her at the command and in the name of the great Friend of Sinners, who was commanded to preach penitence and the forgiveness of sins, since she has in her the signs of true penitence and faith in Jesus.

I prayed with her and read to her the dear words of the Lord: "Thou hast burdened me with thy sins, etc., ... I blot out thy transgressions."[2] She solemnly promised our dear Lord that, if she recovered again, she would serve Him with a sincere heart and begin an entirely new life. Such a sincere confession has the added advantage that one learns to know other people who were accessories in the sin and knows with what forbearance God puts up with the sinners and fences their paths with thorns and puts obstacles in their way through His holy and marvelous providence so that they will not plunge into them even worse. Oh, what is sin that rests and sleeps for a while; if it awakes in the conscience, what pain and disquiet it makes; and it can only be attributed to God's unfathomable mercy if it does not end up as with Cain and Judah.[3]

---

[1] "God will provide."

[2] Isaiah 43:24-25.

[3] Allusion to Judah unclear.

Through their example our people are sincerely warned against the deceit of sin and of Satan.

Yesterday afternoon on the plantations I had the pleasure of being at the mill; the new mill house is already entirely constructed, and there is new hope that the rice and barley stamp will be completed in about two weeks. While I was visiting some families, their little four-year-old children recited for me the Bible verses they had learned, and I gave them a small gift to encourage them to diligence and obedience. An eight year old boy could recite for me without stumbling all the introit verses that we have contemplated publicly in this church year. I rightly admire his active memory.

The parents know how to use such children with their smaller ones in light house work. This I consider a kind of compensation for the great troubles we have had with them and serves them well in their great lack of servants. Those parents who cannot read or who have weak memories gradually learn the Bible verses through the help of their children.

Saturday, the 23rd of March. Someone has shown us gratitude by setting fire to and entirely burning a large fence that stood between Abercorn and our plantations. Our people are accustomed to water their cattle that have been running around a great deal in the forest. They sometimes wander more than a day's journey, and therefore they could be kept together here at night. Some time ago some men took the trouble to burn away the grass with the expectation of being safe from fire.

Our people in town and on the plantations have acquired silk worms in the hope of gradually learning silk culture and through it to earn some money for their needs. However, it appears that in this spring they will not much achieve their purpose. While the mulberry trees were full of leaves because of the warm weather at the middle of this month, a very heavy frost and a strong and ice-cold wind arose that damaged most of the leaves so badly that the trees are not yet sprouting new leaves. Also, the cool weather has lasted rather long in this month so that the leaves that were still remaining on some of the trees have been hindered in their growth to full size.

It seems amazing to us that the leaves on some trees have been thoroughly damaged and ruined by the cold, whereas some standing not far away have remained green and unharmed. As a result no leaves are left on some plantations, while on some a few are left, indeed, whole trees full. When the young foliage gradually sprouts, it still cannot be used for the already grown worms because they get sick and die from new young foliage. It would be good if the people had a large quantity of mulberry trees so that they would not have to rob them every year, which is harmful for the trees and worms. If God grants His blessings, it is an easy and pleasant occupation to raise such worms if only the necessary arrangements have been made for it.

A widow in the neighborhood who has her trees nearby attests that she is raising many thousands of worms without much effort and can make silk with the help of only a grown-up maid. It was an error among us that the people did not plant enough trees, for, while they would not rejoice in the fruits, they could rejoice in the benefit that accrues fom the leaves in their silk making.

Some time ago a certain gentleman[1] commissioned me to take up a nearby plantation and to have it cultivated, and I am planning to do this. It will not only be cultivated in German fashion as a model for our inhabitants but I will also have mulberry trees planted on it so that, if he comes here as he wishes to, he will profit from the trees and will be able to employ industrious women and children.

Sunday, the 24th of March. We are now having warm weather both day and night and, because we have had no rain for a week, the soil has been greatly dried out from the wind and hot sunshine. As in all times of difficulty, it goes as in Hebrews 2:13 "I will put my trust in him." These words were made useful to us today in the introit when we were treating the regular gospel for Laetare concerning trust in God in times of distress.

In the afternoon I treated the dear and important dogma of Holy Communion, and I pursued very simply the words as they appear in Luke 12, from which God granted us much edification. It was most necessary for us to instruct our people very thoroughly concerning the dogma of our church on every occasion that we put the texts in their hands so that they will be in a position to meet with meekness and patience all those who try to burden our church with great absurdity regarding our dogma of Holy Communion. With all my strength I warn against disputing and squabbling about the love feast of Christ, from which arise only bitterness of spirit and sin against God. On the other hand, I help as much as I can to enable every member of our congregation to reply thoroughly, when they are asked, concerning our Evangelical faith that is based on God's word. There are many people here from

---

[1] Baron von Reck, the commissioner of the first and third Salzburger transport. The name was deleted in the manuscript.

Zweibrücken[1] and other regions of Germany who live right profanely and godlessly or at least have not a trace of living recognition of, or love for, Christ.   These are godless disputants and blasphemers of Holy Communion, with which the Reformed minister in Purysburg[2] agrees as often as they wish, untested and without distinction.   This makes me shudder when I think of it.

If the people of a certain region[3] do not get a pious and experienced man as a minister but are allowed to burden themselves with one of their own kind, this will be a great and well deserved judgment on them. A certain matter will require me to report in my next letter to the praiseworthy *Societät de promovenda Christi Cognitione* [4] something about the ecclesiastical situation of the German people, through which some good could be accomplished through the Lord's blessing.

Monday, the 25th of March.   Yesterday after the evening prayer hour, rain clouds gathered and a storm arose, from which we received a right penetrating rain that lasted into the night. God be praised for this great blessing! May He direct His heart and eye for ever to us and our fields so that all harm will be averted and all the blessings that please Him will be turned to us. Everything looks very joyful in the fields and gardens, and everywhere one finds much material for the praise of God.

The tailor[5] would like me to confirm his two children, a boy and a little girl, and then let them go to Holy Communion. Since the father asked me about it and I did not answer as he wished, he became very angry about it, as his wife told me a few days ago. However, I later indicated to him that I was only seeking the children's good through the postponement. If in the case of these and other children who are visiting the preparation hour and other good opportunities I recognize some clear signs of a change of heart, they will be allowed to go to confirmation and to Holy Communion. Otherwise we like to have the confirmation ceremony on Good Friday, but we cannot bind ourselves to this time, even though it is very edifying. Rather we must act according to the spiritual condition of the children.

----

[1] The name of the town is deleted in the manuscript.

[2] Jean François Chiffelle, a minister whom Boltzius considered too worldly and greedy.

[3] The original text had read: "in and around Savannah."

[4] Sic. Boltzius and others referred to the Society for Promoting Christian Knowledge by a variety of truncated names, often confusing it with its sister organization, the Society for the Propagation of the Gospel in Foreign Parts.

[5] The original read: Metzger and his wife.

Wednesday, the 26th of March.   A captain of the Rangers on the Ogeechee River[1] sent his boat here to buy twenty bushels of corn and have them ground, and this will be permitted him.[2]   He wishes to establish a town on the said river with some people brought from Virginia; and he told me that he had seen a very beautiful region that he would gladly grant to our people if I would send some of them to visit it.   However, I sent him word that we did not desire any more land, certainly not so remote.   Especially now that our industrious workers are convinced that the previously scorned pine lands can be made fruitful with God's blessing through work with the plow, in which we have now had some experience.

We are impatiently awaiting the plowshares that our patrons are to send by ship from England and the northern colonies; and I wish that such a number would be brought here that every householder would have his own plow and be able to cultivate his field himself.   This would be of great benefit.   God doth everything in His time[3] and will let this blessing befall us at the proper time.   A couple of neighbors have trained a pair of young tame oxen to pull, which they are now using for carting. When they become stronger and are well accustomed to pulling, they will also be harnessed to the plow.   I hope others of our people will follow them in this.

Wednesday, the 27th of March.   Last week the German people of our confession in and around Savannah asked me to come down to them to preach on the Holy Day and to give them Holy Communion.   I have always been willing but have just waited for them to be serious, and therefore I departed from here yesterday at about noon and arrived in Savannah toward evening.   I took with me the verse "I will put my trust in him";[4] and on the way I told my traveling companions that from now on this would be a watch word at the mill and in other needy circumstances in the community.   Our gracious God will not let me be put to shame because of it, and therefore it is good and very good (that is why

---

[1] Their headquarters was at Ft. Argyle, now on Camp Stuart near Hinesville, Ga.

[2] This proves the great attraction of the Salzburger mills.   The boat would have to go many miles down the Ogeechee, cross Green Island sound, go through the Skidoway Narrows, past Thunderbolt and Savannah, and proceed another twenty-five miles up the Savannah River.   This would surely require at least four or five days each way.

[3] Allusion to Ecclesiastes 3:11.

[4] Hebrews 2:13.

it stands twice in Psalms 118)[1] to trust the Lord and not to rely upon men, who are only tools of His marvelous governance and providence.

I had not yet reached the house of my friends at which I am accustomed to lodge before an acquaintance told me that a letter to or from Mr. Vigera was there. It was soon handed over to me. It was from Mr. Peter Mayer in London with a letter of instruction addressed to Mr. Vigera. In it, however, there was a most friendly letter to me and my late colleague [Gronau] from the worthy Mr. Mayer saying that certain merchandise was going to be sent here by this great benefactor.[2] He was going to lend us the money gained from it for two years without interest for the use of the congregation; afterwards, if God grants him health and life, he will dispose of it further.[3]

Captain Buttler, who brought the goods in several barrels along with dried fruit and other gifts for us, delivered the letter himself in Savannah and has sailed to Frederica with his large ship full of meat, butter, and other things. A pious merchant in Savannah [Habersham], who is managing the money of our dear Mr. [Thomas] Jones while he is in London and who wishes to enter into business with our dear Mr. N. N,[4] took the bill of lading from me and will see to it that the goods are brought as early as possible from Frederica to Savannah. So marvelous is our heavenly Father in His governance over us. Who would not set his trust upon Him?

Several householders in the community have asked me to acquire from the Council some young oxen for drayage, and God granted us luck in this. I was given hope that we are to receive a pair of young three year old oxen from the Lord Trustees' cattle for the said purpose. God be praised for all this!

Thursday, the 28th of March. Yesterday I had time to write to an honest and serviceable merchant in Charleston who has received a commission from Mr. Vigera to receive the goods from our esteemed Mr. N. N. when they come and to send part of them to him in Philadelphia and part to me. I informed him of the arrival of these goods with

---

[1] Vv. 8, 9.

[2] The great benefactor was not Mr. Mayer, but Christian von Münch, the Augsburg banker and patron of the Salzburgers, whose name is suppressed here and elsewhere, but not consistently so.

[3] This appears to be one of the many attempts of Ebenezer's patrons to take advantage of the special status of the Salzburger settlement to gain a foothold in the colonial trade.

[4] The N. N was substituted here and in the following references for the name of von Münch.

Captain Buttler and also of the order of Mr. N. N., who knew of the departure of Mr. Vigera. I also sent him a letter to Mr. Verelst for quick forwarding to London. In addition I wrote a letter to Pastor Mühlenberg in Philadelphia in which I notified Mr. Vigera, if he is still with him, of the arrival of the goods. As soon as these have been brought here, I am planning, with God's help, to report it to the proper places in Europe.

Yesterday only a few people came in from their plantations, and with them I held the prayer and edification hour concerning the first part of the Passion story and concerning the Hymn *O Welt, sieh her, dein Leben...* It rained very hard yesterday and afterwards a very strong northwest wind arose and brought bitterly cold weather. I visited a young family and tended to my business.

At about eight in the morning the German people assembled in the church, and after the hymn and prayer we contemplated the little verse: "I will set my trust in him." After the service an eight day old baby was baptized that had been brought in from Vernonburg. Holy Communion was held in good order with thirty persons, and the entire service was ended with the verse: "These things I command you, that ye may love one another."[1]

I had brought some edifying little tracts down with me, which the people accepted with longing and joy and took back home to their families. Several of them asked me for Arnd's *Christianity*[2] and for New Testaments, which are to be sent to them. I would be so pleased if they would bring their Bibles or testaments, which are easy to carry, to church with them as our people are accustomed to do to their benefit.

Towards noon I boarded the boat and departed with my traveling companions under the governance of God and, even though the cold wind was against us, at about five o'clock we came safely to Abercorn, from which I rode home with a Ranger and even held the evening prayer hour in the Jerusalem Church. At the mill I found everything in very good order, and there I informed the builder about the Lord's providence over our fortunately progressing construction through the orders of our most worthy Mr. N. N. "Now bless the God of all, who in every way doth great things."[3]

Friday, the 29th of March. This morning the smith Leitner advised me that his stepdaughter Sophie Arnsdorf had died yesterday at about

---

[1] John 15:17.
[2] See p. 164, n. 1.
[3] Sirach 50:24.

two o'clock. Several years ago she had scabies, which her mother cured with the usual salve. Since that time one could see by looking at her that she had become consumptive, and she also showed symptoms of it. A few weeks ago she had an exhausting fever and violent cough for which, to be sure, she took some medicines, but they had little effect. On Sunday she was in church and had begun to help her parents with light work, but she was attacked by a swift and violent fever of which she died even before she herself or her parents expected it. She had a calm and fine disposition, and her father attested that she had profited from a certain edifying example of a pious virgin who is one of those before the throne of the Lamb. She would gladly have died according to the will of God, yet she would have considered recovery a blessing of the Lord. Tomorrow morning she will be buried in the town cemetery. At the funeral we contemplated the hymn *Gott lob, die Stund ist kommen, da ich werde aufgenommen*, in which a pious child is very beautifully presented when taking moving and loving leave of her parents.

This spring the weather has been very inconstant and mostly cold. A heavy rain fell on Wednesday and then a very cold wind arose and everything was frozen. Toward evening today it is almost as cold as it was yesterday evening. The leaves of the mulberry trees are remaining small, and those that have lost their leaves a couple of times from the cold cannot foliate again, and this is causing difficulty this year in the silk making. We are waiting to see whether the grapes and the barley, which is now sprouting ears everywhere, will be damaged by the cold and frost. In the future we will probably not sow the barley so early so that no harm can be caused by the late frost.

Saturday, the 30th of March. This morning I had a good opportunity to send a letter to Pastor Driesler with an Englishman who is taking horses there. I asked him to help us see that Mr. N. N.'s merchandise that arrived there will be sent with a safe opportunity to Savannah. In it is a little barrel of hemp seed, which should already have been sowed by this time. If this letter reaches Mr. Driesler safely, as I do not doubt, he will probably send me a little sack full at the first opportunity to a certain fort[1] between Savannah and Frederica, from which it can be brought to Savannah in a few hours. In this way we could at least sow some hemp at the right time this year even if the rest had to remain still longer in Frederica. I allowed Pastor Driesler to take out as much hemp seed as he wishes for himself and other good friends but to send the

---

[1] Ft. Argyle on the Ogeechee.

remainder here well protected. We have waited for hemp seed for a long time. What we received previously did not come up, the reason for which I do not know. Flax grows here very well, both tender and good; and I hope the same for hemp. We have all sorts of land here, and one of them would surely be suitable. We have been hoping for all kinds of good things for our congregation from Pennsylvania, but correspondence is very slow. This I can attribute to nothing other than the embargo and the danger at sea. Mr. Vigera and Mr. Mühlenberg have promised to help us to all sorts of things that we desire for the good of our congregation, but nothing has followed. As long as he has had no assistants, Mr. Mühlenberg has surely had his hands full in his four scattered congregations.

The Englishman who picked up the letter to be delivered to Frederica appeared amiable and grateful for the good that he had received from our inhabitants. They had helped him find his runaway horses that he was driving through Old Ebenezer for sale in Frederica, for which service he also promised to pay. He said that he had not expected so much kindness from the German people. He revealed to Bichler that the people in Old Ebenezer had rather implied to him that our people were unfriendly and not helpful. However, Col. Stephens' son [Newdigate] had assured him of the opposite. Bichler explained to him from where such calumny came, apparently from envy, meanness, and ignorance. We tolerate no disorder such as drunkenness and shouting from either our people or from strangers; they hated our good order. Sometimes our people would gladly be of service, but they are unable to do so and have to spend their time on their own work, for they wish to support themselves honestly and without debts.

Sunday, the 31st of March.[1] In this now ended month our good Lord has again shown us ineffably much spiritual and physical good, among which the following fourteen blessings especially belong. 1) That we have been able to celebrate our Commemoration and Thanksgiving ceremony in calm and contentment and to the great edification of our souls, even though we are now in a dangerous time of war and hear many sad tidings from many places. 2) That not long before the said ceremony, and therefore to our greater preparation, our marvelous God has let most enjoyable letters from Europe come to our hands in which news was given us about all sorts of necessary gifts that have been packed up for us in Augsburg and Halle and also about the great

---

[1] The letters N(ota) B(ene) were added by a European reader, to draw attention to the content of this entry.

benefaction of the £15 Sterling for continuing the construction of the mills. 3) That He has let us see in both healthy and sick people, also in some small children, very noticeable signs of the grace of the Holy Ghost and has thus crowned my ministry with some blessing. 4) That in this blessed Passiontide and also on Sundays, as well as in the weekday sermons and daily prayer hours, He has granted us right much edification from God's word and especially from the current Passion Story that is being examined verse by verse in the prayer hours and weekday sermons. 5) That He has kept in check wicked people, as tools of Satan, who like to cause disquiet and trouble in this Passiontide and has kept them from causing offense and disorder. The sprouting seed of disunity between some and the sins against me and my ministry have been quickly dampened and destroyed. 6) That He has granted us right fruitful and desired weather, because of which the European grains in the fields by the town and on the plantations are standing most beautifully and pleasingly. 7) That He has let the mill construction proceed well and has always granted some means to be able to pay the workers correctly and to their satisfaction. The rice and barley stamp will surely be completed tomorrow; and this, along with other mill works, has an exceedingly beautiful appearance and is built to last. 8) That He has, to be sure, imposed some tribulations and minor sufferings, which, however, redound to our good. 9) That He has granted some means to help the poor in time of need. 10) That He has let the goods of our dear Mr. Münch, that have been so long on their voyage, arrive safely in Frederica according to His and our wish. Our congregation and mill will have great use of them according to the orders of this prominent benefactor. Captain Buttler, who brought the goods, saw no enemy on the entire voyage but probably wished to meet a Spanish or French ship because his ship had twenty cannons and some seventy soldiers. I was glad to hear that he saw no enemy, for divine providence surely ruled in this. 11) That He inclined the council in Savannah to advance our good, whereas we previously noted a lack in this. 12) That He has granted me, poor and unworthy man, enough physical and mental strength to carry out my office and related business. I have not had to miss a single prayer hour or anything else because of sickness, even though a sickness sometimes seemed underway. He has also graciously strengthened Mr. [Ludwig] Mayer in his vacillating health so that he has been able to be of use to me in many ways. Praised be the glory of God on its place!

APRIL 1745

Monday, the 1st of April, 1745.[1] I asked a man on our plantations who knows about vines to take over my vineyard, which has suffered harm because I have had to use all kinds of people for working in it. He was astonished that the leaves and young grapes on my vines were not frozen; he did not save a single plant, rather all the leaves and budding grapes[2] were ruined by the freeze that we had several times last month. I can not give any natural reason for this since it is usually warmer on the plantations than in town. Also, it is a special providence over Kalcher and his family that not one of his mulberry trees lost its leaves because of the severe freeze. Otherwise he would have lost all the work that had been done for the silk worms.

Some cocoons are already ready, and I must admit that in no year have I seen such beautiful, large, and healthy worms and such large, firm, and tender cocoons as now. Without doubt this will encourage our inhabitants still more to apply themselves to silk manufacture, which is an easy task for women and children if one just has enough trees on hand. They are seeing more and more the advantages of undertaking it, and therefore everything is getting easier for them and the profits are becoming greater.

In addition to the great satisfaction I had today in the orphanage in seeing the silkworms in their cocoons, I had another pleasure in the afternoon from God's goodness and providence. The carpenter Kogler sent me word that the rice and barley stamp would function today for the first time, for which reason he would like to see me there. In the afternoon I went out there, and steps were taken to begin stamping. In the long and thick beam there are seven holes in the form of an upright egg, as the holes usually are in the rice stamps in Carolina. Every hole, in which a pestle falls, contains more than a bushel of rice or barley, which can be stamped white in something more than an hour and prepared for use and sale. All seven pestles go as regularly one after the other as if seven men were threshing.

I had a pocket watch with me so that I could exactly measure the time of stamping. In twenty-four hours more than a hundred and fifty bushels of rice can be stamped in these holes, and a man has no other work than to put the rice or barley into them and to take his grain out again after the passage of a good hour and to strain it and take it home.

---

[1] Again as on March 31, the abbreviation N(ota) B(ene) is added.
[2] Boltzius uses the word "seeds" (*Saamen*).

It is an incomparably useful machine that is driven by a single water wheel that stands next to the mill wheel.

Today only a bushel of rice was at hand so that I could see only a single pestle operate. But tomorrow, God willing, so much rice will be brought together that all seven holes will be filled and all pestles set in motion. As soon as I can I shall ask Col. Stephens when it will be opportune for him to come up to us. Our people will bring him up to Abercorn in a few hours, and from there he can ride here on a good horse in the company of a guide. He should see this very useful mill himself and report the matter as he has seen it to the Lord Trustees. It speaks for itself and needs no praise. We rightfully praised the Lord in our prayer hour today for this new and very great physical blessing. We shall also do it tomorrow in the Zion Church. May He, for the sake of Christ, be pleased with our humble praise. Now our inhabitants will plant rice, for which they have enough land. Until now they have planted hardly as much as they need in their own households because they had to spend almost a day and consume much energy in stamping a single bushel. Therefore almost no rice has been for sale at our place.

Tuesday, the 2nd of April. In today's sermon in the Zion Church our kind God granted us much edification and pleasure in our contemplation of His word and in the great blessing which He has shown our congregation through the mill and rice stamp. We praised Him for His mercy and loyalty in song and prayer, warned one another against sin in general and especially against a certain sin that is becoming the mode among common people, and we encouraged one another to a God-pleasing practice of the verse: "But seek ye first the kingdom of God, and his righteousness."[1] Then the blessing of the Lord will remain with us and our children.

After the confession I again made suggestions concerning the just completed stamp mill as to how our dear people should arrange their farming and silk culture easily and conveniently for the good of their wives and children if some time, according to God's will, they should become widows and orphans. I sincerely offered, as far as God grants me the means, to help for the better arrangement of both matters. These suggestions are, as they must admit to themselves, very practicable in the easily workable piny woods if only they will break in oxen for plowing because horse drayage is too expensive for us poor people. After dinner I rode to the mill again and found Mr. [Ludwig] Mayer and other men

---

[1] Matthew 6:33.

and women already there to see for themselves this important work, which praises itself. All seven pestles were stamping rice and this was very pleasant to see. I wish it could be written over the door of the mill in metal letters the words: "The works of the Lord are great, sought out of all them that have pleasure therein."[1]

Today I paid the carpenters for the last work they did on the stamp; and I am, to the best of my knowledge, not indebted one shilling for all the work done. Praised be the good providence of the Lord! Now the carpenters are returning to their own household tasks. When the water in the river drops and warms up, they are planning to build the millrace so that it will grind at very low water, and all preparations have been made for this. They hope to be finished with it in two weeks. This millrace will be a great blessing for our community; for, when rain is lacking for a long time in the summer, the water in the river gets so low that the present mill must stand still. But then the millrace that is soon to be built will do its duty so that they can convert their European grains to meal before it is at all damaged by worms and little weevils (as can easily happen in these warm countries). Also, strangers can have their crops ground whenever they wish and will never come in vain.

Wednesday, the 3rd of April. A pious woman told me that she had been dangerously sick last week and that disquiet and doubts arose in her spirit as to whether or not she would truly find grace. Yet our dear Savior again came to her aid. In times of affliction such true souls soon feel the least mote of sin in the healthy and tender eye of the conscience; and then it is a great mistake if they wish to seek their inner peace by making good their blunder and in other ways since they have blood and water in Jesus for cleansing and sanctification.[2] The punishment lies on Him if we are to have peace.

The people in the congregation are very happy that the worthy NN[3] has sent all sorts of bolts of inexpensive linen here, and they have asked me not to sell them all in Savannah but to have a good deal of it brought here, and this shall be done, for they are without shirts and other things.[4] May God let all these goods arrive safely in Savannah. He will be

---

[1] Psalms 111:2.

[2] Boltzius is preaching Luther's dogma of salvation through faith alone. It is a sign of pride and a snare of the devil to try to achieve justification through good works rather than through the blood of the Lamb.

[3] N.N. again replaces the name von Münch.

[4] This sentence was underlined, but the words "for they are without shirts and other things" were struck out.

thanked in Ebenezer for this blessing, too. Also, it is Christian and just if all the creatures of God are sanctified with God's word and prayer. Also, such trade is a seed toward eternity, to which all believing sellers and buyers should strive. I once wrote that I hoped our dear Lord would know how to protect our most worthy NN [Mr. von Münch], our great benefactor until now, with the goods he is sending, even if shipping is very uncertain and even though Mr. Vigera, who was commissioned to sell them, has departed from us; and I still have this hope.

Last night God again granted us a good but rather cold rain. To be sure, it did not rain much during the day, but it was always dreary and also quite cold. In the past nights it was also rather cool, yet the freezes at night appeared to be entirely past, and this is very good for the barley and rye, which are now in blossom. One cannot look at the European crops without pleasure and praise of God, if one has a Christian spirit.

Thursday, the 4th of April. Because Leitner's oldest daughter died last week and his wife is sickly and unfit for field work, he has had to take back his second daughter from the Italian woman in Savannah,[1] where she, along with another girl, is to learn to reel silk. In her place we will send Rieser's youngest daughter, who is likewise a quiet and industrious girl. I therefore wrote to Col. Stephens and asked him not to be opposed to this change, which I had not been able to see in advance. I reported to him that our rice stamp has been completed. Because he recently expressed a desire to see this useful work, I am asking him to determine the day on which our people can fetch him in our boat and bring him to Abercorn, where horses will be standing ready for him and other friends who wish to come.

After this letter had been written, two men told me of an unpleasant matter about which I must write to Col. Stephens, to the Anglican minister Mr. Bosomworth, and to a captain at Mount Pleasant. Namely, some three weeks ago our people had brought home some cattle out of the woods. Among them were two young bulls that Zant thought were those that he had lost a couple of years ago. However, he had not wished to appropriate them because he had forgotten the marks on their ears[2] until another man had assured him that he knew one of the oxen and that it belonged to Zant, and there were conjectures that the other

---

[1] Mary Camuse, at the filature in Savannah.

[2] In addition to a brand, the cattle were identified by various slices made in their ears, as is indicated in the Cattle Brand Book that was issued ten years later and is still available.

also belonged to him.   He thereupon appropriated both, marked and branded them, and let them run loose.

Now the cattle manager in Old Ebenezer pretends that the one belongs to Mrs. Musgrove, who has married the Anglican minister,[1] and the other to the captain at Mount Pleasant; and he and his people are making a great fuss about it although the man is entirely innocent. He did not do well in having no cattle brand of his own at first, instead he had just made all sorts of cuts, which he himself can no longer remember. He is a dyer and was not brought up with cattle, and therefore all this happened only through simplicity and ignorance.   At the time he appropriated the two oxen he promised he would gladly let them go again if someone should come who could prove his right better than he.

Friday, the 5th of April   N.[2] was with me and revealed to me that he was determined to sell his plantation and to move into town, for which move he was motivated by several causes. Most of all, his wife is urging him. She wishes to live in town rather than in the country and, because her wish cannot be granted, she has become sick. I advised him strongly against this planned move because it is connected with much difficulty.   However, he loves his wife very much and he promises himself an easier life style in town than in the country, and that is why he is trying to put his plan in motion. He is going to plant a lot of mulberry trees and his wife will apply herself to silk culture, but he is planning to establish a plantation in the piny woods near the town. He complained that, since he obtained his plantation, he has lost some thirty hogs, seven at one time a short time ago, for out there in the thick forest there are bears and tigers.[3] Also, hawks were doing much damage to both old and young chickens. I am sorry for the poor man and I would gladly see him helped because he would like to support himself honestly and live content and peacefully with his wife. She is not as industrious as he is, otherwise they would fare all right.

A wild young ox came into the field of two Salzburgers and could not be caught except by being shot, and its meat was divided among fifteen needy people in town and on the plantations. Yesterday I sent a lad on horseback to Captain Barnard in Mount Pleasant with a letter addressed to him, and this afternoon he brought me back a letter from

---

[1] Soon after marrying Mrs. Musgrove, who owned a prosperous trading station on the Altamaha, Bosomworth resigned his position as minister.

[2] The name has been stricken out but is legible as Bischoff (Bishop), an English lad formerly indentured to Boltzius.

[3] Mountain lions (cougars or pumas) were then called tigers.

him which was just as I had wished in the matter reported yesterday. Like us, he sees it as a mistake and will make no more of it. He advises our people to slaughter the bull and to pay him for it what they think it is worth so that there will be no more misunderstandings because it has both his and Zant's ear marks on it. I have several proofs that this man is behaving like a good neighbor, as I shall mention to General Oglethorpe some time. I wish the Lord Trustees' cattle manager in Old Ebenezer were so disposed toward us, for we have shown him all possible services.

Saturday, the 6th of April. I met a righteous Salzburger who had fetched mulberry leaves for his silk worms. He recited for me the verse: "I had many troubles in my heart, but thy...,"[1] the important content of which he could attest from personal experience. He thanked our dear God diligently for His gracious governance with respect to the easy farming with plows, with which large fields have been cultivated with German grains, for there is no work from the time of sowing to the harvest. This very man, as well as others, has lost almost all his strength through the hard work with the hoe and would not have been able to hold out much longer if God had not granted means and courage to begin the work with the plow, even on poor soil. He said that, if he had a team of horses, a plow, and a wagon, he would take up a plantation (if he did not already have one) right in the piny woods on soil that had been scorned until now and that he would easily earn his bread from it with God's blessing.

In this forest they can give their horses or oxen much more work than in the so-called leaf forest, where oaks and other kinds of trees stand with thick and numerous roots that often grow out again. For already in the next year they can extend their fields as far as they wish while the trees are still standing and plow the land around and between the trees often. For, as experience has shown, through much work with the plow they can make the land good and fruitful without using any manure on it. From now on with God's help we will try many things to alleviate our community.

In this country nothing is so lacking as loyal servants. How much could be accomplished if every householder had even one loyal servant, since work can go on unhindered in both winter and summer. I am assured that this land has great advantages if the inhabitants do not forfeit the Lord's blessing through their sins in the great freedom of this

---

[1] Psalms 94:19. The King James version differs greatly in wording.

country. Every householder wishes to have his own plow. Therefore, even if I acquire fifty plowshares from England or the northern colonies, I can still not serve them all as they wish. In England a plowshare with a plow-knife[1] would not cost much more than five shillings, which would be a small amount for the Lord Trustees, yet it could accomplish very much good for the support of our place.

Sunday, the 7th of April. The last time I was in Savannah, I was told that the young minister Zubly is reported to have said that he had a letter that I had sent to London in which the number of German people in and around Savannah was reported as so small that the Lord Trustees were hesitating to give Mr. Zubly to these few people as their minister. To be sure, I inquired about this untruth but could find no grounds for it. Toward evening yesterday I received from Savannah a little letter from this Mr. Zubly in which he assured me that he had not said anything of that kind. He had also been told that, from John 15:17: "These things I command you, that ye love one another." I had admonished my listeners to hearty love for one another and for other members of their confession and to cease all useless disputation and squabbling about dogma and Holy Communion. This teaching method pleased him greatly, and he thanked me for it. I have not yet seen him; but I hope he has a good disposition and will be my friend.

A pious man in Savannah told me that, if this Mr. Zubly diligently teaches the dogma of rebirth to the German people and attacks mouth and name Christianity, he will soon be scorned and considered mad. Thus I and my late colleague fared with most of the Reformed and Lutherans [who then found refuge and comfort with the Reformed minister in Purysburg. If I did not allow them to go to Holy Communion and did not wish to marry them under disorderly conditions, he did so; and thus I have no means left for church discipline.][2] Should Mr. Zubly become the regular minister of the Reformed in Savannah and be anointed with the salve of Mr. Lucius,[3] then we will easily get along together, and thus much good will arise under God's blessing.

Monday, the 8th of April. Today a small boat went down to Savannah on which Kalcher and some other people were sending a part of their silk. More than twenty of Kalcher's large trees were damaged through the carelessness of a neighbor who set fire to the grass in a

---

[1] *Pflug Messer*. This instrument is not described.

[2] The Reformed minister in Purysburg was Henri François Chifelle. The bracketed part of the paragraph was deleted in the text.

[3] This reference is unclear and may be due to an error by the scribe.

strong wind. Therefore he has had a shortage of leaves this year; and, because he had to gather wild or very young leaves that had sprouted again, many of his worms died just a few days ago even though at first they had been in a very good condition.

Mrs. Gronau has also made a beginning with silk worms this year and, because she had her trees nearby in my and her garden, it was more of a pleasure for her than an effort to make several pounds of silk. Her worms remained in a very good condition from the beginning to the end and made lovely, big, yellow and white cocoons. Kalcher's worms also grew rapidly, whereas others in the town and on the plantations remained small; and this has come about partly because they could not be kept warm enough through lack of an oven and partly because there was a shortage of leaves because the cold had frozen many of them and the trees were prevented from sprouting leaves by the cold nights. A large number of trees and warm rooms will be required if silk making is to make any progress. Through love for widows, children, and other needy people, I intend, God willing, to have a great number of trees planted next winter that will have to be cared for every year until they are fully grown, which will, indeed, cause some expenses. I hope, however, that, with time, the profit will also be great.

If God should grant us the sawmill, the people would gradually acquire warm rooms, but we will leave this up to divine providence. God will surely do it.[1] Our carpenter Kogler wishes and hopes that he will meet a man expert in construction with whom he might build the sawmill. He does not understand mills that work with nine or six saws at one time because he and his father only built simple mills with one saw. The wood and ironwork we received from the ruined sawmill in Old Ebenezer is adjusted for many saws. If God should lead General Oglethorpe to this country and to our place, he would surely know what advice to give when he saw the good situation of our mill enterprises.

Tuesday, the 9th of April. The widow Kurtz[2] has established herself on her husband's plantation and wishes to begin her own farming. However, she would have done better if she had remained either in the orphanage or in my house, where she would have had a very easy service. She is sickly and is living on a land where very much work

---

[1] Allusion to hymn by Johann Daniel Herrnschmidt beginning *Gott wills machen, dass die Sachen.*

[2] Matthias Kurtz and his wife Anna and his daughter Gertraut were the last Salzburgers to reach Ebenezer. They had been for years in Cadzand in the Netherlands and in London and were brought to Georgia by H. M. Mühlenberg.

must be done if anything is to grow. She is stuck alone deep in the forest, and therefore she will be more plagued with bears, deer, and other harmful animals and birds. She has her little girl with her, but her two stepdaughters are in service with Christian people and are well provided for. In this country everyone wishes to establish his own farm, and therefore servants, hired hands, and maids are very scarce. The people can't even get a boy to guard their cattle; and therefore, with great difficulty and neglect of their business, they must find their cattle in the woods every day and drive them home.

Loyal servants are as necessary in the land as anything, yet one is glad not to get entangled with such as were sent here in past years. Surely no one in Europe can imagine their disloyalty and wickedness because such perverse servants are not to be found there. To some degree one can envisage them in the people who go to the lord's farm and have to do mandatory labor, when one sees not a whit of the spirit expressed in Colossians 3:22-23. If anyone is not a farmer himself and cannot do the work with his own hands, he cannot establish any plantation, vineyard, or orchard because the expenses would greatly surpass the profit. No common worker in this country works for less than eighteen pence and, if I should maintain a single day worker all year to cultivate the fields and chop wood, he would cost me more than £23 Sterling.

In Savannah the daily workers receive more than eighteen pence, and in Carolina no servant who is assigned as overseer over the Negroes serves for less than £14 Sterling. He also receives subsistence, and the work does not mean much because they use Negroes there for work. The high cost of labor is the reason that I myself can not undertake anything in my family's farming and can not make any experiments and tests in some matters as a good example for the community, for this would cause me to fall into debt. One has so many expenses for indispensable work on practical matters that it is difficult to imagine.

The community is poor and the merchandise in this country is so excessively expensive that I cannot expect anyone to work for us gratis or for a low wage, even if they are willing. Some communal labors are indispensable, and these are assigned in turn. I cannot impose any burdens on them, except for those that contribute to their own good, but I shall wait and see what more our marvelous God might do. For a short time I have remembered the words: "God is able to do exceeding abundantly above all that we ask or think." ... "I have put my trust in the Lord God."[1]

The day laborers cost the Lord Trustees excessively much all year, yet nothing is accomplished by it. I would still hesitate if they offered me their large garden in Savannah for the one that I have had planted behind and near the parsonage and which costs very much money every year. For several years now General Oglethorpe has maintained a Swiss in his vineyard on his barony near Pallachocolas and he paid dearly for his meager work. However, I know of no other profit than a bottle of vinegar that came from the wine that the gardener made last week. He gave me the vinegar because he did not know what to do with it. I shall advise him of this in my report to him. This good gentleman fares similarly with his cowpen on his barony.

Monday, the 10th of April. Some time ago a couple of children of a German widow dwelling near Pallachocolas were in our school but afterwards they had to help for a while in her work, and now they are coming back here again. The boy still needs some schooling, but the little girl will probably take service with someone among us. The mother is no friend of Ebenezer. However, almost against her will God so ordained that the oldest daughter, while her father was still alive, was married to a pious Salzburger, Simon Reiter.[2] General Oglethorpe sent her two sisters to Ebenezer also as serving girls and they were instructed here. Since then they love Ebenezer and would not have left here if their mother had not insisted, especially regarding the second daughter.

A few years ago another German girl was taken away by her wicked parents without my knowledge just while she was attending the preparation hour for Holy Communion. Afterwards she got into all sorts of disorder just like her parents and other siblings. The last time I was in Savannah I was told that she had married a young Reformed man, from whom she has already run away. Almost everywhere there is great confusion among the German people, most of them were not worth much in Germany. During their years of service here they have heaped up their measure of sin, which is followed by all kinds of judgments. I have written letters to the praiseworthy Society and to the Lord Trustees and given the reports I owe concerning the circumstances of the

---

[1] Ephesians 3:20; Psalms 73:28. Hebrews 2:13.

[2] This was Magdalena Gebhard, daughter of Philip Gebhard, who had been indentured at Frederica.

congregation; and now I hope to have an opportunity to send them along with the English diary.[1]

Thursday, the 11th of April.   A German man from Carolina asked me to send a petition for him to a certain planter in Carolina,[2] and this gave me an opportunity to write some other points to this righteous man, whom I respect. 1) I advise him of the death of my worthy colleague, and I thank him for the affection he showed him while he was spending a few days with him during his sickness. 2) I wish to learn from him whether sheep can be obtained inexpensively in his area and at what season the planters prefer to sell them. Some of our inhabitants are showing a great desire for sheep, for which they have sufficient meadows. They are eating almost nothing but pork, sometimes (but little) beef. If in its place they could gradually start enjoying mutton, they would doubtless become healthier. To be sure there are many bears and wolves, also tigers,[3] but they devour the swine just as well as the sheep, therefore the sheep must be kept on the meadows on the plantations. For this the piny woods are very good because one can get large fields in a short time and extend them greatly. 3) I also informed this friend that God has now also helped us to a right desired rice stamp.

Now, under God's blessing, we wish to build a sawmill, for which we now have the best opportunity and also much ironwork and lumber. We are lacking only a builder who has already built such mills with several saws. Kogler will not undertake this burden unless necessity demands, for only then he would risk it. However, I do not think much about that because I have no money for uncertain risks. I have been told that this friend to whom I am writing, or his righteous brother,[4] has insight into and experience with hydraulic works. Therefore I am asking them to aid us with advice and deed or to recommend us to some other knowledgeable and honest man.

Yesterday our dear God graciously aided the righteous wife of the likewise righteous Hans Flerl in her delivery and granted her a healthy little daughter that was baptized in the Jerusalem Church. They are both believing people. Formerly she has had difficult hours and danger in giving birth, however (as I have been told) she placed her trust in the

---

[1] The continued references to an "English diary" are surprising. See n. 2, p. xi.

[2] This was either Hugh or Jonathan Bryan.

[3] See n. 3, p. 217.

[4] See note 2 above.

Lord and surely believed that He would graciously help her through, as He did.

Good Friday, the 12th of April.   We have again celebrated this day as a great Holy Day of grateful remembrance of our Crucified Love, and for this my dear congregation gathered in the morning and the afternoon in the Jerusalem Church. Just as in the past year our loving God granted us much edification in the reconciliation celebration of the New Testament, we have cause also today to praise His unmerited kindness. It has been an especial day of grace for me in that the sweet manna of the gospel concerning the savory words of the introit: "Behold the Lamb of God,"[1] and about the Passion text Luke 22 describing the severe inner spiritual sufferings of the innocent and immaculate Lamb of God, has been proclaimed to my poor heart.

The important material we had begun could not be finished for lack of time, but with God's help this is to be done after the celebration in the prayer hour and weekday sermon. In this now ended Passiontide at our meeting we have contemplated the Passion Story word for word according to the gospel of Luke, and at the beginning of every hour we have repeated the presented points by question and answer. This has had, praised be God, great benefit even though for this reason we could not complete the entire story of the suffering and dying of Christ and will therefore have to continue with it to the end after Easter and have to put aside the contemplation of the story of the Old Testament. In this way we have experienced that it is true what an old minister of our church said of the entire Holy Scripture, consequently also of the most important part of it, namely, of the story of all stories, of the suffering and death of Christ: It is a living well; the deeper one digs, the more it wells forth.

In the evening prayer hour we again communally praised the Lord of the Harvest for the great blessing that He has sent to our dear friend Pastor Mühlenberg by sending him a righteous pastor and two like-minded catechists.[2] This was occasioned by the letters that I received yesterday out of Pennsylvania from Pastor Mühlenberg, Pastor Brunnholtz, and Mr. Vigera, which I have already answered. I hope with certainty that He will also hear our prayer and grant me at the right time a loyal helper in my ministry.

---

[1] John 1:29.
[2] See p. 186, n. 1.

Meanwhile God's kindness to me is very great, and through it I always find myself more strengthened in body and mind than perhaps at any time before in Ebenezer. It is well written: "He is able to do exceeding abundantly above all that we ask or think," and therefore I will place my trust in Him. Mr. Mühlenberg wrote, "I consider it an entirely special Providence and gracious Governance that not a single word of all the letters you have sent me has been lost. I attribute it to your and to so many children of God's prayers that our exceedingly gracious and merciful God in Christ has not wished to let me, a foolish sinner, sink and perish. And, most of all, that our highly praised God has looked on me, miserable person, and my poor congregation so graciously that we have received an ordained minister and two catechists from our superiors in Halle and London. They arrived here safe and sound, and God has carried them through everything unharmed on eagle wings."

Pastor Brunnholtz wrote as follows:

We can now also report that God the Father, whose eyes see through all lands in order to strengthen those who heartily trust in Him, has let me and my two brothers arrive safe and sound in Philadelphia on the 15th of January. On September 10 of last year we departed London and went aboard ship. We were actively tested and trained in the eighteen weeks in the ship. However, the word of our living God was our comfort and light. I have already been in all four congregations and have given, as it were, a trial sermon. My most worthy colleague has already put much in good order. One catechist is in the rural congregations and one in Philadelphia.

These two letters were dated the 8th of February of this year.

Saturday, the 13th of April. Mr. Vigera has sent our congregation two useful plows. One of them has the wooden parts and all attachments, and from it our people can see what kind of plows are used there. He promises to send us another pair in a short time, and these will be most welcome. In his letter of 25 January he wrote:

I must report to you with much joy and praise of God how, three weeks ago, the long awaited help for our most honored friend Pastor Mühlenberg arrived here safely from London, namely, Pastor Brunnholtz with two sincerely pious catechists.

Mr. Zwiffler is said to be suffering from dropsy.

Col. Stephens, whom I invited to inspect our rice and barley stamp, let me know in his answer that his circumstances do not allow him any travel at present but he hopes to seize the opportunity another time. The Anglican minister Bosomworth wrote me that he was going to do nothing more about the confusion that occurred with his ox since I could attest that the man who took it is an honest man. Praise be to God who has graciously saved us from this vexing matter and has stopped the mouth of those enemies who have already made much fuss about it in Savannah and Old Ebenezer. For the raw silk that was sent down I received a recompense that amounts to £54. The people there would hardly believe that it was made at our place. Because of lack of leaves Kalcher had to give the worms newly sprouted leaves (which is a poison for them), with the result that many thousands died all at once to his great loss. This will make him and others cautious.

Sunday and Monday, the 14th and 15th of April
were the Holy Easter Days

On this feast of joy God has given us good rest, health, and edification. Therefore laud, praise, and glory are due Him. On the first day of Easter I treated the regular gospel concerning the gracious reward of sincere and upright love of Jesus and on the second day of Easter I treated the living recognition of Christ our Savior. The verses of the introit were Psalms 69:33 "The humble shall see this, and be glad and your heart shall live that seek God"[1] and John 17:3: "This is life eternal, that they might know thee the only true God, and Jesus Christ, whom thou hast sent."

Old Jacob Kiefer's Reformed son-in-law traveled down to Purysburg on the first day of Easter. Whether he went to Holy Communion there or whatever else he wants to do, I do not know. His wife tried to persuade him to remain here and to enjoy what God will grant us on the holy Easter Day, but no remonstrating did any good. I must be very gentle and cautious with such people if they are not to suck poison from the flower and become bitter. It appears that he is not happy at our place, and that is probably the reason he has wished to move away again for some time, to the sorrow of his wife and parents-in-law. However, he cannot harm us. When we accept such people into our place and let

---

[1] Psalms 69:32 in the King James version.

them enjoy the good that God has granted us, then they and their kind see that we live in the love for the teachings and the example of Christ and truly seek our salvation. However, one can not avoid calumny and misinterpretation of our actions, especially if one does not do what they wish in every way in their false intent, which would harm their neighbor.[1]

Tuesday, the 16th of April. Before the Easter celebration I wrote letters to some of our Fathers and friends in Europe, and today I am busy adding them to the others that are to be sent tomorrow along with the diary in the English and German languages to a good friend in Savannah, who will forward them at a safe opportunity to a merchant in Charleston, Mr. W. Hopton, to whom I am also writing. Last week Col. Stephens wrote me that he had received news that Captain Thomson was on his way to Frederica with soldiers, money, and other things. His arrival is being painfully awaited because of the great lack of money. We hope that he will have the crate from Halle and letters for us in his ship. We greatly desire letters. Because those that were written to us last summer did not reach us properly, they must have been lost. This will be the first time it has happened as long as we have been in this land. If only we knew how things stand with the packets that we have sent. From the recently arrived letters we have learned of nothing but the arrival of a single packet which contained the first months of last year.

I was required to send a letter to the cattle manager in Old Ebenezer in which I asked in a friendly way not to make any disturbance at our place as he once did on Pentecost Monday and yesterday and during the evening prayer hour. He had two men with him, all three were drunk and shouted on the street at the top of their lungs like Indians so that we were disturbed in our prayer, for we did not know who or what was happening. I wrote the letter in the most friendly manner I could, and asked whether perhaps he did not know that we were in church. But Constable Bichler had told him, and one of them beat on our doors and windows so hard that he frightened the little children who were at home alone with a small girl. I am also writing this letter in the English diary, from which the Lord Trustees may be informed of this disorder.

---

[1] This entire paragraph was deleted in the manuscript.

APPENDIX I

Sunday, the 31st of August [1746].[1]   During the prayer hour yesterday evening my dear colleague came home again in health,[2] and we praise the Lord for having graciously turned sickness and misfortune from him and for wishing to use him again as a tool to do good among the German people of our confession in Charleston, of which there is quite a large flock. He enjoyed much good from good people, who also aided him against Curtius' cunning and deceit,[3] and thus we were spared great loss and bother. I could not imagine that Curtius (or Kurtz, as his name should really be[4]) would wish to reveal himself to me and my congregation as a liar and fraud, since he had received so much spiritual and physical good in our community and also experienced the power of the word of God emphatically in his heart.

He always conducted himself among us very well and in a Christian manner, he loved the means of salvation, he attended the sermons and prayer hours regularly and prayed very zealously; and he regretted, lamented, and loathed his former godless life. He solemnly offered himself with body and soul to God his Lord, who had pursued him as a very great sinner with ineffable forbearance, patience, and many benefactions. He also affirmed with emphatic words that he considered it an especial providence of God and great blessing that he had come to Ebenezer and that, through the prayer hours and sermons, he had come to a recognition of himself, of the Lord Jesus, of His treasures of grace and the order of grace through the powerful effect of the Holy Ghost.

In gratitude for these great benefactions of the Lord he wished to let himself be used as a tool and to apply himself and the very good gifts he had received from the Lord for the good of the children and the

---

[1] The Halle copy at this point is headed "Extract from the Ebenezer Diary". Who made the "Extract" and how accurate and inclusive it is, is unknown.

[2] Assuming that Boltzius is writing, the colleague was Hermann Heinrich Lemke, who had come to Ebenezer in January 1746.

[3] Curtius (Kurtz) was a con-artist who fleeced the people of Ebenezer, particularly Thomas Bichler, in a big timber operation.

[4] Latinized names, which should have been used only by clergymen and other Latinists, were often affected by ambitious people.

congregation through the introduction of a useful timber business and, in return, inexpensive merchandise. For this he desired only his necessary subsistence.   In the matters performed here in the school and congregation he proved himself right loyal and diligent and merely wished to help me in every way.

The first time he went away with great emotion and with the intention of going to Charleston and from there to his friends and close relatives in New York in order to discuss and make arrangements concerning a timber business he was going to bring here. However, he did not travel there, rather he remained at least six weeks or longer in Charleston and claimed that he could arrange everything through letters. Some other things came to my ears that made me doubt his honesty. However, when he had returned from Charleston to Ebenezer, he again made a very good impression, and he also produced a letter from his cousin, a merchant in New York, from which I could see his intention to send merchandise here and accept our lumber in boards, barrel staves, hoops, shingles, and dressed boards.

This man, who has a very good natural intelligence and a glib tongue, confirmed all this with many additions and was very zealous in bringing said timber to the river with wagons and afterwards down the river with boats and a large raft. Our inhabitants were willing to let themselves be used for this and expected to be paid later with inexpensive merchandise after the sale of the timber. I thought they were already paid, for, before shipping the goods or money, this Kurtz wished to give me the money himself.

His cousin's vessel was to come to Frederica and sell the wares it had brought but let some of them come to us. Afterwards the vessel with our previously mentioned timber would either go back to New York or be loaded directly for the West Indies. Meanwhile, he said, his cousin had promised him that he would receive some goods in Charleston for paying the initial costs of establishing the business. He had to travel there again to fetch them. After his first return from Charleston he could well notice that I had lost some of my trust in him. Because of that he made bitter complaints against my family, my dear colleague, and others, and in order that I might not doubt his honesty so much, he earnestly requested that my dear colleague and our knowledgeable constable and publican Bichler travel with him and see everything with their own eyes and receive the goods that were brought from New York.

He assured me that this trip would cost them nothing and that it would further the matter if they would travel with him. He also planned a marriage with a German widow in Charleston, and because of this marriage he wished to have my dear colleague with him. He would arrange this marriage only with necessary precaution and after receiving permission from the authorities there, if anything was to come of this marriage. Now who could have thought that such fraud and deceit could lie behind such good appearances and efforts as they have now been revealed.

It is, to wit, not the least bit true that he will receive goods from New York that are already prepared for loading or that he had rented a vessel. Meanwhile he so cunningly blinded the eyes of Mr. Lemke and Bichler with the image of readily available merchandise that they believed him and allowed themselves to be put off for a long time, under all sorts of pretexts, from seeing the least piece or even knowing the name of the merchant who was said to have it ready.

To come closer to his harmful purpose he sent the knowledgeable and usually so cautious Bichler with 500 bushels of corn, which he bought on our account without my knowledge and consent. For this he cunningly persuaded my dear colleague to have it ground as soon as possible in Ebenezer and to send some of the meal back to Charleston in the vessel in which the pretended New York goods are to be sent here. Now, since he had only Mr. Lemke with him, he wished to persuade him to buy in his and my names £100 Sterling worth of goods or to vouch for as much as he (Kurtz) wished to buy and to sign a contract.

Our dear Lord, however, steered Lemke's mind and let him profit from the good counsel of good friends so that he did not do it but at the same time discovered the deceit that they were nothing but Charleston goods, most of which he wished to buy from others; and I was to pay for them within six weeks in two payments with bills of exchange. The payment for the freight would also have fallen upon me, as happened to me in regard to the corn, whose freight cost me £5 Sterling.

Because it was old corn and was brought here now during the harvest of the new corn, it caused no little loss, especially since it cannot be ground for a long time because only the second mill wheel is operating and our inhabitants' wheat, rye, and barley and new corn must be ground. The European crops do not keep but must be ground promptly at the request of our inhabitants. To say nothing of the fact that much of the corn has become very wet and also that in bringing it up from Savannah Bichler made a mistake which greatly increased the costs. Kurtz had also rented a vessel to carry our lumber, who knows where, and the cost of the freight would have fallen on me if our dear Lord had not prevented it.

The travel expenses for these three men, namely Mr. Lemke, Bichler, and Kurtz, the horse's fodder, and quarters in Charleston also amounted to a good deal, which my dear colleague had to pay. Now the miserable Kurtz is at our place again, and we are afraid he would have ridden away with the horse that belongs to us if he had not become dangerously sick on the way and were not now under Mr. [Ludwig] Mayer's care. I am ashamed of my lack of caution and regret that it was only in the past two weeks that I have received letters from Mr. Vigera and Pastor Brunnholtz from Pennsylvania, in which this Kurtz is described as an arch-hypocrite and deceiver and also as an adulterer and very evil person. This I have seen not in the past but in the present, and I was unable to believe that he wished to deceive us until matters became clear upon the arrival of Bichler and even more after the return of my dear colleague.

In the past Bichler has had him in his house; and, because he saw much good in him, he lent him money and has suffered great loss. May God convert him before his measure of sin is full and he is torn away and there is no more counsel. May He also be gracious to us and let us see His help. May he let this sad affair contribute to my wisdom. But I wished so much to help our dear congregation who would like to support themselves honestly in this money-scarce time, to have some earnings in our place because they cannot subsist by agriculture alone. It is for this reason that so many barrel staves, hoops, shingles, etc. have been prepared, which Kurtz wished to take in his cousin's vessel to the West Indies while providing inexpensive goods in exchange for them.

APPENDIX II

Lutheran Dogma Versified for Children[1]

Die drei Haupt-Stücke des Glaubens wahrer Christen nach dem
geoffenbahrten Worte Gottes

Melodie: Lob sey dem allerhöchsten Gott

Der erste Articul des christlichen Glaubens:

1) Ich glaub an Gott, der Vater heisst,	2 Corinthians 8:5-6
an den Sohn und Heilgen Geist.	Matthew 28:19
Er ist der Schöpfer aller Welt,	
der Herr, der alle Ding erhält.	Acts 17:24:25
2) Der erste Mensch war Gottes Bild	
mit Licht, mit Lieb und Gnad erfüllt.	Genesis 1
Sein Sünden Fall riss ihn von Gott	
in Finsterniss in Zorn und Tod.	Genesis 3

Der zweite:

3) Und doch war Gott von Gnad so gross,	John 3:16
gab her den Sohn aus seinem Schooss.	
Der ward ein Mensch, heisst Jesus Christ,	1 Timothy 2:5
durch den der Riss geheilet ist.	Luke 30:31, John 44
4) Denn er ward Bürg, gabs Lösegeld	1 Timothy 2:6.
und litt, ja starb für alle Welt,	Hebrews 2:8-9
erlöste uns von Zorn und Schuld,	
versöhnte Gott, erwarb die Huld,	1 Thessalonians 1:10
5) stand auf vom Tod, verliess die Welt,	
fuhr auf zu Gott ins Himmels Zelt,	Luke 24:51
ist aller König der Seinen Hirt	Ephesians 1:20

---

[1] This versified version of the Apostles' Creed, included under the entry for March 3, 1745, was composed by Court Chaplain Friedrich Michael Ziegenhagen as a mnemonic for children. It was printed in the American Lutheran hymnal for 1786.

auch Richter, der recht richten wird.	John 21:15, Acts 10:22?
	2 Corinthians 5:10

Der dritte Articul des christlichen Glaubens:

6) Der heilge Geist erneuert das Hertz,	Titus 3:5
bestraft die Sünd, wirckt Reu und Schmertz,	John 16:6-9
giebt helles Liecht von Gottes Rath,	
von seinem Sohn und dessen Gnad.	Ephesians 1:16-18
7) Er ists der uns den Glauben schenkt,	2 Corinthians 4:13
auch Lieb zu Gott ins Hertze senkt.	Ephesians 3:16
Durch ihn wird Gottes Bild erneurt,	Titus 3:5
des Fleisches Sinn im Grund zerstört.	Romans 8:9
8) Wer nun durch ihn in Kraft und That,	Romans 8:13-14
Buss, Glauben, Lieb im Hertzen hat,	
der ist aus Gottes Geist gebohren,	
ist Gottes Kind, geht nicht verlohren.	
9) Wer aber nach dem Fleische lebt	Romans 8:13
und Gottes Geiste widerstrebt,	Acts 7:57
ist Satans Kind und sehr verblendt,	John 3:8
muthwillig er zur Höllen rennt.	Romans 8:6

Schlussgebet:

10) Ach Vater in dem höchsten Thron,
nimm uns doch auf in deinem Sohn.
Dein Geist mach bey uns alles rein,
dass ewiges Leben unser sey.

Nöthige Selbst-Prüfung nach den Haupt-Stücken des Glaubens eines
wahren Christen.

Erweg mein Hertz was ist sein Gut,
auf welchem Dein Vertrauen ruht?
Von welchem Wege hoffest Du,
dass er Dich führt dem Leben zu?

Antwort:

Mein bestes Gut soll Gott allein
in Christo meinem Mittler seyn.
Den Lebens-Weg mir niemand weisst,
nur Gottes Wort und Gottes Geist.   Psalm 119:103, 143:10

TRANSLATION

The three main articles of faith of true Christians according to the revealed word of God. Melody: *Lob sey dem allerhöchsten Gott*

The first article of Christian faith:

1) I believe in God, who is called Father,
and in the Son and Holy Ghost.   2 Corinthians 8:5-6
He is the Creator of all the world,   Matthew 28:19
the Lord who maintains all things.
2) The first man was in God's image
filled with light, with love, and grace.   Genesis 1
The fall of man tore him from God
in darkness, wrath, and death.   Genesis 3

The second article of Christian faith:

And yet God's grace was so great   John 3:16
He gave His Son from His bosom.
He became man, was called Jesus Christ,   1 Timothy 2:5
through whom the rent was healed.   Luke 30:31, John 44
He was ransomed, gave redemption   1 Timothy 2:6
and suffered and died for all the world,   Hebrews 2:8-9
redeemed us from wrath and guilt,
reconciled God, won His grace   1 Thessalonians 1:10
5) arose from death, left the world,
rose up to God in the vault of heaven,   Luke 24:51
is King of all, Shepherd of His people.   Ephesians 1:20
and Judge, who shall judge rightly.   John 21:15, Acts 10:22
                                               2 Corinthians 5:10

The third article of Christian faith:

6) The Holy Ghost renews our heart,   Titus 3:5
punishes sin, causes remorse and pain,   John 16:69
gives bright light from God's counsel,

from His Son and His grace.	Ephesians 1:16-18
7) It is He who grants us faith,	2 Corinthians 4:13
and sends love for God into our hearts.	Ephesians 2:16
Through Him God's image is renewed,	Titus 3:5
and carnal thoughts are all destroyed.	Romans 8:9
8) Whoever, in strength and deed, has	
remorse, faith, and love in his heart	Romans 8:13-14
through Him, he is born of God's spirit,	
is a child of God, will not be lost.	
9) But he who lives for the flesh	Romans 8:13
and struggles against God's spirit	Acts 7:57
is Satan's child and very blinded.	John 3:8
Wittingly he runs into hell.	Romans 8:6

Concluding Prayer

10) Oh, Father on the highest throne,
take us up in Thy Son.
Let Thy Spirit make all clean in us
so that we shall have eternal life.

Necessary Self-Examination according to the Faith
of a True Christian

Awake, my heart, what is the Good
on which thy Trust doth rest?
From what path do you hope
that He will lead you to Life?

APPENDIX III

Hymns sung by the Georgia Salzburgers in 1744 and 1745.

All identified authors are listed in Albert Friedrich Fischer, *Kirchen-lieder-Lexikon* (Gotha, 1878, reprint Hildesheim 1967).

Alle Menschen müssen sterben ... (All people must die), by Johann Georg Albinus. p. 175.

Auf! auf! mein Hertz mit Freuden... (Up, up, my heart with joy), by Paul Gerhardt. p. 128.

Aus tiefer Not schrei ich zu dir ...(From deep distress I cry to Thee), by Martin Luther. p. 135.

Befiehl du deine Wege und was dein Hertze kränkt ... (Commit thy ways unto the Lord), by Paul Gerhardt. p. 126.

Christi Leben tröstet mich, mir ist ein erwünschtes Leben ...(Christ's life comforts me, mine is the life I wish), anonymous, found in Freyling-hausen's songbook. p. 24.

Christus, der ist mein Leben... (Christ is my life), by Simon Graff. pp. 24, 27.

Danckt dem Herrn ihr Gottes-Knechte ... (Thank the Lord, ye servants of God), by Count Heinrich Georg Reuss. p. 154.

Denn seelig seyd ihr doch ihr Frommen ... (Then blessed are ye pious), Author unknown. p.178.

Der Bräutigam wird bald rufen ... (The bridegroom will soon call), by Johann Walther. p. 175.

Der wahre Gott und Gottes Sohn ... (The true God and Son of God), by Abraham Hinkelmann. p. 134.

Die Feind sind all in Deiner Hand ... (The enemies are all in Thy Hand), Author unknown. p. 92.

Er mag das Haus, das aus der Erde ... (He can ... the house that from the ground), Author unknown. p. 178.

Erwach, O Mensch, erwache! ... (Awake, oh man, awake!), by Bartholomäus Crasselius. p. 89.

Es ist das Heil uns kommen her ... (Salvation hath come here to us), by Lazarus Spengler or Paul Speratus. pp. 114, 145.

236

Freue dich seh, O meine Seele ... (Rejoice greatly, oh my soul), by Christian Weise. p. 168.

Gleichwie sich fein ein Vögelein ... (Just as fine as a little bird), by Martin Rutulius. p. 90.

Gott hat alles wohl bedacht ... (God hath thought out all things well), by Gustav von Mengden. p. 118.

Gott Lob, die Stund ist kommen ... (Praise to God, the hour is come), by Johann Hermann. p. 210.

Gott wills machen, dass die Sachen, ... (God will ordain that things...), by Johann Daniel Herrnschmidt. p. 220.

Halleluja, das Leben ist erschienen ... (Hallelujah, life has appeared), by Johann Ludwig Conrad Allendorf. p. 132.

Halleluja, Lob, Preis, und Ehre ... (Hallelujah, Praise, and glory), attributed to Bartholomäus Crasselius. p. 189.

Hallelujah sei dir gesungen, O holder Hirt, O süsses Lamm ... (Hallelujah be sung to Thee, oh dear Shepherd, oh sweet Lamb), Author unknown. p. 128.

Herr Gott Zebaoth tröste uns, lass leuchten dein Antlitz über uns, so genesen wir ... (Lord God Zebaoth comfort us, let Thy countenance shine upon us, then we will recover), Author unknown. p. 178.

Herr, so du wirst mit mir seyn ... (Lord, if thou wilt be with me), by Christoph Jacob Koitsch. p. 135.

Hier kommt ein Schüler in die Schule ... (Here comes a pupil into the school), Author unknown. p. 137.

Jesus Christus, Gottes Lamm ... (Jesus Christ, our Lamb), by Johann Joachim Breithaupt. p. 189.

Jesus Christus unser Heyland, der von uns der Gottes Zorn ... (Jesus Christ our Savior, who saves us from God's wrath), by Martin Luther. p. 58.

Lasset uns den Herrn preisen und vermehren ... (Let us praise and magnify the lord), by Christian Jacob Koitsch. pp. 16, 189.

Lobe den Herrn, den mächtigen König der Ehren ... (Praise the Lord, the mighty King of glory), by Joachim Neander. pp. 16, 127.

Lobe, lobe, meine Seele, den der heisst Herr Zabaoth ... (Praise, praise, my soul, Him who is called Lord Zabaoth), by Hermann Reinhold. pp. 16, 190.

Man lobt dich in der Stille ... (We praise thee in quiet), anonymous, often attributed to Joachim Neander. Based on a hymn by Johannes Rist. pp. 6, 16.

Mein Gott, du weisst am allerbesten ... (My God, thou knowest best of all), by Israel Clauder. pp. 45, 177.

Mein holder Freund ist mein ... (My dear Friend is mind) by Ulrich Bogislaus Bonin. pp. 135, 136.

Nun bitten wir den heiligen Geist ... (Now we beg the Holy Ghost), by Martin Luther. p. 189.

Nun dancket all und bringet Ehr ... (Bring thanks and glory, all of you), by Paul Gerhardt. p. 15.

Nun Gott Lob, es ist vollbracht ... (Now praise to God! It is finished), by Hartmann Schenck.

Nun lasset uns den Leib begraben ... (Now let us bury the body), by Michael Weisse. pp. 22, 162, 178.

O dass ich tausend Zungen hätte ... (Oh, had I a thousand tongues), by Johann Mentzer. pp. 15, 123.

O Jesu, Du bist mein ... (Oh, Jesus, Thou art mine), by Count Heinrich Georg Reuss. p. 1.

O meine Seele, erhebe dich ... (Oh my soul, arise), by David Denicke. p. 54.

O Welt, sieh her, dein Leben ... (Oh world, see here, thy life), by Paul Gerhard. p. 209.

O wie selig sind die Seelen ... (Oh, how blessed are the souls), by Christian Friedrich Richter. p. 145.

Sei Lob und Ehr dem höchsten Gut ... (Praise and Glory to the Highest Good), by Johann Jacob Schultz. p. 4.

So bin ich nun nicht mehr ein fremder Gast ... (So now I am no longer a stranger), by Johann Eusebius Schmidt. p. 178.

Solt es gleich bisweilen scheinen ... (Even if it sometimes seems...), by Christoph Tietze. p. 26.

Solt ich meinem Gott nicht singen? ... (Should I not sing unto my Lord?), by Paul Gerhardt. pp. 16, 72, 189.

Stilles Lamm und Friede Fürst ... (Quiet Lamb and Prince of Peace), by Christian Friedrich Richter. p. 128.

Wenn dein hertzliebster Sohn, o Gott, nicht wär ... ... (If Thy dearest Son, oh God, were not ...), by Johann Heermann. p. 139.

Wie wohl ist mir O Freund der Seele ... (How well I fare, oh Friend of the soul), by Wolfgang Christoph Dessler. p. 178.

Wo ist mein Schäflein, das ich liebe ... (Where is my little sheep that I love?), by Juliana Patientia von Schullt. p. 105.

INDEX

This Index, prepared by the editors, includes the names of all persons mentioned anywhere in the text and footnotes, as well as all subjects and places of significance. Abbreviations used in the index are as follows: d=daughter, fr=from, Pal.=Palatine, s=son, Salz.=Salzburger, w=wife, wid=widow, ...=unknown first name. Spelling was still somewhat fluid at this point in history, and there are inconsistencies in spellings of names throughout the German original.

A Der Mühlfluß, welcher ein Arm des Savannah-Flußes ist.
B Die erste Mehlmühle, und Stoßmühle zum Reiß mit ~ Stämpfel; da
Mühle ihre eigene Waßerräder hat, die durch gewiße Schleußen un
nach des Müllers Verordnung können gehend oder stehend gemacht
C Die andre Mehlmühle, welche bey mittelmäßige u. niederm Waßer des
die andre Mahl-u. Stoßmühle mahlt u stoßt bey niederm u. hohem Wa
D Die große Schleuße od Thor eines Gangs, um dadurch das überflüßiwe Waßer
E Ein Trog zu der Sägmühle, 6 Zoll weit, nach der Weite od Breite des Waßerra
F Die Sägmühle, welche eben so viel Waßer als die erste Mehlmühle
braucht, und mit 2 Sägen ungemein wohl arbeitet.
G Eine lange u. sehr starcke Brucke, bestehend aus langen u. dicke
eingeschlagene Pfälen v. rothem Fichtenholz, viereckigten
Stücke u. langem Zimerholz, gelegt in 4 Reihen von
dem hohen Lande H.H.H. bis zu dem Boden der
Sägmühle, so das viele Stäme Holz ganz leicht zu
den Sägen gebracht werden können.